A TALE OF TWO SEASONS

A TALE OF TWO SEASONS

The Fall and Rise of Heart of Midlothian

Steve Weddell

First published by Pitch Publishing, 2015

Pitch Publishing
A2 Yeoman Gate
Yeoman Way
Durrington
BN13 3QZ
www.pitchpublishing.co.uk

A CIP catalogue record is available for this book
from the British Library.

ISBN 978 178531-069-0

Typesetting and origination by Pitch Publishing

Printed by Bell & Bain, Glasgow, Scotland

Contents

Dedicated to the memory of Brian J Alps

Acknowledgements

FIRSTLY, I should thank my granddad, Alf, for setting me on the road to becoming a Jambo. He took me to my first game when I was ten – a 1-0 home defeat by Partick Thistle back in November 1978. Each botched attempt at goal was lamented with a forlorn 'Willie Bauld would've scored that', setting me on the road to years of wistful disappointment and tailored expectations.

Next, I have to say that without Ross Millar there wouldn't have been a book to speak of. In 1995 I left Edinburgh to spend nine years as a student in Liverpool and, as a closet Red, found the lure of Anfield irresistible. Ross made sure my links to Tynecastle stayed intact, always sorting me out with tickets and a place to stay. So for that, for your generosity and for taking the time to read my drafts – offering great feedback, plus a line about Ryan Stevenson and tattoos that still makes me laugh. Thanks Ross!

Thanks also to Grant Young and his wife Carolyn for being full of kindness and positivity about my project and for being there with me when we lost those 89th- and 92nd-minute goals up at Ross County. I'm not kidding guys, I seriously could not have faced making that journey back on my own. Thanks too to Jack Millar for reminding me always to bring my notebook to games and for never peeking.

I flagged a bit (after the League Cup semi-final defeat to Inverness), so thanks to George Kinnear for suggesting I kept at it since, as he puts it, I 'dae fuck all anyway'. Thanks also to the Old Team for always taking an interest in my progress: Alec Young, Jim Ollason, Tam Jones and Bill Young.

Thanks to all the people down through the years who have had the misfortune to attend Hearts' games with me as I go pink-cheeked, talk gibberish and shout myself hoarse by half-time: Ian Millar, Stephen Shearman, Keith Smith, Stu Millar, Shawn Millar, Andy Ewing, Alan McDermaid, Ian Cadogan, Graeme Kay, Ryan Simpson, Paul Millar, Colin Andrew, Scott Hutchison, Alex W. Neill and many others.

Special thanks to Neil Fraser with whom I went to my first away game, up at Tannadice on 18 February 1984. The two of us had a blast back in the day, dodging all manner of projectiles from Vienna to Montrose and I look back at those days with genuine fondness.

Big thanks to Scott Wilson for kindly agreeing to write the foreword and for looking over my early chapters – it really was greatly appreciated.

Also, thanks to Pitch Publishing for agreeing to publish this, to Bob Swan for coming up with the title and to London Hearts for their statistical expertise.

And, finally, thanks to my long-suffering wife, Janey. Eighty-three games in two seasons can't have been easy for her but I'm struggling to remember a cross word. She certainly never used the term 'football widow' to describe herself. Pretty sure I'd have remembered something like that.

Introduction

THE origins of this book can be traced back to drunk talk, sweet beautiful drunk talk, at a Hearts fundraiser in the Gorgie Suite at Tynecastle in early July 2013. Our beloved team had been declared financially insolvent with debts of around £30m, triggering a 15-point penalty, so Ross Millar, Grant Young and I swore an allegiance to attend every game until we reached zero points. Ross even went further and suggested I wrote a book about it. Alas, *Bravo 'til Zero* outgrew its title as the tale that ultimately emerged stretched to two crazy, unforgettable seasons.

Like every other Hearts fan we'd spent the 2013 close-season on tenterhooks, squirming in painful anticipation of how low we would need to stoop before bottoming out and beginning the slow pull back to the level we perceived ourselves to belong.

Jambos flocked in their droves to be at the bedside of their cherished, ailing patient, pledging thousands in season ticket sales to keep that big heart beating. The prospect of losing so precious an institution, an establishment that played such a crucial part in so many people's daily lives had a rousing, galvanising effect.

Secretly, I suppose, we'd all been preparing for the day we would get this call to arms. We'd had a rehearsal of sorts back in November 2012 with a flurry of fundraising activity and the share issue. For my part, I attended a bash at the Gorgie Suite and bought a signed photo of Gary Mackay scoring versus Clydebank in 1986 and a signed, match-worn Steven Pressley away shirt. My wife got the top framed for my Christmas and I re-donated it for the July fundraiser. It felt nice to give something back and, besides, Pressley's a big unit: that framed XXXL shirt would've brought the wall down.

An indication of how mobilised and motivated the Hearts support was came at East End Park exactly a week later, with a joint fundraiser against Dunfermline Athletic. Like many others, arriving at the ground in good time, I found the stand behind the goal locked, packed to the rafters with a swirling mass of maroon. By the time the teams emerged I had found a seat across from the tunnel in the north east stand and it was immediately apparent how utterly overwhelmed the players were with this stirring show of support. It felt truly momentous. It felt like we were all in this together and you just wanted to applaud everything the players did on the pitch, even the passes that never came off.

The sense of shared spirit and camaraderie was resounding: you had the crop of youngsters, rightfully being lauded for bearing the club's immediate future on the pitch on their young shoulders and you had the older, more experienced pros who'd volunteered to take a wage cut.

It felt poignant and, in the sweltering Fife sunshine, 'The Hearts Song' caught in my throat. The club I loved seemed to be skirting around the very edge of oblivion. I was so glad I'd come through. I'd been avoiding the truth. It suddenly occurred to me there may not always be a Hearts to follow and I cursed myself for all the times I'd freewheeled as a supporter. All the times I'd lazily kept half an eye on *Final Score* or *Soccer Saturday* from afar. For years I'd coasted, I'd taken my team for granted and, who knows, they might now be playing out their final few games. Ever.

Forgetting zero points and whether or not I'd always have company in the car, I pledged that day to support my team the best way I could – by following them home and away, the length and breadth of the country. I'd reacquaint myself with all the away grounds I hadn't been to in years, plus a fair few newies. I'd stick with it until the club were back where they belonged and on an even keel again: and, if this were to be Hearts' swansong, their last season as a going concern, I wouldn't miss a kick. The following account was written, game-by-game, as seasons 2013/14 and 2014/15 unfolded.

Foreword

AT the end of November 2013 I received an e-mail from a Hearts fan who said he was writing a book about the club and would I oblige him by letting him know what I thought about the first few chapters. I was delighted to be asked and happy to help but, as is typical of my busy life, the e-mail arrived some months later and sat forlornly in my inbox while I criss-crossed Europe.

I finally got around to it while sitting in an airport and my fellow travellers must have thought I was strange as I kept on laughing out loud at the content. When I wasn't laughing I was trying to stifle tears as I read about the football club that is so dear to my heart.

The end result is a beautifully written tome about the travails of Heart of Midlothian Football Club during the 2013/14 and 2014/15 seasons from the year in administration where we all sang that we were staying up but few really believed it, to the remarkable Championship-winning season just gone.

Steve captures every golden moment and transports you back to that day; you remember the sights, the smells, the noise and the joy of following Edinburgh's big team.

This book is beautifully written, grammatically perfect and a fantastic keepsake to dip into whenever you need a wee pick-up and to remember just why God made you a Jambo

Enjoy.

Scott Wilson

Part One:

Though We Sometimes Go Down

1

St Johnstone away, McDiarmid Park, 4 August 2013, 3pm

THERE had been genuine frissons of anticipation regarding the season's opener up at McDiarmid Park. Whether they came about as a result of the unbridled relief that we still *had* a team to participate in the big kick-off or through a desperate desire to see the side chip away at that points deficit, or a combination of both, the air crackled with a bullish defiance and an almost heady optimism.

The 6,174 crowd was made up of 3,335 Hearts fans, meaning three of St Johnstone's dinky little Lego, toy-town stands were bouncing with sections of maroon. Just before kick-off the dim-witted stadium announcer was imploring similar attendance levels for Thursday night's visit of Minsk, but I'm guessing most people inside the ground had already made alternate plans.

Our game had final billing, so by the time the players took to the sun-drenched pitch we were already staring up greedily at the dangling legs of the opening-day stragglers: St Mirren, Kilmarnock, Hibs and Ross County who'd succumbed, respectively, to Inverness, Aberdeen, Motherwell and Celtic. Friday night had seen a dogged Partick Thistle hold off Dundee United, much to anyone in maroon's ill-concealed disappointment. Rightly or wrongly many felt Hearts' Premiership survival would hinge upon Partick's perceived frailties. A point relayed triumphantly to Jamie Walker via Twitter, post-match, 'Every point for Partick is another nail in Hearts' relegation coffin.'

The opening moments felt breathless, Hearts scurrying to win possession and then frantically trying to force the ball forward to the twin battering rams of Callum Paterson and Ryan Stevenson. A pumped-up Jamie Hamill, his eyes on stalks, was barrelling around the midfield like a tumble dryer on a super-charged spin cycle. When Hearts won their first corner I almost expected to see Jamie charge over and boot the advertising boarding in celebration. Unfortunately, as with virtually all of Hearts' set-piece delivery on the day, the corner came to nothing.

A criticism often levelled at Hearts the previous season was that they'd tended to overplay when in possession and ended up going nowhere. It takes a supremely talented set of players to pass the opposition off the pitch, yet here were a bunch of graduates from the Under-20s attempting to do so against seasoned SPL campaigners. We'd often look lightweight and flimsy, especially once Paterson's foot injury sidelined him for the season.

Against St Johnstone, however, there seemed an acceptance that this ploy wasn't necessarily the way forward facing such a well-drilled, robust side and Hearts set themselves the task of trying to match St Johnstone physically.

The problem with that, however, was two-fold: firstly, it isn't a style of play Hearts are necessarily that comfortable with and, in attempting to win possession back high up the pitch, fouls were being conceded and possession squandered cheaply and, secondly, the Europa League qualifiers had St Johnstone up and running early and Hearts simply couldn't match their pace and power.

Allan Preston took this a stage further on *Sportsound*, suggesting that other than Celtic this fixture represented the toughest challenge Hearts could've faced. Hard to know whether that was actually true or whether Preston was just being kind about two sides he'd once played for. The caveat to that was surely the tiny matter of St Johnstone's Thursday night date in Belarus and the mere two days' preparation this left them to prepare for Sunday. Most Hearts fans felt this gave their side a distinct advantage and had been relishing the prospect of the Perth curtain-raiser.

Hearts had small flurries where they were able to scuffle together enough possession to make Mannus look lively and both Stevenson and Paterson had half-decent efforts from distance. But these were mere minor diversions as St Johnstone pounded forward at every available opportunity, Chris Millar and David Wotherspoon pulling the Hearts defence apart at the seams with probing balls and tireless forays into the channels.

Stevie May, looking like a cross between Toadfish from *Neighbours* and Albert Kidd on steroids, was borderline unplayable, bullying and harrying defenders and embarking on galloping, lung-bursting runs. A St Johnstone goal seemed inevitable and unsurprisingly it was the impressive May who played a starring role. On 25 minutes he took a pass from Steven MacLean wide left and looked to be heading towards the corner before jinking back inside and sweeping a right-footed curler past the flailing Jamie MacDonald. The referee's assistant on the far side immediately flagged for offside against Wotherspoon for possible interference with play but referee Steven McLean (no relation) refused to be swayed, barely even listening to what his assistant had to say before re-signalling the goal.

The *Sportscene* trio of Jonathan Sutherland, Steven Thompson and Michael Stewart pored solemnly over the replay footage with all the enthusiasm of forensic pathologists picking over a mutilated corpse before – seeming to bore of the exercise – Stewart unhelpfully offered up that it had probably been meant as a cross anyway.

As the match worn on it became patently obvious Hearts weren't going to trouble St Johnstone, despite Billy King looking bright when replacing an out-of-sorts Walker. Full time duly arrived and as the St Johnstone fans made hastily for the exits and evening milking, the Hearts support stayed behind and delivered a rousing ovation. It would have been easy to have been disheartened as our side had been fairly comprehensively outplayed, but that would have been missing the point somewhat.

There *were* positives to be seized upon. The biggest being that we were still alive, still fighting and, judging by the scenes at the end, most definitely still all together. And, besides, better Hearts sides than this XI had been turned over at McDiarmid Park.

On the pitch, too, there had been signs of hope for the future. MacDonald had made three quite phenomenal saves and seemed to be carrying forward his brilliant form of pre-season, Kevin McHattie never missed a tackle and was resolute and powerful, while Danny Wilson and Brad McKay both looked commanding at the back, although that might have been as much to do with the fact that it had been well nigh impossible to tell them apart from halfway up the Ormond stand.

Further forward it was clear a little tweaking would be needed. The game had seemed to pass Scott Robinson by as Hearts often bypassed the midfield and questions remained as to whether 4-3-1-2 got the best out of Walker and Paterson. And a way would surely need to be found to fit Jason Holt into the starting line-up.

The answers would come in time. St Johnstone had undoubtedly been very impressive and, as Gary Locke put it post-match, but for a disputed offside goal it would've been 0-0.

So, one week in, and 15 points remains the gap to our closest rivals. And long before the final whistle sounded at McDiarmid Park the spectre of the next challenge, the derby at Tynecastle, began to loom large in people's minds.

2

Hibernian home,
11 August 2013, 12.05pm

CALLUM Paterson's 72nd-minute derby winner, a bludgeoning header from an exquisite Dylan McGowan cross, transformed the mood, not only of all associated with Hearts, but also of the wider footballing public. Hope had been ignited and it sparked euphoric scenes of jubilation in the 16,621 crowd, bringing Hearts to within 12 points of three sides: the vanquished Hibs, stuttering Ross County, who had lost 3-1 at home to surprise package Partick Thistle and St Mirren, whose match with Celtic had been postponed to allow the latter to play a Dublin friendly against Liverpool.

In the days following that narrow defeat up at St Johnstone there had been an unmistakably sanguine drop-off in expectation levels regarding Hearts' chances for survival. At the close of the distinctly patchy fundraiser, The Trial of Gary Locke, on the Monday night, our eponymous hero spoke from the heart of the miracle that would be needed. This was echoed in a pre-derby interview Tosh McKinlay gave *The Sun* where he opined that Hearts were in danger of getting a doing and suffering a heavy defeat since it was a case of boys going into a man's game.

And Toshie wasn't the only pessimistic former employee, a befuddled Peter Houston eschewed the basic laws of arithmetic to wonder aloud on *Sportsound* whether *any* side would drop the requisite 15 points to allow Hearts to climb to safety. A similarly morose Graham Spiers then delivered a critique of his own that was peppered with such pearls of positivity as 'next to impossible', 'divine intervention needed', and, my personal favourite, 'cannon fodder'.

So it was from beneath this stifling blanket of negativity that Hearts emerged, shortly after midday on Sunday. What was clear above all else was that this derby would shine a light on what could realistically be expected, one way or another, from the season.

The cold, hard facts told us that come full time we'd either be 12, 15 or 18 points behind our city rivals. But we all knew the ramifications would run far deeper. This match felt pivotal, with the power to shape the mood and alter the landscape of the unfolding season. Defeat would see Hibs and their putrid smoke bombs almost certainly disappear, gloatingly, over the horizon but, more significantly, it would also cast serious aspersions on our ability to garner together enough points at Tynecastle to make a fist of survival.

However, instead of Hibs grabbing the initiative and going all out for this eminently attainable prize, Pat Fenlon sent out a fretful and disjointed XI, seemingly focused more on intimidation than inspiration. One particularly bone-juddering challenge by the agricultural Rowan Vine on Ryan Stevenson saw the stricken Hearts man stretchered off with suspected medial ligament damage.

Pat Nevin played glowering headmaster to Steven Thompson's giggling sixth form prefect as they pored over footage of the tackle on *Sportscene*, condemning its inherent nastiness, although in all honesty the match had been punctuated by far worse fouls, most of which were perpetrated by the combative Scott Robertson. Like many of his team-mates, Robertson had taken full advantage of referee Craig Thompson's desire to prove those internet sceptics wrong and show, beyond all reasonable doubt, he most definitely was *not* a Hearts fan.

The first half had been largely uninspiring if somewhat tousy with Jamie Hamill's limitless energy knitting the midfield together alongside the scurrying Scott Robinson. It was Hamill who'd also looked Hearts' best bet for a goal, shooting on sight and forcing Ben Williams to dive smartly to his left to keep out his net-bound free kick.

Hearts had switched to a conventional 4-4-2 with Jason Holt, who came in for Jamie Walker, playing just off Paterson. The second change saw David Smith come in for Callum Tapping in an attempt to provide the width that had been lacking in Perth. Stevenson's unfortunate injury gave Walker an early opportunity to come on and make amends for the previous weekend, although it was hard for anyone to shine in a first half devoid of shape or fluidity.

And this muddled lack of cohesion continued into the second half which at least had the benefit of being slightly more open. Despite Hamill's swirling 30-yarder which Williams plucked spectacularly out of the air, play was tending to swing more and more towards Jamie MacDonald's goal. This period of play culminated in Hibs coming within a bawhair of breaking the deadlock. Liam Kelly skipped clear on the left and hooked an inviting ball into the path of the in-rushing Tom Taiwo. Thankfully for Hearts – with the goal gaping – Taiwo fluffed his lines, sliding in to strike the ball which skidded up off the turf and bounced harmlessly to safety.

Within minutes of this reprieve Hearts had their precious winner and the visceral roar and tumultuous scenes at full time were the pure, living embodiment of hope and relief. The victory, the removal of a chunk of the points deficit, gave a voice to the whispered shred of hope that we all still clung to. Perhaps it wasn't delusional, despite our better judgement, despite what the media were telling us, to still believe.

Of course, the reality of our predicament is a paper-thin squad, so to have any chance of building the momentum that's going to be needed, the footballing gods will have to shine down on us: ensuring Ryan Stevenson doesn't have too much company in the treatment room.

Motherwell fans love to reminisce about the time, in administration, they were asked to donate long-sleeved shirts on the eve of a game. Well, a bad run of injuries for us and any kitted-up Hearts fans might also be needing to step up to the plate. However, they might just find themselves with a place on the bench, lacing up a pair of ice-blue Nike Mercurial Vapors while Lockie decides whether or not Jordan McGhee can run off that ankle knock.

A week which began with Gary Locke pleading for a miracle ended with Steven Thompson glibly predicting our deficit would be gone altogether within a few months. One victory against a choking and lacklustre Hibernian is patently insufficient to justify such a radical swing in our perceived fortunes. The point is, no one has the slightest clue where this thrilling, intoxicating fightback will take us.

All we do know is that next up is a Friday night date in Maryhill with Partick Thistle. And right now it feels like the games just can't come quickly enough.

3

Partick Thistle away, 16 August 2013, 7.45pm

FOR this match I drove through to Glasgow, parked up on Garscube Road and, after a short walk, clambered up the steep, darkened steps into the rickety old main stand at Firhill. I don't own a souped-up De Lorean with a flux capacitor but on entering that creaky, crumbling edifice, I could have been Marty McFly with the time circuits set to 1978. All that was missing was a check-jacketed Arthur Montford, the *Scotsport* cameras and a heroically moustached Drew Busby doing his level best to smash Alan Rough into the net.

The Friday night fixture had been a relatively recent innovation and it was only a matter of time before Hearts' number came up. Just how unfortunate a coincidence it would prove to be that five of our first-team regulars had received call-ups for the Scotland Under-21s against England at Bramall Lane on the Tuesday night would remain to be seen. Thankfully, all five (Kevin McHattie, Brad McKay, Jason Holt, David Smith and Jamie Walker) were deemed fit enough to start, although this was no thanks to Raheem Sterling who needlessly left his studs in on McKay.

It is fast becoming clear that this is a season like no other. The points deficit has obliterated any comfort zone. Hearts sides in the past have given the impression of coasting through certain run-of-the-mill games. Not this year. The word meaningless has no meaning. From the first whistle, every single second assumes vital importance.

And, from the stands, the level of support is frenzied, relentless, unyielding. There is a sense, in the perpetual cacophony of noise, of the fans wishing to reach out and physically drag the players out of this predicament. Richard Gordon called it right on Friday night's *Sportsound*, 'Every point will be treated like a trophy win.'

Thistle began with all the confidence you would expect from an unbeaten side with the chance to go top with victory. Their high-tempo, pressing game was no match for a misfiring Hearts and they dominated the first half pretty much from start to finish.

It had taken until Thursday morning before Gary Locke had his full quota of players back for training and this may have contributed to Hearts' uncertainty and hesitancy.

While Partick were efficient and well organised and stuck rigidly to an obviously well-rehearsed game-plan, Hearts gave the impression they were making things up as they went along, muddling together little clusters of passes before either mis-controlling or overrunning and being crowded out.

Thistle's slick passing led to wave upon wave of attacks as the first half became excruciating to watch. Partick's number nine, Kris Doolan, was giving Danny Wilson a torrid evening, firstly having a goal correctly ruled out for offside and then, moments later, glancing a gift of a near-post header wide from inside the six-yard box.

An agitated and fraught Hearts support desperately counted down the minutes to half-time. The hope being that Gary Locke and Billy Brown might be able to galvanise the players during the break, re-jig the system and send the side back out reinvigorated.

And, indeed, the second half saw a decent improvement. Robinson got closer to Hamill as 4-3-3 became more of a 4-2-3-1, allowing Hearts to keep the ball better. In the early moments of the half it became clear Thistle's rhythm had been disrupted and they resorted to pumping long, occasionally aimless, balls towards Steven Lawless and Doolan. Hearts were able to pick up possession relatively cheaply and this sequence of play culminated in a flurry of corners for the Edinburgh side. From the last of these Wilson had a wonderful chance to nick a priceless goal, but his diving header from ten yards missed the target.

Despite Hearts' improvement Thistle still seemed liable to carve them open at will and Jamie MacDonald repeatedly kept his side in it, with a string of top-class saves. He flung himself to his left to claw away a James Craigan header, next up he dived right to fist away a piledriver from substitute John Baird and, finally, with only five minutes left on the clock, he was at full stretch once again, this time to tip away a ferocious Lawless 20-yarder.

A bruising and hard-fought point looked to be tantalisingly within Hearts' grasp but, from the resultant corner, slack marking left Baird free in the box. In Jamie Walker's haste to get back, he was adjudged to have bundled over the Thistle striker. From high in the main stand, with its obstructive pillars, the decision appeared highly contentious, a feeling only exacerbated by the furious reactions of Lockie and Billy Brown below us.

Brown came bouncing out of the technical area looking like Bob Mortimer's Councillor Roy Evans from Aldington-On-Sea. Thankfully he stopped short of getting referee Bobby Madden in a headlock and calling him a 'fat bastard', but he still did enough to earn a stern rebuke. Tellingly, however, Jamie Walker simply strolled disconsolately to the edge of the box, his head bowed.

With the minimum of fuss, Aaron Muirhead stuck the ball on the spot and smashed it straight down the middle. The howls of derision that had been directed at the officials as play restarted quickly faded to be replaced by a raucous rendition of 'The Hearts Song' and roars of encouragement from the 2,000-plus who'd made the journey.

The clock was ticking down, with only a couple of minutes remaining, and Hearts became frantic in their quest to find an equaliser. Walker, yearning to make amends, nicked the ball off Gary Fraser to win back possession. McKay picked up the loose ball and fed Hamill who threaded an inch-perfect through ball back to Walker who'd spun and was sprinting goalwards. A drop of the shoulder took him around Conrad Balatoni and then, from 18 yards, he crashed a spectacular rising shot high past the despairing Scott Fox to trigger scenes of utter jubilation among the travelling hordes.

So another point had been dug out and another small step taken towards attaining positivity as we hit the -11 mark. And the following day's Premiership programme delivered another boost with Ross County demolished 4-0 in Perth to leave them still pointless after three matches.

Elsewhere, in the games that directly impacted upon Hearts, St Mirren and Kilmarnock drew one-all, as did Hibs and Dundee United.

On the face of it we might have preferred Hibs and St Mirren to have been beaten, rendering them pointless along with Ross County but neither Kilmarnock nor Dundee United had started their seasons well, so there was merit in having the both of them not too far out of sight on two points.

Thankfully, Walker's priceless late equaliser had allowed the momentum from last weekend's derby win to continue to build. Ground had again been made and we trailed Ross County by 11 points, Hibs and St Mirren by 12 and Kilmarnock and Dundee United by 13.

This, coupled with the Foundation of Hearts receiving preferred bidder status two days earlier created a mood of cautious optimism. 'This is an important day in the pathway towards putting Heart of Midlothian back on its feet,' said the foundation's chairman, Ian Murray MP. 'We are proud that the bid backed by the Foundation of Hearts has been named preferred bidder. Let us be clear though. The journey is only beginning. Our bid has not yet been accepted, albeit we are hopeful an agreement can be reached. Now, for the first time, the fate of Heart of Midlothian really is in the hands of us, the supporters of this remarkable football club. It's a big day for the football club and hopefully now we can move forward.'

The supporters were throwing their full weight behind the foundation, pledging to pay a set amount each month. Of this Gary Locke noted, 'It'll be Hearts people running the football club and that's the most important thing.' Yet any deal to exit administration via a company voluntary arrangement (CVA) still needed to be agreed with the major creditors of the club so we were all very much aware how much still needed to happen before we'd be free to celebrate.

4
Aberdeen home,
24 August 2013, 3pm

WHEN the dust finally settles on 2013/14, irrespective of where it leaves Hearts, the sheer, heart-stopping drama of this pulsating encounter will live long in the memory. This was a ferocious victory for a gutsy, tenacious ten-man Hearts side that simply refused to accept their fate when one point, let alone all three, seemed beyond them. This summer, Hearts were the football club that refused to die and this pugnacious obstinacy is being taken out on to the pitch. In the words of Aberdeen legend Willie Miller, 'If they can pull a victory like this off, then anything's possible.'

The swell of Aberdeen fans that flocked south clearly did so harbouring high hopes of breaking a dismal run of results at Tynecastle. Not since a 3-0 victory in January 2010 – that signalled jotter time for Hearts' then manager Csaba Laszlo – had they managed even a goal in this troublesome fixture.

There was no indication of the spikiness and animosity that was brewing as the minute's applause for Hearts winger Johnny Hamilton was generously extended to include former Aberdeen goalkeeper Fred Martin who'd also passed away in the week leading up to the game.

Hearts elected to start with the same team and formation that had finished at Partick, meaning David Smith's place went to the impressively quicksilver Billy King and Hearts kept their favoured 4-2-3-1 shape.

Later that night, Twitter would be rife with stories of Derek McInnes's pre-match rhetoric as his players took to the field, where he'd apparently been overheard urging that his players 'show these boys who the men are'. Either Aberdeen had mistakenly thought Hearts planned to follow Shakhter Karagandy's lead and slaughter a live sheep just before kick-off or McInnes saw a fragility and vulnerability in Hearts that he felt could be turned to his side's advantage with a few uncompromising tackles.

In fact, Aberdeen's alehouse defending was directly responsible for an early, gilt-edged chance for the reassuringly cumbersome Scott Vernon. A lusty clearing header by Mark Reynolds put him clean through on goal but, thankfully for Hearts, the striker was held back by the invisible tractor he seemed to be dragging and eventually he scuffed a weak effort straight at Jamie MacDonald.

Having weathered that mini-storm, Hearts took the lead on 18 minutes with a beautifully crafted and executed goal. From right-back, Dylan McGowan fed Callum Paterson in the centre circle. Paterson's cushioned lay-off was controlled by Jason Holt who pinged a crisp diagonal ball into the path of Jamie Walker on the left. Walker advanced with purpose to the edge of the box before cutting inside and driving sweetly past the helpless Nicky Weaver.

The remainder of the first half passed without incident, although there was still time for Vernon to squander another relatively simple chance. Weaver, surely a poor man's Ian Walker, took a goal kick that carried through to the big Mancunian. He held Danny Wilson off before sclaffing the ball wide from around the penalty spot.

With half-time came a rousing speech from Ian Murray MP, chairman of the Foundation of Hearts, revealing the heartening news that 7,000 had now pledged their support to the foundation. The massive Hearts following in the crowd of 15,218 applauded this vociferously while the mean-spirited away support sung pointlessly throughout the whole speech drowning much of it out. Any pre-match camaraderie, it would seem, long forgotten.

Midway through the second half the match boiled over with the first of a clutch of contentious decisions. Aberdeen substitute Calvin Zola fell in the box under a strong challenge from Kevin McHattie and referee Ian Muir delivered the shattering double whammy of a penalty and a red card.

Boyhood Don Liam McLeod may or may not have been sitting in the BBC studio, fine-tuning his recorded commentary, in an Aberdeen bobble hat and Gothenburg 1983 commemorative hoodie, but he was unequivocal in his assessment that McHattie 'had a lot of Zola as well'.

Equally, a bristling and vaguely sinister Barry Robson, looking like he'd stepped off the set of *Taggart* or *River City* where he'd been playing the head of a Glasgow crime syndicate, felt it was a clear penalty for his side. His sidekick on *Sportscene*, a slightly fearful-looking Peter Houston, nodded along enthusiastically but short of putting him in witness protection and giving him a new identity it was impossible to know what he really thought.

However, Gary Locke felt, categorically, that McHattie had won the ball cleanly and after some deliberation Hearts opted to appeal the red card, with a supporter commendably volunteering to stump up the £500. An offer the club turned down. You'd imagine reluctantly.

Niall McGinn slotted home the spot-kick before being booked for celebrating over-zealously in front of the Wheatfield Stand. It was hard to take any offence, though. He seems to be cupping those big ears of his every other weekend, so it clearly wasn't anything personal.

Prior to McHattie getting his marching orders, Brad McKay had reluctantly left the field with blurred vision after suffering a head knock, to be replaced by 17-year-old Jordan McGhee. McGhee had gone to right-back with McGowan slotting in at centre-half. Therefore, McHattie's red card meant an already reshuffled back division would require a further tweak and Callum Tapping came on for King, allowing Jamie Hamill to fill in at left-back.

Aberdeen sensed blood and stepped up a gear. Peter Pawlett went surging, at speed, into the Hearts box before being cleaned out by a reckless, scything Walker tackle. Muir took a long, hard look before waving away the sustained appeals. Pawlett, his reputation for histrionics notwithstanding, did himself no favours whatsoever, embellishing the contact with a very peculiar swan dive that just made it easier for the referee to also book him for simulation.

There was a simmering sense of injustice from Aberdeen as play raged on and Hearts were hanging on to parity by the merest of threads. Gregg Wylde and Josh Magennis were thrown into the fray alongside McGinn and Zola, giving Aberdeen a four-man strike force: the intention being to bludgeon Hearts into submission. And, on 85 minutes, Wylde flew past McGhee down the Aberdeen left and swept in an inch-perfect cross for McGinn who headed over when a goal seemed inevitable.

In a rare escape from their own half, with two minutes to go, Hearts broke and won a free kick midway inside the Aberdeen half on the right. From Tapping's looping delivery, ten-man Hearts sensationally reclaimed the lead. Wilson jumped with Weaver, and as the ball evaded them both, substitute McGhee gleefully planted a firm header into the empty net before wheeling away in delight.

This sparked wild scenes of unconfined joy as Tynecastle erupted in celebration. Tempers that had been fraying on the touchline all afternoon reached breaking point with Billy Brown's triumphant jig taking him into the Aberdeen technical area. McInnes reacted angrily, giving him a hefty shove, and both men were forced to see out stoppage time in the main stand.

This altercation, along with the earlier sending off, meant that when the board eventually went up it was to signify five added minutes, much to the dismay of the home support whose nerves, by now, were totally shredded.

Aberdeen continued to pound forward, lumping ball after ball into the box and winning a succession of corners. But Hearts clung on to the lead as if their lives depended on it, with Wilson, McGowan and Hamill repeatedly repelling the fierce onslaught.

Deep into stoppage time, Magennis had a close-range header that McDonald did well to push over for yet another corner while, right at the death, Zola could quite easily have won his second penalty of the afternoon, when Paterson appeared to tangle with him at the back post, to howls of protest from the away end.

At long last, the whistle finally sounded and the bloodied, battered Hearts players sank to the turf in exhaustion. The match had been played out at a breathtaking pace and Hearts had triumphed through sheer force of will, digging another three-point chunk out of the 15.

The drama didn't end with the final whistle, however. Hearts captain Wilson, bursting with pride at the resilience of his young side, was unable to resist thumping on the door of the away dressing room to see whether McInnes and his players cared to re-evaluate their opinion of him and his team-mates. Wilson, it is said, has little time for McInnes after the pair clashed during the skipper's short loan spell at Bristol City and so the victory would have tasted all the more sweet.

Unfortunately, for Wilson, despite the omnipresence of industrial language on the pitch, the referee's advisor – the in-no-way priggish and wilfully petty Iain Brines – took a dim view. Wilson was subsequently charged with 'using language deemed offensive and insulting directed at the opposition' and given a one-match ban.

So far this season Hearts have surpassed all expectations with seven points amassed from four matches. There is an almost feverish desire to succeed. However, a drawback of that irrepressible desire has been those two red cards, not to mention the concession of two penalties.

Perhaps this is the only way forward for Hearts this season. A pumped-up, tightly-knit bunch of players, buzzing with nervous energy: accumulating points as quickly as possible before the inevitable burn-out. Without question, though, a balance is going to have to be found.

For the fires of this remarkable fightback to still be burning at Christmas, up to and beyond the split and, who knows, through the play-offs, we're going to need better luck with injuries and a cleaner disciplinary record. Otherwise, the number of players Gary Locke has at his disposal each week will slowly dwindle away, as will our challenge.

Mercifully, thus far, a number of our rivals appear to be floundering. This weekend, those sides closest to us were conveniently involved in a couple of mini play-offs. St Mirren lost 3-0 away at Ross County leaving them on the one-point mark, nine ahead of us with a game in hand, while Ross County remain 11 clear. And Kilmarnock lost at home to Hibs meaning they're now ten in front of us on two points with Hibs still 12 points clear.

5

Inverness Caledonian Thistle away, 31 August 2013, 3pm

IT would have been fanciful not to have thought there'd be days like this. This fixture always stood out as a severe test for Lockie's kids, even before two of Hearts' first-choice back four were made unavailable through suspension. In actual fact, the first half was a lot closer than the scoreline suggested and Hearts were simply undone by the predatory brilliance of Billy McKay. The second half, however, was a completely different story with Inverness Caley Thistle moving through the gears impressively and steamrolling Hearts.

There's a scene in the film *Dances With Wolves* in which Kevin Costner, after being captured and brutally interrogated by his former US Cavalry compatriots, is written off as having 'gone injin'.

There has to be whole swathes of middle England who look upon Terry Butcher in much the same way, deciding that he's 'gone Scotch'. They'd have a point, too. Butcher has unquestionably found his spiritual home in Caledonia, reinventing himself as some sort of honorary chieftain of the Highland clans. Maurice 'miss-pass' Malpas fulfilling the role of faithful 'ghillie' with aplomb, laying out the cones and phoning ahead to Auchterarder, after away matches, with the boys' chippie order.

A laudable travelling support of 1,165 made the trek north to the Tulloch Caledonian Stadium. Kevin McHattie's failed appeal and Danny Wilson's one-match ban dictated that Hearts took to the field with a defence as makeshift-looking as ICT's flimsy and dust-blown south stand. Right-back Jordan McGhee made his first league start and stand-in captain Jamie Hamill filled in on the other side as he had done throughout the latter stages of the Aberdeen game. Elsewhere, David Smith made his customary switch with Billy King and started on the left with King benched.

Hearts, resplendent in all-white, were bright and inventive from the kick-off and nearly went ahead in the opening few seconds. McGhee surged forward and found Jason Holt in space on the edge of the box. Holt quickly nudged the ball sideways to Jamie Walker who whipped his first-time shot into the side-netting.

In previous campaigns, tricky away fixtures, such as this one, would often see Hearts adopt an ultra-cautious, safety-first approach. They would go with, perhaps, only one up front and concentrate on being tough to break down. This season, however, Hearts are in dire need of the points and are throwing caution to the wind, increasingly going toe-to-toe with opponents.

While refreshing, this is a policy that can sometimes leave the team exposed and with only eight minutes on the clock ICT scored from their first real attack of note. David Raven played the ball into space for Aaron Doran down ICT's right. Doran pulled the ball back intelligently for McKay who thrashed the ball home from 16 yards despite the valiant efforts of Jamie MacDonald.

Hearts dusted themselves down and restarted play, keen to pick up where they'd left off. They had a stiff breeze swirling in from the Moray Firth at their backs and at times this played havoc with the Inverness central defenders. On 25 minutes, Callum Paterson, looking like a precociously over-developed primary seven gatecrashing a primary three gym class, rampaged into the box and set up a chance for Walker. Agonisingly for Hearts, his shot ran across the face of goal and past the far post.

At this point the game was wide open, swinging from end to end and Billy McKay, in particular, was revelling in the freedom. His general movement, on and off the ball, was creating a major headache for Dylan McGowan and Brad McKay and it came as no real shock to see him grab his and ICT's second after half an hour. Hearts made heavy weather of clearing their lines after McKay had raced clear and once Doran and James Vincent both had shots blocked the little Ulsterman swept home with the minimum of fuss.

In the dying embers of the half, Hearts came within a whisker of giving themselves a fighting chance for the second half. Walker robbed left-back Graeme Shinnie and advanced, only to see his right-footed shot smack back off the upright and away to safety.

At half-time the game looked to be out of reach. The previous weekend, though, Inverness had squandered a 2-0 lead at Celtic Park and it was this faint hope that we clung to as the teams re-emerged for the second half. However, it immediately became clear ICT were in no mood to relinquish the three points and two minutes after the restart Gary Warren bounced a header off the Hearts bar with MacDonald nowhere.

The tone was set and time and time again ICT swept forward only to be denied by a combination of profligate finishing and the heroics of MacDonald. McKay was desperate to add to his tally of five goals for the season and became involved in a personal duel with MacDonald, with the Hearts keeper repeatedly defying him.

With ten minutes to go McKay was presented with the perfect opportunity to complete his hat-trick in highly dubious circumstances. Nick Ross, taking a break from presenting *Crimewatch*, swung the ball in from the left and from point-blank range MacDonald bravely denied Richie Foran. As the ball spun free on the edge of the six-yard box, McKay's close-range hook shot cannoned off the head of Hamill. Momentarily stunned, the Hearts skipper scrambled groggily to his feet, ready to repel the next ball into the box. As he did so, referee John Beaton ran across and showed the incredulous Hamill a straight red for deliberate handball.

This was quite simply a staggeringly awful decision. From where I was seated behind the goal, slightly to the left, you could practically make out the word 'Mitre' imprinted on to Jamie's big shiny head.

On *Sportscene*, Stuart Lovell smiled winningly at the camera and called the decision a 'headscratcher' while Mark Wilson went a stage further, saying that even if it had been handball it would've been a very harsh decision given how little room Hamill had to manoeuvre himself out of the way.

Thrillingly, MacDonald thwarted McKay's spot-kick with an instinctive dive low to his right, before clutching the rebound to howls of defiance from the Hearts fans behind him who'd amassed in the inexplicably large concourse between the first row of seats and the perimeter wall at the away end.

Of course, the season has really only just begun but already Hearts seem to have suffered their fair share of harsh refereeing decisions. It's hard to see, as the conspiracy theorists on Twitter would have you believe, that an SFA-led agenda exists to make sure Hearts are relegated as punishment for falling into administration, but there's certainly a case to be made for all three red cards being marginal calls that could have gone either way.

Thankfully for Hearts, this reversal didn't prove as costly as it might have. Partick Thistle came from behind to beat St Mirren and Motherwell saw off Kilmarnock, meaning we still trail St Mirren and Killie by nine and ten points, respectively. Ross County fought out a spirit-crushing 0-0 draw with Hibs at Easter Road leaving those sides 12 and 13 points, respectively, clear. And, finally, Dundee United lost 1-0 at home to our next opponents, Celtic, leaving them also 13 points ahead of us.

6

Celtic home,
14 September 2013, 12.30pm

HAVING spent a number of years living on Merseyside, attending a decent quantity of Liverpool games, it's impossible to escape the genuinely high regard people south of the border have for the Celtic support. They seem especially taken with what they perceive to be the Bhoys' loyalty, passion and generosity of spirit. Indeed, the merest mention of Celtic's unshakeable support, post-Hillsborough, is enough to reduce many a staunch Red to tears and, in the week leading up to this Tynecastle league match, a packed Parkhead paid tribute to Stilyan Petrov with a deeply poignant benefit match.

The flipside to this, and one of the principle drawbacks of the demise of the old Rangers, is our reluctant promotion to the position of enemy number one in the eyes of these same loveable rascals. You can see them when they come through to Tynecastle, furiously, dare I say hopefully even, scanning row upon row of home supporters for the odd Union Jack scattered here and there, craning their ears for snatches of half-hearted sectarian chanting.

Their need to define us in this way is truly insidious since, as far as they are concerned, it then gives them full licence to indulge their odious repertoire of Republican bile. We aren't the enemy. The vast majority of Hearts fans reject their tedious stereotypical image of us with every fibre of our beings, but a Celtic support in full self-justification mode is about the closest thing you'll get to spontaneous combustion.

Celtic had opted to leave behind their new toothpaste-inspired home strip and instead took to the pitch wearing the Norwich City kit.

Whether it was a result of the early kick-off time or a quiet sense of dread about the potential for a drubbing, the atmosphere at kick-off was slightly less fervently upbeat than it had been for the previous two home games. To our dismay, mild trepidation tinged with reduced expectation levels proved not the only parallel with our last league outing, up in Inverness. Then, as with today, Jamie Hamill fell victim to a bewilderingly inept penalty call, this time from Willie Collum.

Seventeen minutes in and Anthony Stokes got a firm head on to Kris Commons's in-swinging corner. Hamill, a matter of inches from the striker, leapt to try and block the net-bound effort and the ball grazed his hand from what was essentially point-blank range. BT's Gary McAllister, reacquainting himself with refereeing incompetence on a scale he hadn't encountered since exiting Fir Park for Leicester City in the summer of 1985, struggled to get his head around the decision, 'How are you meant to know where your hands are going there? Very fortunate to get that.'

Commons calmly waited for Collum to disdainfully shoo the incredulous Hearts players out of the box and blasted the ball home to a crescendo of booing from three sides of the ground.

Half-time came and went and Hearts, despite surrendering large chunks of possession to their opponents, still carried a considerable threat on the counter-attack. And, on 56 minutes, the roof nearly came off Tynecastle as Hearts made one of those breaks count with the equaliser.

Jamie Walker teased Mikael Lustig wide on the left and the ball broke to Kevin McHattie on the edge of the box. His shot was half-blocked by Virgil van Dijk but only came out as far as Jason Holt who insolently rapped the ball past Fraser Forster from 20 yards. The flailing Celtic keeper resembled a badly sprung ironing board as the ball flew in.

So, despite losing out 70-30 in the possession stakes and having been picked apart in the first half by a preening, at times almost showboating Celtic, Hearts had pulled level. Their unquenchable spirit and desire had kept them in the game and from high up in the Wheatfield Stand it was clear this turn of events had left the champions shaken. The triumphant olés that had rung out as Celtic stroked the ball around the pitch were suddenly not quite so audible.

As Celtic visibly wobbled, Tynecastle rose, scarves fluttering, maroon smoke billowing. Billy King darted like a whippet along the 18-yard line only to be crudely upended by van Dijk. While Hamill and McHattie deliberated over their options Forster bounced up and down on his goal line, gurning nervously.

What followed, however, only made doubly certain that any post-match analyses would have no choice but to revolve around the bewildering incompetence of Collum.

Hamill's effort was poor, the latest in a long line of disappointing set pieces from the otherwise impressively dogged midfielder. However, after harmlessly rebounding off the wall the ball reared up and struck the hand of the inert Efe Ambrose. Hamill sprinted after the singularly unimpressed Collum, disbelief scorched across his face. You could clearly make him out imploring 'but it was the same as my one!' but Collum was unmoved.

Once *Sportscene*'s Jonathan Sutherland and Billy Dodds had finished wetting themselves over Hamill's latest penalty-related mishap, the Hamill/Collum interface was faithfully re-enacted in the studio with Mikey Stewart playing the role of Hamill and Billy Dodds filling in as Collum. Luckily, for the BBC, the role of petty, diminutive, west coast fusspot proved not too much of a stretch for Doddsy and the boys agreed to disagree about both decisions.

But the game roared on and, moments later, the ever-impressive Stokes was put clear by a nifty Commons header and duly lashed the ball high into the net, much to the relief and delight of the fans packed into the Roseburn Stand.

Irrespective of the odd half-chance carved out at the other end – substitute David Smith floating a free back-post header into Forster's arms – the game looked to have gone. An increasingly ragged Hearts, weakened by enforced substitutions, were chasing shadows in the closing stages and it came as no real surprise when, with five minutes left, Celtic got the third goal their obvious superiority probably warranted.

New signing Teemu Pukki came off the bench to head home from close range. The goal came after Stokes had made the most of a lucky break off Scott Robinson before extravagantly looping the ball into the air for a simple Finnish.

Given our current financial plight it was hard not to feel a slight twang of jealousy as we'd watched Celtic prepare their new £2.4m Finnish striker for action. Although, having said that, the monumentally dull, utterly predictable path these protracted deals take would always have grated, irrespective of our parlous state.

There's the crushingly monotonous 'will he/won't he' tabloid speculation, moving in tandem with a complete mini-series of bland, non-committal responses from an array of faceless club spokespersons. Then, once the player is finally satisfied his agent has wrung every last euro out of the negotiation process, Sky Sports News takes charge, endlessly looping footage of the player blinking shyly into a bank of flashbulbs, a wrinkled XXL replica top pulled crudely over his everyday clothes and a cheap monogrammed club shop scarf held aloft.

And, last of all, there's that ancient custom beholden of all overseas players inducted into either half of the Old Firm, the ceremonial bestowing of a suitably *weedge* nickname, 'Aye, pure brand new eh, you're wan of us now Shuggie/Tam/Eck/Billy,' etc.

Anyway, there is little doubt that the best side won. But the fact that it took two highly questionable refereeing decisions to ease them to that victory leaves a decidedly sour taste in the mouth. Even more so when both are viewed not as isolated incidents but within the context of all the other contentious calls we've suffered thus far this season.

Happily for us, though, we'd earned another reprieve as, for the second week in a row, both of our closest competitors – St Mirren and Kilmarnock – lost, to Motherwell and ICT, respectively. Both remain within touching distance, nine and ten points clear. And, encouragingly, our next opponents, Ross County, were also defeated: 4-2 at home to an ever-improving Dundee United, leaving them a mere 12 points in front.

Taking points from either ICT or Celtic was always going to be a tall order for Hearts and in many ways it comes as no shock to remain stuck on -8 for another week. However, our next three league matches see us pitted away against Ross County and then home to Dundee United and St Mirren. These are matches that come into a different category altogether.

It would be nice to think, with these nine points up for grabs, we could take ourselves a good deal closer to that hallowed zero-point mark.

7

Ross County away,
21 September 2013, 3pm

IT was sickening enough when Melvin de Leeuw powered home an 89th-minute equaliser at the Global Energy Stadium but fate had an even crueller twist in store for Hearts as Richard Brittain snatched an injury-time winner to leave them shattered and distraught on the Highland turf. A season that has already produced Callum Paterson's majestic derby winner and crucial late strikes from Jamie Walker and Jordan McGhee now has Hearts on the receiving end of late drama.

Once more it was a privilege to see, first hand, Hearts' indomitable spirit and swashbuckling sense of adventure and the south stand was packed full (all the way from Row A up to Row N) with a boisterous away support. Sadly, it was this raw impetuosity that proved Hearts' ultimate undoing. At 1-1, when the prudent course of action might have been just to take that late choker of an equaliser on the chin and slink away with one point in the bag, Hearts fatally charged back upfield in search of the victory.

For all of Ross County's first-half possession much of their play was stuttering and directionless. Their ploy of knocking diagonal passes over the top for unkempt wideman Ivan Sproule, in the vain hope that at some point he'd stop overrunning the ball and getting tackled, failed miserably. Kevin McHattie shackled him admirably and snuffed out his one and only sniff of goal with a bone-crunching block tackle.

Derek Adams felt his side had enough of the ball to have definitely deserved something from the game. Tellingly, however, despite the *Sportscene* highlights package having Jane Lewis announce each and every Hearts attack as 'coming against the run of the play', they neglected to show even one save from Jamie MacDonald.

In truth, Hearts never looked unduly troubled. Beyond looking for Sproule, County's other mode of attack suggested some half-assed form of group hypnosis had taken place, whereby Adams's men had been led to believe they were the Brazilian World Cup side circa Spain 1982. Every opportunity for a pop from distance was taken and the fans behind the goals were repeatedly forced to duck for cover.

The Ross County blueprint for success was personified by the stooping, lumpen Mihael Kovacevic. Whenever he ambled forward, lining up a shot, the biggest threat was to the bodywork of the cars parked outside the stadium. He hoofed the ball out of the ground so many times that at one point it was impossible to make out the referee's whistle over all the car alarms going off.

Underpinning Ross County's muddled style of play was the urgent need to win back possession as quickly and uncompromisingly as possible. Red-haired centre-half Scott Boyd, looking uncannily like Lomper, the security guard in *The Full Monty*, was particularly culpable, clambering all over Callum Paterson at every available opportunity.

Appeals from fans for fouls on Paterson, though, are becoming increasingly half-hearted since referees appear stubbornly resistant to awarding them. Both opposition centre-halves could bring the big man down with piano wire strung across the 18-yard line before finishing the job with a cast iron frying pan and the referee would still take a long, hard look before deciding, on balance, that Paterson had probably played for it.

But, it wouldn't matter, because within a matter of moments you'd see a groggy-looking C-Patz, pitchside, preparing to come back on, toilet paper stuffed up each nostril.

It was Paterson who gave Hearts the lead midway through the first half. McHattie swung a vicious free kick in from the right and the big number 12 timed his run to perfection to knock the ball home from six yards.

The second half followed much the same pattern, plenty of clunky, fruitless possession from County's random assortment of big-eared boys with Hearts eager to break swiftly and test Mark Brown in the Staggies' goal.

Twice Hearts were desperately unlucky, having carved County apart, and both times Jason Holt was heavily involved. Firstly, on the hour, he latched on to a favourable ricochet from a Paterson piledriver and advanced dangerously into the box. However, his cutback was fractionally behind the in-rushing Paterson and the ball spun high and wide with the goal gaping.

Then, ten minutes later, Billy King and Walker combined neatly to find the Hearts number 15 midway inside the Staggies' half. Holt bamboozled two defenders with a cute body swerve before stinging Brown's palms with a rasping drive from the angle of the box.

As the minutes counted inexorably down it became impossible not to cast tantalising glimpses forward as to the potential ramifications of victory here: hitting the heady heights of -5 and moving to within six points of the still-floundering, beaten-again St Mirren.

Unfortunately for Hearts, County continued to plug away and got the first of their late double after De Leeuw outjumped Dylan McGowan at the back post to convert Brittain's hanging cross.

From the restart Hearts were clearly keen to repeat the trick they'd pulled off at Partick Thistle, piling forward for an immediate riposte to the concession of a late goal. With gaps at both ends the game was poised on a knife edge. Virtually all of the three minutes of added time had come and gone when play broke down between Scott Robinson and Jamie Hamill deep inside the County half. The Staggies surged forward and there was an air of merciless inevitability about Brittain's headed winner.

John Robertson, covering the game for *Sportsound*, relayed as much of the unfolding spectacle as he could before his pitch became so high that only dogs and certain species of bat were able to pick up the identity of County's winning scorer. A sombre, white-shirted Craig Gordon provided a sharp contrast to this on *Sportscene*, respectfully exuding an air of quiet contemplation like a choirboy or an apprentice undertaker.

Travelling all the way back down the A9 this defeat felt utterly soul-destroying but throughout a season every team suffers this sort of last-minute heartache, it's just become far more intensified by the state we find ourselves in. The fact remains that we're still only seven games in and nothing conclusive will have been decided on the back of a few catastrophic minutes at the end of a match we probably should have held on to win in Dingwall in late September.

8

Queen of the South home, League Cup third round, 25 September 2013, 7.45pm

HEARTS have developed something of a penchant for turning these League Cup ties into mini-epics. Last season's quarter-final and semi-final went all the way to penalties as did this season's second-round tie against Raith Rovers at Starks Park. It should, therefore, have come as little shock to see every last second wrung out of this third round tie at Tynecastle before Hearts thrillingly triumphed 4-2 on spot-kicks.

At kick-off there was a crowd of 8,381 inside Tynecastle which, on the one hand, was maybe slightly disappointing given the attendances we've seen for league games but, on the other, was still over 2,000 more than Hibs had for their tie against Stranraer the previous evening.

The echoey applause and occasionally audible shouts from players and coaching staff offered up a sobering glimpse into what life might be like for Hearts should that quest to remain in the Premiership falter.

Hearts made one change from the Ross County game with Gary Oliver replacing David Smith up top while the Queen of the South line-up contained that customary smattering of familiar names and faces that you always get when you come up against a team from the lower leagues.

A sizeable and vocal contingent had made the journey north from Dumfries, heartened not only by Morton's heroics at Celtic Park on the Tuesday night but also by the opportunity to add the scalp of last year's beaten finalists to that of the winners, St Mirren.

Unfazed, QotS started in confident fashion, stringing decent numbers of passes together and making Hearts work hard to get the ball off them. It was therefore a very pleasant surprise to see Hearts take the lead from their first attack of note. Kevin McHattie seized upon a loose ball and, very much in the mould of Lee Wallace, muscled his way into the box before finishing confidently.

Hearts' lead lasted for only four minutes. Ian McShane, keen to show there's more to his game than simply making menopausal women feel a bit flushed as *Lovejoy*, sent in a dangerous corner which Ryan McGuffie converted at the second time of asking after Jamie MacDonald brilliantly parried his first effort.

At this stage of the proceedings QotS were in the driving seat and a goal before half-time would certainly have put a serious dent in Hearts' hopes of progressing into the quarter-finals. And perma-tanned number nine Derek Lyle should have given them that lead but somehow contrived to miss when clear in the six-yard box. According to NASA his ballooned effort entered the stratosphere at 2053 hours and will remain in near-Earth orbit until the synthetic leather perishes.

Hearts came out for the second half with renewed vigour and within five minutes had regained the lead from what Chris Waddle would've called the 'pelanty spot' had he been co-commentating. Jamie Walker raced on to a Jamie Hamill through ball and ended up in a crumpled heap on the deck after tangling with both McGuffie and Chris Higgins. Hamill had the air of a man who knew he was about to score and calmly slotted his penalty past Calum Antell with consummate ease.

In his post-match interview Gary Locke would bemoan his side's inability to consolidate a lead and, as with the game in Dingwall, Hearts were once again pegged back when trying to add to a lead. This time it took QotS ten minutes to draw level, Lyle peeling brilliantly off Dylan McGowan to set up ex-Aberdeen forward Michael Paton.

At 2-2 the smart money was probably on QotS to win it in regulation time. They appeared to grow in strength while Hearts became fretful and loose in possession, rushing even the simplest of passes and squandering a number of presentable chances to hurt QotS on the break.

Allan Preston on *Sportsound*'s 'Open All Mics' felt Queen of the South were unlucky to lose on the night and that Hearts got lucky. Perhaps a tad harsh given that within the first minute of extra time Hearts had taken the lead for a third time. Walker's corner from the right was pulled intelligently back for Hamill, loitering 25 yards from goal. His anaemic effort turned into an inch-perfect pass for Danny Wilson who elegantly clipped the ball into the corner of the net from 16 yards.

A pattern had been established whereby Hearts raised their game sufficiently to take the lead and then in their hastiness to put the game to bed became panicky and subsequently wasteful, letting QotS back in. So we were all familiar with the script when, with three minutes of extra time left, the Doonhamers equalised yet again. Higgins clogged an unstoppable drive into the top corner after his initial shot was blocked.

So it came down to yet another penalty shoot-out. Jordan McGhee and Lyle both scored before Hamill sent his effort bouncing into the seats at the Roseburn end. QotS had the advantage but only if Mitchell could score. He couldn't, though, and his attempt smashed back off the bar before he impressively caught it. This was the point at which the contest crucially swung Hearts' way. Sandwiched between successful strikes from McGowan and Billy King was an effort from Paton that was brilliantly pushed away by MacDonald who, it has to be said, loves a penalty.

All of which meant that it came down to Dale Carrick to score and send Hearts through and he obliged in some style, nervelessly beating Antell.

The following day at Hampden, Hearts were paired with Hibernian at Easter Road on 29 or 30 October and suddenly a competition that thus far had been a mildly diverting interlude from the unrelenting intensity of the league programme, became something far more serious.

9

Dundee United home,
28 September 2013, 3pm

IT was hard not to feel more than a little cheated after this hard-fought 0-0 draw in front of an impressive 13,970 punters at Tynecastle. While Dundee United showed, in momentary bursts, just exactly why they'd racked up ten goals in their previous three games, we had to contend with yet another deplorable decision from the officials, this time inexplicably denying Hearts a perfectly legitimate goal.

This was Dundee United's first trip back to Tynecastle since December of last year. On that occasion they were more like gooseberries than tangerines, their decision to start Rudi Skacel rendering them mere bit-part players in his emotionally charged homecoming.

Hearts showed a couple of minor tweaks from the previous league outing up in Dingwall with Billy King and David Smith resuming their job share of the wide attacker role. Thus far, the routine has seen them switch over at or around the hour mark, the replacement generally impressing enough to earn a place in the first 11 for the following week. The unexpected but nonetheless welcome sight of Ryan Stevenson on the bench may signal the end, for the time being, of the Smith/King cycle.

The second change saw Jordan McGhee come in at right-back with Dylan McGowan taking Brad McKay's position alongside Danny Wilson. McKay may have struggled at times against Queen of the South but far more prescient is the vastly improved shape the side has when McGhee is included, both defensively and going forward.

Despite similarities between the two sides in terms of a youthful emphasis on attack tempered by the odd defensive lapse, the slow burning first half ended up as something of a stalemate. While Hearts were far more threatening from set plays, it was from open play that United looked to prosper.

The first half impasse was most notable for each side having a goal chalked off. The United effort, on 28 minutes, was ruled out for a David Goodwillie push on McGowan as the ball was en route to the prolific Nadir Ciftçi. Television footage also picked up, just for good measure, a clear handball from Goodwillie immediately after his nudge.

Meanwhile, at the opposite end of the spectrum, the decision for the Hearts goal was truly atrocious. Countless replays, from a host of different angles, showed nothing untoward whatsoever when Radoslaw Cierzniak mistimed his jump and ended up flapping ineffectually at Callum Paterson's gargantuan throw into the six-yard box.

Referee Steven McLean certainly saw nothing amiss and, after McGowan tapped home, he signalled for the goal before being halted in his tracks by a flag from his stand-side assistant, signifying a push on the keeper by Jason Holt.

There now exists an ever-growing montage of mystifying refereeing decisions that have gone against Hearts this season that BBC Scotland seems unwilling to put together or even allude to in vaguely ironic fashion. With music. There was the harsh award of a penalty against Aberdeen and subsequent sending off of Kevin McHattie, not to mention Danny Wilson's red card for swearing, post-match. And where do we begin with all Jamie Hamill's tribulations? Suffice to say there are prisoners in Guantanamo Bay with 'Justice for Jamie Hamill' t-shirts underneath their orange boiler suits.

This reluctance is either borne out of the need to skirt around potentially controversial issues and keep things bland and upbeat or it's because Jonathan Sutherland has no short-term memory, like Guy Pearce in the film *Memento*. If it's the latter then a tattoo artist will need to be commissioned to cover Sutherland's upper torso with images of Jamie Hamill (3), Kevin McHattie and Danny Wilson in time for whatever joys lie in wait from Craig Thomson at Tynecastle next Saturday. At least we could rely upon a whiskery Craig Levein to nail the utter incompetence of the assistant referee, 'I saw nothing wrong with it at the time and I see nothing now.'

The second half saw Dundee United sweep exuberantly forward with increasing regularity, Hearts' chances coming sporadically on the break. At times, play flitted like a particularly frenzied game of five-a-side, indeed this analogy even extends as far as United repeatedly booting the ball against the boards.

At the heart of most of their attacks was the swarthy Ciftçi. The former Turkish Under-19 international, who looked to have secured diplomatic immunity from being booked until McLean risked the wrath of the embassy late on, cannoned the ball off the base of the upright on 65 minutes with MacDonald transfixed.

Two minutes later Jackie MacNamara pulled off what he probably felt at the time was a managerial masterstroke when the positively foetal Ryan Gauld was taken off to be burped and given a Farley's rusk and replaced with the much-feted Gary Mackay-Steven. The United number 11 virtually pirouetted his way on to the pitch, relishing the prospect of unleashing his full gamut of flicks and drag-back turns on the rookie McGhee.

The reality, however, was the footballing equivalent of that scene in *Raiders of the Lost Ark* where Indy just shoots that overly flamboyant, showboating swordsman as McGhee repeatedly emerged with the ball, frowning quizzically at the ease with which he'd just robbed his counterpart.

In the end, and especially after last week's gruesome finale, this was a point that was pocketed gratefully. However, similarly with last week, there was also the sense that a hefty dose of misfortune had cost us all three points and instead of now sitting on minus seven we could have been on minus two.

Yet, of course, it's crucial we stay upbeat. Kilmarnock lost 5-2 at home to a rampant Celtic side so a point was gained on them, bringing us to back within ten, and next in town are St Mirren for the mother of all six-pointers.

10
St Mirren home,
5 October 2013, 3pm

THIS fixture, above all others, was the one we'd had our eye on for weeks but, when St Mirren finally came calling, the Hearts players gave the impression they'd rather be anywhere else but out on the pitch.

What we'd needed was for our team to come roaring out of the blocks, seizing the initiative and picking apart a St Mirren side that had only two measly points to their name: a side that would, ordinarily, have been rooted at the foot of the table. Instead, what we got was a pitiful whimper. This performance was devoid of spirit and desperately disappointing given what was at stake. Hearts seemed to wilt under the expectation, shackled by nerves, while the Buddies thoroughly merited their 2-0 victory.

Before the end many Hearts fans had seen enough and begun to drift away, the triumphant taunts of an underwhelming away support ringing in their ears.

Back in March and what now feels like a lifetime ago, these two sides contested a cup final. Since then the fortunes of both have plummeted to the extent that an altogether different cup final was now being played out. It was testament to St Mirren's malaise that, despite Hearts taking just one point from their last 12 – on top of that points penalty – the cushion was still only nine going into this crucial six-pointer.

Danny Lennon has had the air of a man who's known for weeks he's living on borrowed time, while maintaining the façade that it'll all come good in the end. Well, his side certainly did him proud at Tynecastle – sticking with gusto to his game-plan: hustling and harrying to great effect and taking every opportunity to fire as many balls as possible into the box. No one exemplified what St Mirren were all about more than Steven Thompson, the veteran centre-forward delivering a powerhouse performance that clearly unsettled the Hearts defence.

Dylan McGowan, in particular, was as jittery as a Mexican jumping bean, his panic triggering shakiness throughout a defence increasingly incapable of properly clearing its lines. As the ball was fed repeatedly into the Hearts box, something had to give and St Mirren took a wholly predictable lead in the 43rd minute, John McGinn ducking to head home.

Danny Lennon must have felt that noose lifting from around his neck. He'd given an interview on the pitch, for BT Sport, straight after Monday night's 1-1 home draw with Aberdeen that was a truly harrowing spectacle. It was almost as if, off camera, the guillotine was being made ready. A haggard and pursed-looking Lennon, his knuckles white as he clenched the mic, delivered a never-ending stream of barely coherent, platitudinous psycho-babble: his unfocused eyes staring unblinking into the middle distance like an emaciated hostage on Al Jazeera News 24 reading out his captors' demands. To his left, Billy Stark and Eric Black had shifted uncomfortably throughout this plea bargain, unable to even raise their heads and look across.

Of course, it still remains to be seen whether that guillotine can be put properly away in its box and stuck back up in the attic next to the Christmas decorations or whether it'll just get pushed behind the sofa with a throw chucked on top of it. That's because, if we're being completely honest, this encounter didn't ask too much of St Mirren.

After the match, ex-Jambo Ryan McGowan tweeted, 'Besides Stevo, Hamill, Wilson and Jamma none of them would've been first team regulars [18 months ago]! Situation now [sic] is find themselves chucked in at the deep end.'

Got to love Gowser, yet, one of these regulars he spoke of, Jamie MacDonald, dithered around all afternoon and was clearly at fault for St Mirren's second, fatally palming the ball back into the danger area where the lurking Paul McGowan could pounce. While another, Jamie Hamill, was leaden-footed and distracted, paralysed by what was at stake. Who knows, perhaps we'd have seen a more composed performance had we got those two wins we arguably deserved against Ross County and Dundee United. Only trailing St Mirren by four points (instead of nine) might have coaxed a calmer showing out of those two Jamies.

The performances of those two can be contrasted with that of another Jamie, Jamie Walker and, to a lesser extent Callum Paterson, both of whom demanded the ball all afternoon, were fearlessly bright and, despite things not always coming off, fought desperately and never hid.

Back in McGowan's day it used to be that all Hearts needed to do to beat St Mirren at home was roll the ball into the path of Rudi Skacel and sit back as the last vestiges of Craig Samson's reputation disappeared like so many match balls under Rudi's arm. But these days are gone and hankering after them won't make this task any easier. Equally, neither will focusing undue attention on the supposed paucity of experience out there on the pitch.

Under Paulo Sergio's fabled 2011/12 tenure, the era to which Gowser was directly referring, Hearts' away record at one point was officially the worst out of all 92 league sides, with only four goals scored from the start of the season until the end of 2011. The point being that if a side featuring such luminaries as Marius Zaliukas, Andy Webster, Ian Black, Skacel and (not forgetting) McGowan can toil to *that* degree then surely we owe it to the present crop to stick with them come what may.

Hearts have been ultra-close to picking up points in recent weeks. You could understand losing hope if it was a case of the side being outclassed every week but that simply isn't what's been happening. Admittedly, one point from Ross County, Dundee United and St Mirren represents a grim return which leaves us with still a bit of work to do to get to zero, but we are only at game nine. Crucial to our cause, though, is that we all stay together.

Scott Robinson let himself down in Monday's *Evening News* as his frustrations got the better of him, 'On Saturday there, I think it was a case of "I'll just pick on him again and take him off". I didn't think I was the poorest out of the midfield four.'

The case against panicking unduly was put by a genuinely magnanimous Steven Thompson on *Sportscene*. You could have excused him a slight air of smugness, given the result, but other than having the top button of his shirt fastened, a fashion statement last seen on Tom Cruise in *Rain Man* circa 1989, his conduct was above reproach.

St Mirren may have won on Saturday but we made it easy for them and they don't look an especially talented side while, over at Rugby Park, the days of Alexei Eremenko, Conor Sammon and, whisper it, Hamill are but a distant memory. Kilmarnock, who lost at Tannadice, are ten points ahead and our attention turns, reflexively, on to them, our opponents in a fortnight after a little excursion to Fir Park, Motherwell.

11
Motherwell away, 19 October 2013, 3pm

AS each week passes hope turns imperceptibly to resignation. Since victory over Aberdeen was achieved back on 24 August one point has been taken from a possible 18. This is relegation form irrespective of any points deficit. Yet, for weeks, the consequences of this slump have been masked by the equally dire form displayed by St Mirren and Kilmarnock, which has ensured we've at least remained within touching distance of salvation. However, Saturday, and Hearts' 2-1 reversal at Fir Park coupled with wins for both our closest rivals, saw the stark spectre of relegation come sharply into focus for perhaps the first time.

Fir Park, Motherwell can be a grim and soulless place at the best of times so it was intriguing to note that the home fans had undergone a degree of self-reinvention. All these trips abroad, getting their claret and amber arses handed to them in the qualifying rounds of various European competitions, appears to have inspired a mercifully small section of dubious miscreants to style themselves as *ultras*. In the section closest to the away fans a cringe-inducing attempt had been made at recreating one of those enormous Serie A-style banners with a king-sized bed sheet from TK Maxx and some felt-tip pens. Not only that, they had a drum, thumped, spirit-sappingly, throughout the entirety of the game and this complete spanner with a megaphone was leading the chanting. This unintentionally hilarious ensemble was topped off with a Hearts banner one of these daft wee laddies had no doubt snatched which was held upside down to anger the blood of the travelling support.

It's probably just me but there's something inherently wrong with this notion of Motherwell as European aficionados, with well-thumbed passports and a string of exotic pennants pinned up on the boardroom wall. In my mind they'll always be synonymous with garish strips from randomly obscure kit manufacturers, illegible shirt sponsors and John Philliben being owned by the mercurial John Colquhoun in a Scottish Cup fourth round tie played in the midst of a spring downpour at Tynecastle in the early nineties.

Kevin McHattie's illness meant the whole Hearts defence was re-vamped. Jordan McGhee went across to left-back with Dylan McGowan moving to right-back and Brad McKay coming in to partner Danny Wilson. Elsewhere, David Smith and Callum Tapping replaced Scott Robinson and Jason Holt.

For the Steelmen, I'd have gladly wagered dollars to doughnuts that John Sutton would get on the scoresheet. And not only that, but that it would be exactly the sort of finish he'd never have managed in a million years for us. As it happened this would have ended up being a wasted bet but, nevertheless, Sutton proved a major headache for Hearts all afternoon. So no change there, then.

In truth, the first half was a fairly toothless affair devoid of any discernible form or pattern, let alone incidents of note. Even the Coatbridge Clooney, Keith Lasley, who can usually be relied upon to stamp his personality all over this fixture, for once kept his studs to himself.

Motherwell came closest with a couple of Iain Vigurs efforts from distance, one of which caused Jamie MacDonald, wearing an unfamiliar blue goalkeeper kit, to scramble the ball clear.

With the clock winding down to half-time Hearts suddenly stunned their opponents by coming within inches of taking the lead. McGhee put Jamie Walker clear in the box with an exquisitely weighted pass but Gunnar Nielsen got down to Walker's powder puff side-foot before pulling off an even more impressive save, somehow getting fingertips to Smith's pile-driver from the rebound and tipping it over the bar.

Under the likeable Stuart McCall, Motherwell can be formidable opponents, especially at home, and it was hard to envisage them performing quite so listlessly in the second half. Not for the first time that afternoon, indeed this season, we were left to rue what might have been if only we'd taken our chances.

If the first half had ended up looking rather like a cagey dress rehearsal, then the second was undoubtedly the main event. Motherwell re-emerged looking far more like their usual selves and straight from the whistle Hearts were on the back foot, clinging doggedly to parity.

Seconds after the restart Sutton, now free from that nagging affliction of always appearing to be running in very deep sand, nodded a back-post header into the side-netting, causing all the fans in the Davie Cooper Stand to leap to their feet convinced he'd scored. Annoyingly, there was very little time to properly crow about how stupid they'd all looked as moments later an even better Sutton header was clawed away magnificently by MacDonald. Hearts were under the cosh and finding it impossible to clear their lines effectively. This flurry of attacks culminated in yet another flying header, this time from Shaun Hutchison, which Tapping somehow managed to hack clear.

Respite from this barrage only came for Hearts when, after 52 minutes, Callum Paterson signalled that he was unable to continue after coming off second best in an aerial challenge. Scott Robinson, suitably chastened after his ill-advised media outburst post-St Mirren, eventually took his place and the delay seemed to give Hearts time to catch their breath. From a quick breakaway Jamie Hamill drove powerfully at the heart of the Motherwell defence and found Walker. The Hearts striker's first touch was a trifle heavy, though, and he was only able to get a toe on the ball which went harmlessly through to the keeper.

A pattern became established whereby Motherwell would squeeze Hearts back, forcing them into some desperately frenetic defending, but then every so often Hearts would counter with Ryan Stevenson eager to run at the back-pedalling defenders. And, just after the hour, and after somehow repelling a virtually relentless onslaught, Hearts took the lead from one such break. Robinson fed Stevenson tight on the left touchline and with defenders backing off, Stevo advanced, cut inside and saw his shot take a glorious nick off Stephen McManus, fooling Nielsen at his near post.

The 1,253 Hearts fans packing out the upper tier of the South Stand went absolutely berserk at this unexpected breakthrough. Suddenly, watches were being checked and re-checked, phones were being fished out of pockets and the Hearts fans were singing themselves hoarse to try and see their side home.

If anything, Motherwell stepped up the pace and tore with even greater relish into a Hearts side that was defending deeper and deeper with every passing minute. With shots and crosses raining in on the Hearts goal from every angle it seemed inconceivable that Motherwell wouldn't equalise and barely an eyebrow was raised when substitute Craig Moore hammered the ball home from 25 yards with what we later discovered was his first touch.

Hearts' lead had lasted little more than five minutes and with 20 still left to go there was a very real danger that another opportunity to pick up at least a point was going to slip through our grasp. Despite this fear, Hearts countered bravely when they could, relieving the pressure, and substitute Jason Holt had a great chance to restore the advantage but was possibly caught cold and pulled his shot wide.

While Hearts had a tendency to get flustered in front of goal, Motherwell refused to press the panic button and continued their aerial assault on Hearts' six-yard box. Their obvious self-belief coupled with Hearts' vulnerability in the air meant it came as no real shock when, from Motherwell's umpteenth corner, Hutchison rose impressively and bulleted a header into the bottom-left corner of the net.

With only eight minutes left on the clock there was nothing left for Hearts, in this season of do-or-die cup ties, but to throw caution to the wind in search of a barely-deserved late equaliser. McKay, following in the fine tradition of Zaliukas, Pressley and McPherson, pushed up and played out the rest of the game as an auxiliary striker. It was a ploy that so nearly paid dividends for Hearts right at the death. The excellent Sam Nicholson, who'd come on for Smith, won a corner which floated through to Danny Wilson at the back post. He elegantly pulled the ball down but then took an eternity to pull the trigger and the ball was lashed to safety.

Seconds later the final whistle sounded and, leaving the ground, that infernal drum sounded like a death knell.

12
Kilmarnock away,
26 October 2013, 3pm

ON the eve of this match, the plug was pulled on BT Sport's coverage of Ross County against ICT due to the oxymoron of a half-time power failure at the Global Energy Stadium. And still on the subject of morons, the fuse blew slightly too late to spare us an opinion from that deadpan prophet of doom, Stephen Craigan. His unapologetically simplistic assertion that defeat at Rugby Park would make Hearts certainties for relegation set the tone for the rest of what would be a truly dismal weekend. Long before Kris Boyd notched the second of his two goals against a shapeless and slithering Hearts side, the obituaries were being solemnly penned for a season in terminal decline.

There is a school of thought that Hearts' best chance of avoiding the drop this season lies in another side, most likely Kilmarnock, entering administration. If reports are to be believed the Rugby Park side is in dire financial straits and compelled to count every single penny. Well, it certainly took them an age to eventually switch their floodlights on here, an apathetic and dwindling home support eventually illuminated through the murk and streaking drizzle.

Two changes were made from the side which lost at Fir Park with Kevin McHattie and Scott Robinson replacing Dylan McGowan and Callum Paterson as Hearts went for a 4-2-3-1 formation. The readiness of the coaching staff to alter playing systems, not to mention personnel, is definitely to be lauded but as this match unfolded it became harder and harder to shake the image of deckchairs being rearranged on the *Titanic*.

Leading the line was Ryan Stevenson and four minutes in he wrapped his foot around a curling drive from the angle of the box that was dipping unerringly into the top-left corner until Craig Samson scampered back and palmed it to safety.

A clutch of corner kicks then followed which came to nothing, either cannoning off the first defender or being ludicrously over-hit. Once more we were faced with the prospect of failing to sustain a relatively bright start and, to add to Hearts' miseries, Stevenson was lost to a knee injury as he overstretched to get a shot away and was replaced by Paterson.

Kilmarnock gradually eased into their stride and, after seven minutes, Kris Boyd sent out a declaration of intent, flashing a half-volley fractionally wide of the left-hand post. The former Rangers frontman had, in his locker, pretty much everything we were lacking: guile, coolness, presence, confidence, an eye for goal, 20 Lambert & Butler, a

Fray Bentos steak pie and a six-pack of Tennent's Extra. Furthermore, as was the case with another recent thorn in our flesh – Steven Thompson of St Mirren – he's someone who would walk into our side.

For his first goal, on the quarter-hour mark, Boyd ran on to an optimistic punt forward that had sailed in super-slo-mo over the head of an uncharacteristically flat-footed Danny Wilson. Brad McKay, lurching across to cover, lost his footing as he would do, repeatedly, all afternoon, opening up a clear route to goal. Jordan McGhee's aquaplaning intervention was deftly skirted with a subtle feint before Boyd lashed the ball past the criminally exposed Jamie MacDonald.

Slowly and surely there was a building sense of the whole season being on the verge of unravelling in the dank Ayrshire gloom. Not for the first time the rasping peal of the half-time whistle felt akin to the bell that rescues a punch-drunk boxer floundering on the ropes.

The first half had been a long, drawn-out affair as a result of copious amounts of injury time. In addition to the time needed for Stevo's injury there had also been a lengthy stoppage for Killie's Darren Barr who'd sustained the latest in an *ER* box set of horrible-looking head knocks. In many ways Barr's the footballing equivalent of Chip Cobb, the hard-of-hearing stuntman from *The Fast Show*, 'What's that you say, run across the box like 'eadless chicken, miss the ball completely and smash me forehead into the base of the other centre 'alf's skull? Alright, got you...'

When Dazza was eventually placed gingerly on to his stretcher and carried off, the Hearts fans put their rivals to shame, booming out his name while they all sat on their hands.

Echoing the opening 45 minutes, Hearts again began like world-beaters. Jamie Walker wriggled clear of Sean Clohessy and made speedy progress down the right-hand side, picking out Paterson with an inch-perfect cross. The chance was a carbon copy of C-Patz's derby winner but on this occasion his attempt lacked conviction and brushed past the post, much to the consternation of the large travelling support.

For Hearts, perhaps the cumulative effects of heart-wrenching defeats against the likes of Ross County and St Mirren finally caught up with them: there was definitely a hint that the bubbling team spirit, which had served the side so well, was disintegrating in the face of yet another reversal.

Boyd was relishing this match-up against the side he'd supposedly come close to joining in the summer and hovered menacingly like an overweight and malevolent wasp around a jam jar. On the hour mark he found the time and space to grab goal number two, this time exploiting the large area of prime real estate behind McKay. The only real surprise was that his second had taken so long in coming.

Hearts continued to try and play, refusing to give up hope of nicking a goal and setting up an improbable grandstand finish. Walker again made decent headway down the right, his attempt to give Samson the eyes and fox him at the near post foiled by the big keeper's foot.

The final stages of the match were played out in a torrential downpour as a demoralised Hearts scurried and skidded their way through to full time.

When it came the whistle felt like blessed relief.

13

Hibernian away,
League Cup quarter-final,
30 October 2013, 7pm

IN a claustrophobic and at times unspeakably tense League Cup quarter-final at Easter Road, Hearts weathered a raging tempest from Hibernian before slaying them with a searing knockout blow from miracle man Ryan Stevenson.

With Hearts only having taken one point from their previous 24, Hibs came into the match full of ebullience. Yet, by full time, their own fans had turned on them, viciously howling their derision at a side whose will had been broken by Hearts' unbreakable spirit and resilience. And, within days, Pat Fenlon would be gone, a fans' protest forcing the Irishman to accept the inevitable truth about his doomed tenure.

Easter Road beamed brightly like an illuminated bear pit as the players took to the pitch for this 7pm kick-off. Despite Hearts selling out the whole of the south stand it was the Hibs support in the ascendancy, making all the noise. After getting all defiantly misty-eyed over The Proclaimers, they taunted Hearts at length over their financial plight and/or league position ('going down, going down, going down') before finishing off with a perfunctory run through their ever-popular paedophile medley ('paedo-, paedo- paedophile, paedophile' and 'Jimmy Savile, he's one of your own').

If you're a Hearts fan, these excursions to Easter Road bristle with tension and unbridled hostility. It is a shadowy and sinister place full of foreboding and where you are always outnumbered on three sides. And, afterwards, if you aren't ambushed by goblins as you squeeze en masse over the bridge of Khazad-dum then there's always the risk of running into a cave troll in the trees at the corner of London Road and Leith Walk.

From the kick-off, Hearts were pinned, instantly, on to the back foot, making it barely possible to tell where the Kilmarnock performance ended and this one began. Hearts were simply engulfed by a green and white tsunami as Hibernian swarmed all over them, backed by a baying, gloating home crowd. Whenever Hearts cleared their lines the ball would remain out of harm's way for only a matter of seconds before, to another ear-splitting roar of anticipation, Hibs would build again, feeding the ball into the channels for Lewis Stevenson and Scott Robertson to fire diagonal balls into the box in search of Rowan Vine or James Collins. Vine resembled Abe 'Grampa' Simpson and his 15lb beard of bees.

After four minutes, from a Robertson cross, Paul Hanlon rose majestically above Dylan McGowan and thumped in a header that grazed the base of the upright. Seconds earlier, Jamie MacDonald had more or less invited the chance through an ill-advised punch when the catch looked routine. A point he was more than happy to concede as he retrieved the ball from the Hearts fans behind his goal.

On 16 minutes, however, none of us were questioning MacDonald's abilities when he kept Hearts in this tie with a staggeringly brilliant one-handed save. Ten yards from goal, on the right, Robertson smashed the ball goalwards and the whole ground held its collective breath, awaiting the inevitable. Hearts' fans felt a tightening in their chests and braced themselves for the deafening wall of sound while the home supporters were up on their feet, poised to acclaim the goal. But MacDonald had other ideas and, somehow, diving full length, managed to tip the ball up and on to the crossbar with Robertson left to pound the turf in despair.

Four minutes later, as Hibs continued to pulverise Hearts, James Collins weaved and bustled his way into the box only to see his skidding drive pushed away by the diving MacDonald who began berating his overworked defenders before even back on his feet.

The ball was just refusing to stick up front for Hearts and Hibs were giving their city rivals a monumental pummelling. Hearts were hanging on for dear life, hunting after the ball in packs, clinging to the hope of somehow nicking something, anything, on one of their ever-so-rare forays forward.

Robbo slipped into the technical area for a quick word and, not long after, a minor tactical switch was made with Jamie Walker and Callum Paterson dropping back to tuck in as wide midfielders while Stevenson was pushed into a lone central striking role. This cut Hearts a tiny amount of slack with the extra body in midfield and, after a couple of corners and a free kick came to nothing, Stevenson gave Hibs a reason to be wary after 28 minutes, nutmegging Tom Taiwo by the touchline and rippling the side-netting with a drive from the angle of the box.

Five minutes later it became apparent Stevo had simply been finding his range as Hearts sensationally took the lead. James McPake headed a clearance weakly to Jason Holt who instantly fed it forward to the strapped-up Hearts number 16. Without even looking up, Stevenson allowed the ball to roll behind him before wheeling and exploding a 25-yard rocket past the helpless Ben Williams. The close to 4,000 Hearts fans erupted in unrestrained joy and disbelief, tripping and falling over seats in utter, mass delirium.

The whole complexion of the tie suddenly changed with that wonder strike. For Hearts, they had something tangible to hold on to and, if anything, redoubled their efforts to thwart and frustrate their shell-shocked opponents. While, for Hibs, their self-belief visibly ebbed away, it was as if they'd realised, despite all their best efforts, that they simply couldn't break Hearts.

Behind the *Sportscene* plexiglass, a morose Ian Murray was forced to try and sum up where his former club had gone wrong in the first half, his brooding disappointment barely concealed. He'd been bullish about Hibernian's prospects, pre-match, and now looked close to tears. Beside him was a grinning Mikey Stewart who, if his appearance was anything to go by, has been spending those free afternoons with the *Brideshead Revisited* box set, what with his faded cotton jacket and old school V-neck. All Mikey was missing was a straw boater, a poorly strung tennis racket and a cheeky Pimm's and lemonade.

For the second half, Hibs still had enough possession to ensure a nervy time of it for the away support as the minutes were inexorably counted down. Yet the edge had gone from their play and tetchiness and angst from the stands began slowly permeating its way down on to the pitch with Hibs' quick, precise, passing game gradually disintegrating.

While the first half had been notable for the heroics of Jamie MacDonald, as Hibs peppered his goal, the second saw him called into serious action only once. On 73 minutes, Danny Wilson's rushed clearance unexpectedly rebounded off McGowan and the ricochet fell kindly for Liam Craig, putting him through one-on-one with the keeper. Thankfully from a Hearts perspective, he got the shot all wrong and MacDonald was able to get down and smother the ball.

It was clear that the increasingly likely prospect of the tie slipping away, despite Hibs' utter dominance in the first half, was sticking in the craw of many a home supporter. Ripples of abuse became more and more audible as passes were going astray and, on the pitch, frustration boiled over.

With only eight minutes left on the clock McPake was guilty of a heinous two-footed lunge on Paterson. After seeming to meekly accept his fate, McPake walked off, only to return like a pub drunk to further debate the issue with referee Willie Collum and then verbally abuse the Hearts bench on his way past again.

All of which helped see the game out for Hearts, the three minutes' injury time most notable for Pat Fenlon bouncing up and down on the touchline and gobbing everywhere like a hyperactive punk garden gnome. His time at Hibernian had been characterised by calamitous derby defeats and in many ways this one was the daddy of them all.

When the whistle eventually sounded the Hearts players sprinted across to their bouncing fans and all that belief from those heady days of August came flooding back.

14

St Johnstone home,
2 November 2013, 3pm

L AST weekend saw the completion of the first quarter of the season and, despite our tribulations, St Mirren getting humped four-zip at Tannadice tossed a bone in our vague direction. Once more we were back trailing the Buddies by 15 points and, going into this home match with St Johnstone, there was genuine hope that a combination of the next quarter's theoretically winnable home games against Kilmarnock, Motherwell, Partick Thistle, Ross County, ICT and St Johnstone, along with an undoubted boost from that victory in the League Cup at Easter Road, might breathe new life into that push to get closer to our rivals.

Under Tommy Wright – looking like a Hallowe'en-inspired, helium-filled Craig Levein balloon – St Johnstone have earned the reputation for being well drilled and hard to break down as well as a genuine handful up front. While they were a little slow to settle on Saturday, Hearts emerged from the tunnel in customary fashion, buzzing with nervous energy – like hyperactive children that have drunk too many fizzy drinks containing tartrazine.

Three times in the opening ten minutes Hearts threatened: firstly through a Danny Wilson header from a Jamie Walker free kick, then from an angled Walker shot from distance that deviated from goal at the last second and, finally, with a rising Jason Holt volley after Ryan Stevenson had picked him out with a clever glancing header.

Lockie had gone with the same starting line-up as Wednesday night in the hope his side might pick up where they'd left off in Lochend and play with that same fire and belief. And he got his wish up to a point as Hearts' fragile confidence levels appeared to have been replenished somewhat. However, while it was encouraging to see a little of that summer swagger return, it remains a sad fact that in order for this current Hearts side to have any hope of winning football matches, Jamie MacDonald needs to perform minor miracles, bailing out his slipshod defenders.

St Johnstone suddenly awoke with a jolt and with their first attack of note, on 13 minutes, filleted Hearts wide open with the simplest of run and crosses from big, beefy Stevie May. His cut-back found Nigel Hasselbaink in so much space you almost felt it must have been half-time and Teenie and Tynie were going to be bobbing around in the goal. As it was, MacDonald did superbly, thwarting Jimmy Floyd's favourite nephew with his feet.

Back in 1989, the Scotland Under-16s narrowly and controversially lost the World Cup Final to a Saudi Arabia side containing players that had suspiciously well-developed muscles and facial hair. And, not long after, the truth emerged that they had indeed included a clutch of over-age players that afternoon. You just wonder how long until the truth about Stevie May's real identity is revealed. My hunch is he's former Everton, Oldham and Leicester City striker Ian Marshall and is subsisting on a diet of EPO, botox and stem cells in order to give himself one last hurrah. To be fair he looks good on it.

While St Johnstone were now able to build possession without any real pressure on the ball, Hearts had the Saints players snarling in their faces at every turn. And it was this tireless pressing that led indirectly to St Johnstone taking the lead after half an hour. Dylan McGowan coughed up possession in midfield and the ball was seized upon instantly by David Wotherspoon who swept it wide for Chris Millar. The St Johnstone midfielder's cross clipped Kevin McHattie and, as McGowan dithered and, regrettably, held back, Hasselbaink nodded home.

Billy Dodds summed it up best on *Sportscene*, 'After losing the ball Dylan McGowan should be throwing himself at that.' Not for the first time this season the opposition had scored cheaply after McGowan had allowed himself to be bullied in the air.

Taking the lead allowed St Johnstone to settle into the comfort of their familiar counter-attacking game and, despite not having registered an away win in the league all season, they looked in complete control. This trend was only accentuated by their second goal, after 51 minutes, as May curled a delightful shot high past MacDonald after a furious episode of pinball in the Hearts box.

There were decent claims for offside in the midst of the build-up to the goal but after some of the seriously crackpot calls we've seen this season it's become increasingly hard to get worked up at these more modest, common or garden fuck-ups from the officials.

It's hard to know where this now leaves us. The St Mirren game was abandoned with them, hilariously, coasting at two-up, and Killie lost again so – for the time being – no more ground has been lost to those two. But, realistically, our best hope now has to be to stay in contention until administration can hopefully be exited and then, who knows, bring in a few sympathetic ringers from yesteryear like Rudi Skacel and Gary Naysmith in February or another hungry young English striker in the mould of Michael Ngoo.

Failing that, the slump we are now in, with this group of players, would seem to make relegation fairly likely and Gary Locke and Billy Brown have their work cut out keeping the troops positive. It can't be easy, though, when every Sunday night it's a Hearts defeat on *Sportscene*.

Judging from those opening credits we were doomed before we even began, though. While supporters of the likes of St Mirren, Celtic, Motherwell and Dundee United get to see their sides scoring in finals, lifting cups and celebrating madly we get a randomly pointless Derek O'Connor slide tackle from the single most depressing era in Hearts history. Perhaps someone at the BBC was trying to tell us something.

The one ray of sunshine saw a vital step taken this week regarding the ownership of the club with the announcement that a meeting has been scheduled for 22 November in which Hearts' creditors will be given the chance to accept an offer of £2.5m from the Foundation of Hearts to purchase the club's majority shareholding and stadium.

The offer consists of £1 for the 29.5 per cent shareholding of Ukio and the 50 per cent shareholding held by Ubig, which is awaiting the confirmation of administrators in Lithuania. Upon completion of the deal, £2m would be paid up front to secure Tynecastle Stadium, with the final £500,000 delivered after ten months. The deal needs the acceptance of major creditors Ukio Bankas, in administration itself, and Ubig, to go ahead. The Foundation of Hearts would also assume responsibility of the £535,000 of football debt that Hearts currently owes.

Hearts' administrators, BDO, led by Bryan Jackson, said the deal represents the best outcome for creditors of the Edinburgh club, with liquidation likely to realise less from the sale of the land. All we can do is hope that the creditors feel the same way, too.

Ian Murray, chairman of the Foundation of Hearts, said, 'We welcome the news that BDO is progressing the CVA for November 22 and hope that there will be a positive outcome. There is much work to be done, and again I cannot stress enough the importance of supporters who have not yet signed up to FoH, and who are able to do so.'

The bitter sting of relegation, you feel, would be more than soothed if it meant we were free of Lithuanian debt and self-owned.

15
Aberdeen away,
9 November 2013, 3pm

THIS away-day to high-flying Aberdeen was undertaken with fairly modest expectation levels regarding our chances. The league form of late has dwindled away to the extent that the math at the foot of the table is now governed each week by nothing other than whether or not Kilmarnock and St Mirren pick up any points.

The Aberdeen neds were, as Danny Dyer would put it, 'pwoper naughty' and, squashed up against the barrier fence, they yelled 'going down, going down, going down' as if they expected a reaction. All they got were diffident shrugs, people mouthing back 'and?' and more Hearts songs.

However, as this seething, rambunctious tussle lurched towards its charged conclusion, hope flickered and perhaps even reignited. Might the fickle hand of fate have yet another twist in store for us in this compelling tale of redemption?

The early exchanges in the crisp, clear Aberdeenshire air offered nothing to suggest this match was going to turn out any different to any of the others we've endured in this dire run of league games. Hearts flattering to deceive early on before succumbing to inevitable defeat once the opposition gets a feel for the ball and our heroes' enduring frailties.

We even had our customary golden early chance, Ryan Stevenson lashing the ball against Jamie Langfield's legs after Kevin McHattie's cross had found him unmarked in the penalty area, before Aberdeen raced into the lead without appearing even to break sweat. Teams aren't needing to do that much to score against us these days and from his side's first corner, on 25 minutes, Niall McGinn rifled home, the ball bobbing up nicely for him courtesy of a fortuitous bobble off Michael Hector.

From here, you'd have got seriously long odds on Hearts finding a way back into this game. The Dons' fans were almost wetting themselves at the predicament their old foes found themselves in, urging their team to go for the jugular and yelping their dismay at even the most obvious refereeing decision not to go their way. The Aberdeen fans' deluded sense of entitlement really began to grate. At one point I dropped my gloves and I swear half of the Richard Donald stand leapt to their feet, claiming them.

Yet, for all their bluster and bustling possession Aberdeen were finding Hearts in obstinate mood and the ultimate destiny of the game turned on a number of key incidents. Perhaps the most significant of which was the yellow card incurred by Aberdeen substitute Barry Robson for encroaching at a free kick. Indisputably, Robson deserved his card, it just came as something of a jolt to see a side other than ourselves penalised by a referee applying the letter of the law like a religious zealot.

The bleating cranked up a few more notches on 35 minutes when the sheep were adamant they should have had a penalty, a goalbound effort rearing up and striking Dylan McGowan as he stood on the goal line. After studying the replay, Rob MacLean, commentating for *Sportscene*, was convinced the ball had smacked off baby Gowser's face.

Pittodrie bubbled away uproariously, though, as the grumbling natives were incensed at this terrible injustice and this may have planted a seed of doubt in referee Iain Brines's mind as, a matter of minutes later, he gave the Dons an even more dubious penalty than the one he'd waved away, the ball cannoning innocuously off Jordan McGhee's back as he turned to block.

No doubt Derek McInnes turned to his coaching staff at this point and whined about justice being seen to be done, his side getting the penalty they so richly deserved. Certainly, post-match, he carped on about Brines's failure to give the first award, singularly ignoring the fact that his side *got* a penalty moments later and that it was a complete joke of an award.

Stuart Lovell on *Sportscene* was equally blinkered, making a massive deal of the first penalty call and then just chuckling derisorily at the one that *was* given. For me, we lost Jamie Hamill at ICT for a supposedly deliberate handball when the ball had hit his head and then, a week later, saw the same player concede a penalty at home to Celtic for a point-blank handball, it would therefore have been ridiculously unfair for a third of these debatable handball decisions to go against us.

But, thankfully for Hearts, Jamie MacDonald has a truly magnificent record when it comes to spot-kicks and gloriously denied McGinn a second, sprawling athletically to his left. At that moment Jamma's save felt as good as a goal and was certainly celebrated like one by the massive travelling support in the south stand.

Aberdeen may have seen out the rest of the first half on the offensive, quite literally in the case of their supporters, one of whom hit a young kid in the Hearts end with a flying vodka bottle, but it was the maroon contingent making all the noise.

The second half was barely ten minutes old when Robson failed to make his cynical trip on Jason Holt look like enough of an accident to fool Brines and picked up a second yellow for his troubles. Once again a glazed-looking Lovell made no attempt to be impartial, making the case that Robson had been trying to pull out of the challenge. Well, Stu, he needed to try a little harder, given that Holt was racing clear and Robson tripped him.

Lockie and Billy Brown got their heads together and within a few minutes sought to take advantage of the numerical advantage, swapping Callum Tapping and David Smith for Scott Robinson and Jason Holt and switching from 4-5-1 to 4-4-2. Irrespective of the extra man, this represented a bold move from Hearts given the quality of the opposition.

As Hearts took a moment or so to adapt to having one less in midfield, Aberdeen came within MacDonald's outstretched fingertips of sealing the match, Scott Vernon cushioning a volleyed lob over the advancing keeper. This save would prove pivotal as two minutes later Hearts were level.

Switching to two up front meant Jamie Walker could operate in the space just behind Stevenson and create problems for anyone trying to pick him up. From a Danny Wilson knock down, he was lightning quick, controlling the ball with the sweetest of touches and rounding Langfield to thrash home.

The reluctant wisp of optimism at drawing level against ten men was tempered, not only by the surfeit of late collapses we've endured thus far, but also by the fact that at 1-1 this match was now exactly mirroring the first game between the sides back in August. That day, the home side led before having a man sent off. The away side equalised and then, as they went all out to win, were sucker-punched, losing 2-1 to the ten men.

Furthermore, with 20 minutes left, there seemed little danger of Aberdeen sitting back and settling for the point as they flew back at Hearts, setting up a gripping finale. On 70 minutes Dylan McGowan executed a superb last-ditch tackle on Peter Pawlett as he raced in on goal. After the odd shaky moment this season, nothing got past Gowser at Pittodrie. Maybe having his big brother back in town, training with the boys for a few days, was just what baby Gowser needed.

Despite having been here before, losing late on at Ross County and Motherwell after piling forward at 1-1, Hearts swallowed their doubts and fearlessly went in search of the win. And, on 73 minutes, Pittodrie was duly stunned when Hearts surged ahead. Walker, revelling in his free role, took a pass from McHattie on the left-hand side of the box, skipped clear and dribbled along the goal line before pulling the ball back for Paterson to tuck home.

The victory was now so close you could almost touch it and on 85 minutes the Hearts fans were left groaning in anguish when Walker, timing his run in behind the Aberdeen defence to perfection, set up Paterson only to see him slide in and sky it.

These are the sorts of moments that have come back to haunt Hearts this season and Aberdeen's fervent and relentless hunt for an equaliser made for unbearably tense viewing. The board went up showing four minutes of added time and it felt like a hammer blow. While the fans fearfully willed Aberdeen to mess up each time they came forward, at one point nearly lifting the roof off when Russell Anderson sclaffed a 30-yarder high into the stand, the Hearts defenders stood tall and staunch, repelling everything.

Even Langfield got an invite to this injury-time bash and when he got caught on the edge of the Hearts box as the ball was cleared, it was just a question of who had big enough cojones to be Xabi Alonso and fire the ball into the empty net from inside their own half. As it was, Walker was stopped in his tracks before he could pull the trigger, forcing Paterson to change tack and feed the ball into space for Stevenson wide on the right.

With time more-or-less up any thoughts that Stevo might simply take the ball for a stroll into the corner were magnificently dispelled as he powered through on goal and thundered an unstoppable blockbuster of a shot high into the top corner to put the seal on a quite epic victory.

At full time the Remembrance shirts, emblazoned with poppies, got tossed into the crowd as the Hearts fans stayed behind to serenade their heroes. The blow from that 2-1 defeat up at Ross County back in September juddered Hearts, sending them spiralling into a downward vortex. It would be nice to think this result might have the opposite effect, triggering an upturn in both mood and fortune.

For Aberdeen, on the basis of Derek McInnes's post-match comments, that long search for the heir apparent to Jimmy Calderwood would appear at an end, given the sheer gracelessness of the man. No one was expecting a glittering eulogy from Del, especially not after the fall-out from his witless 'come on, let's show these boys who the men are' line back in August, but to suggest Hearts were far and away the poorest side they've faced at home all season just smacked of sour grapes. Defeat, it would appear, doesn't sit well. Yet this isn't a novel concept up here.

On my last visit, Hearts were pumped 6-2 and, with the home and away exits situated, unhelpfully, adjacent to each other, I got hit on the head with a handful of coins on the way out. I remember thinking that if they're that prone to petty acts of violence when they've actually *won*, what happens when these sociopaths get beat? I guess the unfortunate passengers on the Orwell Hearts bus are best placed to answer, given that they had the windows of their coach panelled in after the game.

You stay classy now, Aberdeen.

16
Wolfsburg home,
13 November 2013, 7.30pm

IT was wonderfully charitable of crack Bundesliga outfit Wolfsburg to send over a side for this fundraising match at a bitterly cold Tynecastle. Although, in truth, it was more like hunting dogs than wolves on show as only two – Patrick Ochs and Daniel Caligiuri – started from the 11 that beat Borussia Dortmund 2-1 at the weekend.

Despite this, you could still tell, even from the warm-ups, that the Germans were a class apart and belonged in a different stratosphere to Hearts. At one point a loose ball from Callum Tapping, intended for a team-mate, ended up in the middle of the Wolfsburg half. Instead of just knocking the ball back, the shuttling Bundesliga players steadfastly refused to touch it, surveying it coldly and with deep suspicion. Perhaps this errant pass had deeply offended their precise Teutonic sensibilities, either way the ball just sat there, neglected, for the rest of the warm-up.

The game itself, despite finishing goalless, represented a decent workout, in much the same way as Scotland's international friendly with the USA (another 0-0) would also do later the same week. Adam King and Mark Ridgers made the starting line-up and Brad McKay returned for his first start since spending the whole of the away match at Killie skiting around on his arse.

Hearts more than held their own throughout. For reasons that extended beyond taste in music, barnet and tattoos, Ryan Stevenson did not look out of place in this company while, at the other end of the pitch, Mark Ridgers did his reputation no harm whatsoever, shutting out the sharp-shooting Germans.

In fact, there was only one genuine moment when his goal looked in serious danger of being breached – a 35th-minute penalty awarded by referee Brian Colvin for a nothing tackle by Danny Wilson on Caligiuri – and, for that, salvation arrived in the unlikely form of Jamie 'Roy Neary' Hamill.

Hammy, under the nose of an oblivious Colvin, sculpted a mound of soil on to the penalty spot, very much in the spirit of Richard Dreyfuss's character in *Close Encounters of the Third Kind*. Let's be clear here, this was an act of pure sabotage. Hamill had no intention of using his mound to contact extraterrestrials, even if, from Caligiuri's blazed effort, the ball had half a chance of making some new friends, exploding as it did deep into the cosmos.

You could tell Stevenson clearly fancied his chances from distance and as the wind whipped at his back he tested Grun as the half drew to a close.

Ridgers became the main focal point in the second half as Wolfsburg threatened to overwhelm Hearts. Willi Evseev and Das Bost were both spectacularly thwarted by the big keeper.

A flying McKay header from a Hamill cross offered brief respite with 20 minutes to go but it wasn't long before Wolfsburg had Ridgers in their sights again, Evseev racing clear before flashing a drive wide of the far post.

A subdued crowd of 5,535 helped raise much-needed funds although the word on Twitter, pre-match, had a break-even attendance of 8,000 leading many to conclude this match may ultimately have been a mild misjudgement: one fundraiser too many.

Perhaps the organisers had visions of a packed Tynecastle rocking as it had when the likes of VfB Stuttgart and Bayern Munich came to town. Sadly, this modest friendly was never going to arouse that same passion and intensity and the atmosphere was as far removed from those two nights as it was possible to be.

Furthermore, the rise in crowds both home and away was bound to have an impact on this game. Something had to give, yet you'd imagine the organisers would quite happily take this crowd if it means a few more thousand on the gate roaring us on to victory over Ross County.

17
Ross County home,
23 November 2013, 3pm

THE width of the crossbar deprived Hearts of a stoppage-time winner in this anxious, error-strewn yet endlessly compelling six-pointer at Tynecastle. Whenever Hearts come up against the teams closest to them in the table, the contest becomes as much about them conquering their own nerves and apparent compulsion to self-destruct as anything else. Against Ross County, a skittish Hearts side twice fell behind to pantomime goals before rallying and snatching a point with a late equaliser.

Tynecastle swelled with another highly impressive crowd of more than 12,000, although the Ross County contingent was so paltry I almost expected Scott Wilson to read out their names one by one after he'd finished going through the Staggies' first 11 and substitutes.

Jason Holt's popped fifth metatarsal opened the door for Callum Tapping in the only change from Pittodrie, Tapps slotting into central midfield alongside Jamie Hamill as Hearts went with 4-4-2 and a twin strike-force of Ryan Stevenson and Callum Paterson. Ross County had their own strapping double act up top of Melvin de Leeuw and Kevin Luckassen and they were assisted in this by a rather lost-looking Gary Glen. Whenever Glen comes back to Tynecastle he looks like a little kid who has been accidentally left behind at the nursery.

The early stages of the game were quite poor fare. At times it was as if the dimensions of the pitch were too small to accommodate that many outfield players. An ungainly struggle ensued with neither side capable of retaining possession for more than a few passes. It resembled one of those medieval re-enactments where the residents of some quaint English hamlet gather en masse to fight in a muddy ditch over a massive ball of Wensleydale.

Whenever the ball did emerge from the scrum Hearts looked the keener of the two sides and Jamie Walker sent in a shot from distance that drew appreciative gasps of 'ooooh' from the crowd despite it ending up closer to the corner flag.

As nerves slowly took hold Hearts no longer seemed to trust themselves to play out of defence, choosing instead to arrow the ball forward in the hope of finding Paterson. On 22 minutes these nerves finally caught up with the home side and their punishment was to go a goal down to an undeserving and disbelieving County.

Tapping, for reasons known only to himself, stole the ball off Hamill's toes, 20 yards out and, instead of playing a simple pass forward, attempted to trundle a pea-roller back towards right-back Jordan McGhee.

Unhappily for us, the ball ran straight to the feet of the lurking Graham Carey who advanced and swept the ball underneath Jamie MacDonald.

Falling behind seemed to focus Hearts' minds, firming up their passing, and from the restart Scott Robinson saw a textbook downward header, from a first-time Hamill cross, tipped away at the foot of the post by Mark Brown. Tynecastle was now in full voice and the increased levels of urgency in Hearts' movement, on and off the ball, meant players were better able to locate little pockets of space to exploit.

A number of corners were won to great fanfare only to be squandered. Ironically, from probably the worst of these deliveries, on 27 minutes, Hearts drew level. Robinson's badly scuffed effort barely had the legs to reach the edge of the box. Section G of the Wheatfield Stand were still articulating the finer points of their displeasure when Paterson repeated the trick he'd pulled for the Scotland Under-21s against Slovenia, the previous midweek, and found the net with a truly eye-catching, acrobatic volley.

During the goal celebrations Robinson felt the need to respond to the sporadic abuse he'd been receiving with a couple of internationally recognised hand gestures. While it's worth pointing out that the area around the corner spot *was* badly rutted – which can't have helped the delivery – and Robinson has emerged as something of a target for the boo-boys in recent weeks, it's difficult to see how these petulant little reactions can do him any favours.

Poorly engineered corner kicks notwithstanding, Robinson was definitely having one of his better days, stationed as he was wide on the right side of midfield. On the other side of the pitch, Jamie Walker was giving County plenty to think about. At one point their big, immobile defenders were lining up to obstruct him and knock him off balance. Richard Brittain eventually picked up a yellow from referee Crawford Allan for more or less dry-humping the Hearts number 14 as he beat him for pace.

Gaping fissures were now opening up defensively for Hearts as they sought to keep the momentum going and from a sudden breakaway Rocco Quinn unleashed a blur of a shot that thudded off the bar as MacDonald crouched, transfixed.

It was as if it somehow hadn't occurred to Hearts that Ross County might want their lead back and this sudden realisation had them visibly blanching. Jamie Hamill had some sort of mental aberration and attempted a back-pass even more suicidal than Tapping's, playing in Luckasson from around 40 yards out. The lanky Dutchman did his best to keep the attempt low but was denied by the onrushing MacDonald who blocked his strike.

It felt like half-time came at the right time for Hearts and down in the Gorgie Suite the hope for us was that Hearts had finally got all of those schoolboy errors out of their system. Four minutes after retaking our seats, though, this proved a mere pipe dream as County went ahead for the second time with a carbon copy of the same goal we've been conceding all season.

From a routine ball into the box countless opportunities to clear were spurned as the toothless Hearts defence stood off their opponents, dawdling ineffectually. It was as if they'd all come out for the second half accidently wearing flip-flops. After an age, de Leeuw was set up by Glen and found the far corner from the edge of the box.

As de Leeuw ran over to the tiny knot of away supporters, the Hearts defence stood in silence, almost paralysed with disbelief. Danny Wilson reacted first, venting his anger at Paterson and then giving him a hefty shove when the big striker refuted culpability.

Hearts still had 40 minutes to turn things around though and once again the pressing need for all-out attack appeared to liberate them, causing them to forget all about being nervy. To begin with the Staggies dealt ably with the challenge of keeping Hearts at bay. They broke up play via a highly effective combination of persistent, niggly fouling and shameless time-wasting.

However, by the hour mark, enough yellow cards had been brandished to make this destructive approach unsustainable and, with County suitably softened up, David Smith was brought on for Tapping as Hearts went 4-3-3.

Smith's link-up play and single-minded directness drew players towards him and, in attempting to bail out his over-stretched defenders, Brittain picked up a second yellow for hacking down Walker as he flew into the box.

It was one-way traffic all the way now and the only thing stopping Hearts from running over the top of County was the superb form of Brown in the County goal and he repeatedly denied Hearts with a string of top-class saves. He got down brilliantly to a fizzing Hamill strike and then denied Smith twice in quick succession, once from close range after he'd swivelled quickly and once from further out.

With only a matter of minutes left on the clock and the crowd on their feet willing Hearts on, an equaliser was finally found. Wilson's header from Smith's corner nudged off the post and into the net after passing through a cluster of bodies. In the chaotic celebrations that followed, the goal was mysteriously accredited to Stevenson but common sense eventually prevailed, allowing those clever punters at my table who'd backed Wilson as last scorer to get any monies they were due.

Having at last breached that obdurate County defence anything seemed possible and Hearts were immediately back on the offensive. In the dying embers of the game Paterson got his head to another Smith cross only to see the ball smash back off the bar as the supporters rose in unison.

The award of only three minutes' injury time seemed a trifle stingy given the second half had seen four substitutions, two goals, a sending off and two players booked for blatant time-wasting but, then again,

Iain Brines was the fourth official. Instead of griping about being short-changed we should just count our blessings no one used any foul language on the way up the tunnel.

After the late and lasting sting of the corresponding fixture back in September, it felt deeply gratifying to plunder a late equaliser here. Although, having said that, Paterson's near-miss in stoppage time, Brittain's sending off and the fact that both County goals came gift-wrapped in a big maroon bow, meant this point was very much bittersweet.

Nevertheless, it was enough to pull Hearts back to within 12 points of a moribund Kilmarnock. A point acknowledged rather sniffily in certain quarters, Paul Forsyth in *The Scotsman* and, latterly, Stephen Craigan on BT both making the point that after 13 games Hearts were now only three points closer to 11th spot than they had been when the season *began*.

You could argue that at least we're seeing movement in the right direction. It's not as if we are being cut adrift. We may be struggling to make inroads into the 15-point deficit but we're keeping pace with sides at the foot of the table which is significantly better than many thought we'd be capable of.

Celtic home, Scottish Cup fourth round, 1 December 2013, 3pm

DURING the build-up to this fourth round Scottish Cup tie at Tynecastle the general consensus was we'd either nick it 1-0 with a backs-to-the-wall, smash-and-grab type of performance with Jamie MacDonald playing an absolute stormer. Or we'd be well and truly annihilated. In the end it was the latter as Celtic went all 'Malmo' on our asses.

There's this amusing sequence in *Blackadder the Third* in which Edmund drop-kicks Mildred the cat down the stairs before confiding in Baldrick that this is merely the way of the world: the abused always kick downwards. Upstairs, the Prince Regent had laid into him, so he'd kicked the cat, the cat pounced on a mouse and the mouse bit Baldrick on the behind. We saw another manifestation of this truism on Sunday afternoon: Milan gave Celtic a good shoeing on Tuesday night so Celtic came through to Edinburgh a few days later and offloaded all that pent-up frustration on us.

It's well-nigh impossible to argue against the notion that Celtic ran riot at Tynecastle. That they did so against a defensively naïve, disorganised, hopelessly dispirited Hearts Under-20 side, makes a dewy-eyed Neil Lennon slavering on about football utopia faintly ridiculous to say the least.

Once Kris Commons struck the first a few minutes in it was glaringly obvious which side was going into the hat for the fifth round draw the following afternoon. As a supporter all I was now concerned with was (a) avoiding needless injuries and (b) the potential damage to morale if Celtic went supersize.

But, honestly now, was anyone at Hearts secretly coveting a nice long cup run? I mean, it wasn't as if we were ever actually candidates to win the thing this year, what with our threadbare bunch of bum-fluff desperadoes. It's becoming hard enough for Lockie to find enough bodies each week to fulfil the league commitments, let alone midweek cup replays and all that palaver.

A point painfully illustrated by Ryan Stevenson. Our talisman and main goal threat yanked his hamstring and spent the second half hobbling around on one leg, chasing a cause that had long since left the building. What good is he to us in the treatment room? Especially with the festive league programme *we* have looming on the horizon. It was mind-numbingly stupid of the coaching staff not to hook him. Instead, they just gawped on from the sidelines as he limped around throughout the majority of that charade of a match.

So, Hearts were picked apart, failing even to get the basics right and found themselves five down by half-time. Commons notched his second while Scott Brown, Joe Ledley and Mikael Lustig also got in on the act as Hearts wilted in the face of a supremely motivated Celtic side revelling in the role of flat-track bullies.

It had been such a starkly one-sided exercise, with the Hearts youngsters retreating into their shells, that it seemed inconceivable Lennon wouldn't give all those misfiring million-pound duds of his an airing in the second half in a vain attempt to kick-start their faltering Celtic careers. As it was, only the £2m wood elf, Pukki, got the opportunity to try and fill his reindeer-skin boots. The match may have been football utopia for Lennie but his costly Finn never got a sniff.

Willie Collum was back at Tynecastle also having refereed the league match between the two sides and he achieved the not-inconsiderable feat of emulating that abject performance back in September with yet another needlessly petty penalty award.

At 5-0 he penalised Danny Wilson for a handball that wouldn't have been possible, anatomically, for the Hearts skipper to have averted unless Adidas had decided, on a crazy whim, to add pockets to the home shorts as an optional extra.

Oddly enough, despite Collum adhering with almost puritanical zeal to his zero tolerance on what constitutes handball in the box, he eschewed that same fervent consistency when the issue of inciting the crowd after scoring a goal raised its shaven, pock-marked head.

In the League Cup quarter-final at Easter Road, Ryan Stevenson's cupped ear to the East Stand had incurred an instant rebuke from Collum. In fact he'd raced across to Stevo quicker than some of his team-mates and almost dropped his notebook and miniature pencil in his eagerness to administer the booking.

Therefore, you'd have imagined Scott Brown openly eyeballing and then goading the Hearts fans in the Gorgie Stand after scoring his side's third goal would have meant the simplest of calls for Collum to make: a literal and metaphorical no-brainer? Mystifyingly, however, he chose to turn a blind eye.

Anyhow, Commons converted the spot-kick, completing his hat-trick, and then Brown made it seven with 15 to go. And there endeth the scoring but not the internet-based baiting of Hearts fans which was only just getting warmed up. Most of it stemmed from deeply conflicted Hibs fans who were struggling to reconcile the paradox of actively ridiculing the very same side that, this season, has twice sent them packing.

Besides, for us, it had been a momentous week regarding our immediate and long-term future and it wasn't difficult to use the ramifications of Friday's creditors' meeting as a way of putting the defeat into its true context. Here, a major milestone had been reached with the

CVA being passed by 87 per cent majority. This was followed, an hour or so later, by the shareholders' vote which was passed by 100 per cent. Had either of these two votes failed to go to plan that match on Sunday could very possibly have been Hearts' last ever.

Yet, despite overwhelming relief at this best-possible outcome it went hand-in-hand with the instantly sobering caveat that the probable timescales for the next stages – securing the shares from Ubig, securing a sale and purchase agreement and then completing the deal within a set timescale – will likely mean us remaining in administration until March or possibly even April.

Suddenly the door was slammed shut on that faint hope we'd all been harbouring about reinforcements arriving in February. And seeing free agent Rudi Skacel sat in the main stand was a 'here's what you could have won' moment far more disheartening than any *Bullseye* speedboat.

Losing 7-0 at home to Celtic ultimately meant far more to those out-with Hearts than it did to anyone associated with the club. Graeme Spiers and Michael Stewart led the criticism. The former felt, despite everything, that Locke could be doing better while the latter described Hearts as shapeless, poorly coached and bereft of a recognisable playing style.

For us, it was pure and simple relief that we still have a team left to support and the rest will surely take care of itself.

19

Dundee United away,
7 December 2013, 3pm

TWO late goals skewed the result of this full-blooded encounter at Tannadice, giving the impression of a stroll in the swing-park for United's much-hyped Pampers' prodigies.

Yet for pretty much the entirety of the second half the outcome lay in the balance with each side's youthful attack gleefully terrorising the opposition defenders. As the game drew to a close, however, Hearts struggled to sustain an increasingly ragged push for the equaliser and were caught out by Mackay-Steven (84) and Rankin (90) who applied the gloss to a final score of 4-1.

Visiting Tannadice in its present incarnation is the footballing equivalent of becoming Facebook friends with a little minx from your schooldays and discovering she's now a yummy mummy in Deirdre Barlow specs who's married to a prematurely balding bank manager and proceeds to clog up your newsfeed with tips on jam-making. I mean, time really has not been kind to the place.

A fourth-round Scottish Cup tie here in February 1984 represented my first away game and, as a wide-eyed 15-year-old, it felt like a rite of passage: crammed on to a precipitous, narrow-stepped terrace, teetering on the tips of my toes as the crowd swayed and ebbed like a giant single entity. All the while, at the mesh of the segregation barrier, police hats were being scattered akimbo as supporters surged and baited each other under a barrage of whirring projectiles.

I'm not going all Cass Pennant here and advocating a nostalgia-fuelled return to those dark, terrifying days but surely there's a happy medium to be found. The Tannadice of today is an atmosphere vacuum. It's a pale imitation of that wonderfully evocative, steep-sloped coliseum. It's a place where it isn't enough that the hosts bag a few goals against you, but where they feel compelled to add to your misery by playing 'Love Is In The Air' by John Paul Young after every goal.

And the supporters just seem heavily sedated, borderline mute. They roused themselves ever so slightly when the teams emerged from the tunnel with a drowsy chant of 'United, United!' and then, suddenly noticing we'd all arrived and packed out both tiers of our half of the Jerry Kerr stand, followed it with 'you're going down with the Dundee'. But even that felt a bit half-hearted and pointless. Are we? But you can see them getting promoted, no? But never mind, thanks for trying.

United began with all the irritating precociousness of an 11-year-old games whizz nonchalantly running rings around you on FIFA14. Yet, for all their smoothness of touch and intuitive movement, there was a rawness and vulnerability about them and Hearts quickly realised there was no need to feel overawed.

Ryan Gauld had to have been feeling the eyes of those Liverpool and Everton scouts boring into him whenever the ball came close. Up until the 12th minute he'd been buzzing around impressively but getting the grand sum of nowhere, like a chubby hamster on a giant wheel. But a dipping volley from distance changed all that. Jamie MacDonald was happy to back-pedal furiously and tip his effort to safety.

As is Hearts' wont this season they never adequately cleared their lines from the resultant corner and, despite spirited appeals for offside, United went ahead. Gary Mackay-Steven scooped a sumptuous ball over the top for Stuart Armstrong to run on to. Despite being credited with the goal the ball looked to have eventually been bundled over the line by a combination of Brian Graham and Kevin McHattie.

Dundee United's lead would remain intact for a mere five minutes, though, as Jamie Walker cut in from the left and was cynically chopped down in the box by Mark Wilson. An icy cool Jamie Hamill puffed his chest out slightly further than usual and sent Radoslaw Cierzniak the wrong way, rolling the ball ever so gently into the bottom corner.

The remainder of the first half saw Walker become a magnet for the ball, tying the overworked, retreating United defenders in knots. In the end they resorted to taking it in turns to hack him down and both John Souttar and Mackay-Steven took him out in full flow.

Worryingly, referee Craig Thompson seemed largely unperturbed by this turn of events, failing even to speak to Mackay-Steven. Unchecked, United flew into tackles with even more abandon and Gauld got away with a studs-up lunge at Walker that saw him require lengthy treatment, as well as a sneaky shove on Paterson.

United made a conscious effort to up the tempo after the restart and John Rankin unleashed one of his patented squigglers from distance that was punched away spectacularly by the flying MacDonald. But United wouldn't be denied and direct from the corner Graham sent a header crashing into the roof of the net.

However, as the ball floated in, Sean Dillon had deliberately stepped across Callum Paterson as he'd sought to pick Graham up, in what *Sportscene*'s Mikey Stewart referred to darkly as a 'training ground routine'. Neither Jonathan Sutherland nor Stuart Lovell seemed to know what to say to this so Mikey elaborated, 'I mean, it's definitely a free kick but Paterson could be a bit cuter there and avoid the contact.'

Only Paterson really knows whether or not he could have dodged Dillon's close-range block but the only reason this was even a topic for discussion was because the officials missed a blatant infringement right under their noses. And, when you think we were denied a perfectly legitimate goal in the corresponding fixture at Tynecastle due to an assistant flagging for an infringement that was a figment of his imagination, it just adds to the frustration.

The tone was now set and Paterson saw out the match engaged in a more-or-less constant dialogue with the assistant on the near side, repeatedly chipping away at him, occasionally breaking off to try and get his head on to one of MacDonald's plummeting clearances but then jogging back across to finish whatever point it was he was making. 'Aye, where was I now…?'

Also in keeping with the match at Tynecastle, the second half saw both sides open up and the attacks swung from end to end like a pendulum. United's dazzling array of attacking starlets made this a high-risk policy but in recent weeks Walker has shown himself to be a rare talent and he was desperate to get on the ball as much as possible.

After receiving even more treatment after another unpunished foul, around the hour mark, he picked the ball up and drove fearlessly down the left wing. Confronted by Paul Paton and Mark Wilson, the marauding Hearts winger darted nimbly between the two of them only to be clipped and sent spinning by Wilson. As the former Celtic full-back put his hands to his head fearing a second yellow, Thompson came lolloping over, his ungainly knee-bouncing scamper inadvertently parodying the Craig Beattie©, and flashed a yellow card for simulation in Walker's aggrieved face.

Commentator John Barnes was fairly unequivocal in his appraisal, 'On first viewing I thought he was impeded.' Although this was as far as the biting analysis went as the incident was steadfastly ignored by Jonathan Sutherland and the pullover crew.

With 20 minutes to go Hearts began to run out of legs and the frequency of the United attacks grew. While Walker began to labour and Ryan Stevenson was seriously curtailed by his tightening hamstring, you could see Mackay-Steven and Gauld, at the other end of the pitch, licking their lips at all the space. The only thing keeping Hearts in the game, at this point, was the young duo's touchingly idealistic desire to score the perfect goal.

Hearts had one last chance to nab an equaliser on 81 minutes when Walker was upended for the umpteenth time. However, from the free kick tight on the touchline at the corner of the box, it came as no surprise whatsoever to see a woeful attempt at a cross dribble out of play on the far side.

Cursed annoyance at our repeated and wholly avoidable wastefulness from set pieces was still suspended in a speech bubble above our heads as United broke away from the throw-in and finally got their third goal. Mackay-Steven combined almost telepathically with Gauld before checking inside and rifling a sweet left-footed strike high past the diving MacDonald. The goal had been coming and, having finally secured it, United were keen to add a fourth, giving them four goals in four consecutive home games for the first time since 1936, apparently.

Rankin obliged, although for a player who takes such pride in hammering home spectacular goals from distance it was at least gratifying to see it was a scrappy, deflected effort that barely even reached the back of the net.

Pathetically scant consolation, I know, but Kilmarnock's victory up at Ross County made it a weekend of criminally small mercies.

20

Inverness Caledonian Thistle home, 14 December 2013, 3pm

INVERNESS Caledonian Thistle arrived at a wind-blown capital with a new yet familiar face at the helm. Terry Butcher had vacated his Highland berth, tempted over to the dark side of Edinburgh, and bequeathed his ancient stone bonnet to John Hughes. Yogi is nothing if not consistent, peddling his 'big daft laddie fi' Leith' schtick like an old pro with ill-fitting dentures and a dicky hip returning to the London Palladium for one last hurrah.

Brucey has his 'nice to see you', 'you get nothing for a pair' and 'keep dancing' whereas Yogi holds court with his time-honoured staples of 'you ken me', 'you could'nae meet a more honest bunch ay boys' and 'end ay the day it's aw aboot the shree points'.

The freakish weather had put paid to a few fixtures over the weekend as gales ravaged Scotland. At kick-off the playing arena resembled one of those sci-fi movies in which the airlock has been breached causing the stricken inhabitants of some intergalactic space station to get whisked around violently and then sucked at speed towards a gaping air vent.

In hindsight, Hearts probably picked the wrong day to start with a couple of lightweights in the side with Gary Oliver up front and Sam Nicholson on the right of midfield. There was a distinct danger of either or both ending up snagged on the roof of the main stand or clinging to a piece of driftwood in the Firth of Forth.

A further change saw Jamie Hamill relieved of his midfield duties and shunted to right-back with Jordan McGhee benched. Back in July, Hamill had begun pre-season at full-back only for it to become obvious it wasn't really for him and to the relief of most people he was relocated into midfield where, to be fair, he'd shone for a few games under Paulo Sergio in 2012.

It can be taken as an indication of how far Jamie's stock has fallen of late that it felt like a blessed relief to see him restored to full-back. Back there, he stuck impressively to his task in what were hugely trying conditions. It was then typical of the way this season is panning out for Hearts that his one and only gaffe was pounced upon by the devastatingly prolific Billy McKay and in an instant the game was gone.

After an uneventful first half there had been genuine hope for the second yet, on 58 minutes, Hearts lost that ever-so-crucial first goal. Scott Robinson wanted way too much time on the ball, midway inside his own half, and it came as no shock to see him quickly dispossessed.

The ball found its way to Marley Watkins who looked up and saw a gaping chasm on the right of the Hearts defence as a sleepy-looking

Hamill looked to have momentarily forgotten he was playing full-back. He'd drifted inside and was sitting in front of Dylan McGowan, so by the time Watkins guided the ball into the feet of McKay, on the left of the box, he was stranded, hopelessly out of position.

McKay has pure ice running through his veins and as Hamill threw himself back across to make the block, the ICT number seven coolly shifted the ball from left foot to right and swept it nonchalantly into the far corner with his instep.

A task that was testing enough at 0-0 suddenly got a whole lot harder against a miserly defence that had only conceded three goals at home and eight on its travels all season. Hearts sought to freshen up the attack with first Billy King and then Dale Carrick coming on for the clearly shattered Nicholson and Oliver, respectively.

However, the combination of ICT's clever organisation and rapier speed on the counter-attack proved too rich for Hearts and from a breakaway McKay made it two on 83 minutes, rifling the ball high past MacDonald.

So another game falls by the wayside. Another fixture eyed eagerly from afar yields the sum total of zero points and we remain, cut adrift, on minus three. For as long as the team(s) immediately above us keep on tripping up, earning our side barely earned reprieves, the table won't allow all hope to be lost. Yet, as the weeks pass, any notion that Hearts might feature in the SPL fixture list next July becomes ever more fanciful.

Against ICT, as is so often the case, it was the small margins that dismantled us. Virtually every game we play is tight for long periods, with the outcome hanging in the balance, so it can really take very little to derail us: a defender switching off for a nanosecond here, a striker failing to look up there, an unfathomable refereeing decision, well, pretty much everywhere.

All of which can be attributable, to a lesser or greater degree, to a group of callow youngsters who are being thrust into the limelight week in, week out, irrespective of form and niggling injuries. A group suffering from a combination of burn-out, loss of confidence and a coaching staff perhaps not properly equipped to get the best out of them.

In particular, we seem to struggle defensively. Apparently we have Robbo coaching the strikers or, more accurately, coaching Callum Paterson. How about a volunteer or two to coach the defence? A quick trawl around the Gorgie Suite on any match day and you're bound to run into at least a couple of former Hearts defenders. I'm sure these guys would relish going through a few defensive drills a couple of afternoons a week. 'Boil some black coffee, sober them up, find them a couple of tracksuits and get them out there, come on, we're not licked yet…!'

Because, we are simply crying out for organisation to come from somewhere. We repeatedly switch off and lose opposition players in the box. For heaven's sake, Kris Boyd is due in town on Boxing Day! With his knack of finding space in the box he's probably already practising goal celebrations in his full-length mirror at home, working out which two or three look best.

And, of course, against someone as good as McKay, such naivety and poor positional play was always going to be punished, it was just a matter of when. He was like a squat little vulture perched high above a busy highway, biding his time before swooping down on the inevitable roadkill.

Unless we learn to cope with the smarter strikers this league possesses we'll struggle to pick up any more points. As Billy Dodds put it so aptly on *Sportscene*, 'You don't leave a striker **that** sort of space in front of goal.'

He sounded mildly exasperated. We know how he feels.

18
Celtic away,
21 December 2013, 12.15pm

AFTER my last visit to Celtic Park, back in the mid-1980s, I'd more or less vowed never to set foot in the infernal place again. Prior to that fateful trip it had always been the train for us, so when our coach driver reached his destination earlier than planned and mistakenly parked up in the still empty home car park, we had no way of knowing that a) this was the *wrong* car park and b) he'd up sticks and move to the correct place immediately upon realising the error of his ways.

Anyway, a quintessentially Celtic end to this midweek showdown had seen the hosts come from two down to pilfer the win courtesy of a hotly-disputed 96th-minute pea-roller from Brian McClair. In the darkness and ensuing chaos at full time we fought our way out and found ourselves mingling, inexplicably, with crowds of jubilant Celtic fans getting on to their buses. Thankfully, after retracing our steps, a couple of kindly Bhoys noticed our predicament and ushered us discreetly in the direction of the away buses.

However, on discovering said strip of barren wasteland, we stumbled into hordes of Celtic fans pelting the departing Hearts fans and their buses with a deluge of masonry. A number of coaches were already beginning to pull away, their windows smashed in, meaning we had little option but to move as quickly as possible through the brick-throwing mob.

We were fending off Celtic fans – grabbing at us and swinging punches in our direction – all the while ducking as every now and again a retreating Hearts fan would lob the odd half-brick back at their aggressors. Eventually, soaked in sweat and out of breath, we located our bus and clambered gratefully aboard, noting a fair quantity of Hearts fans nursing bloody head wounds.

In truth, I needn't have worried. The landscape of Scottish football has altered dramatically since those days. Glaswegian stand-up Kevin Bridges put it best, reflecting that our much-maligned two-horse race can now best be characterised as 'showjumping'.

With Rangers still lurking in the shadows, you get the sense that none of these home games actually means anything anymore. Previously, Celtic would always be mega-paranoid about letting their guard down, even for a split second, lest a momentary lapse be seized upon greedily by their ugly sister from across the city. All of which lent an unmistakably rabid air to proceedings. Now, however, unchallenged, the home fire no longer burns in their bellies.

Of course, the pyrotechnics-obsessed hardcore away support continue to whoop it up on the road, ruffling feathers and bending plastic seating as they go but at home all you are left with are bloated, disinterested hosts.

On Saturday, my seat had me tight against the flimsy strip of high-vis ticker tape that passes for segregation in these parts but all that my proximity to the Celtic fans put me in mind of was a visit to the zoo, just after the lions have had their bi-weekly feed.

During gaps in the play I'd steal the odd glance across at my apathetic, complacent counterparts as they yawned, picked distractedly at their teeth and checked their phones to see how Liverpool were getting on at home to Cardiff.

As their side clunked jerkily through the gears, the sparse Celtic support, scattered disparately throughout their hulking stadium, barely flinched. Their side may ultimately have inched tediously closer to yet another hollow title with their pedestrian 2-0 win, yet they were insufficiently moved even to offer a token nod to our predicament, to us 'dyin' with the Rangers' as they are wont to put it. At the Tynecastle Scottish Cup tie three weeks ago they had been, quite literally, falling over themselves to inform us of this fact and, of course, 'what a shitey home support' we were. Well, quite.

Celtic's undeniably vast superiority meant that for perhaps the first time this season, Hearts went purely for damage limitation. Dylan McGowan was stationed in front of the back four and his transformation from shaky centre-back to reliable midfield enforcer had echoes of Darren Barr. Jamie Walker and David Smith had orders to doggedly track back to double up with their full backs so it was left to Callum Paterson to hunt down lost causes and harry defenders.

You know that for your side to successfully grind out a point in such improbable circumstances, it'll take a number of things to go your way: a supremely committed effort; your goalkeeper to be truly inspired; decent portions of luck; and a referee that doesn't just play it safe and give all the borderline calls to the hosts.

There was no doubt that the first two could readily be ticked off. Callum Tapping went monobrow to monobrow with Scott Brown and his impressive smothering of the Celtic captain had echoes of another successfully-shackled monobrow Celtic skipper: Paul McStay nullified by Chuck Berry.

With Brown constantly being harassed and forced to check back, much of Celtic's attacking verve came down the wings with Emilio Izaguirre on one side and Kris Commons on the other. Their treacherous deliveries into the box meant Jamie MacDonald was under intense pressure right from the first whistle.

Luckily for us, MacDonald matched his masterful League Cup quarter-final performance and pulled off a flurry of barely believable saves. At one point Anthony Stokes paused to nod appreciatively as a reflex save from Jamma saw the ball tipped on to angle of crossbar and post from eight yards.

A save from a similar range courtesy of a Joe Ledley diving header had the tiny knot of Hearts fans squirrelled away in the deepest, darkest recess of the ground desperately believing this might be one we could somehow tough out.

The second half produced more of the same as Hearts strung themselves across the pitch to close down space and Celtic enjoyed 74 per cent possession. MacDonald was still being called into more-or-less constant action and somehow got his hand to a blistering Commons drive after the Celtic man had spun cleverly in the box.

On 63 minutes, though, Celtic finally earned a breakthrough that their half-asleep fans could barely even be bothered to acknowledge. No one could say it hadn't been coming but after standing up so resolutely to everything Celtic could muster and on a day where we were so down to the bare bones that we couldn't even fill our bench, it rankled somewhat that the goal came from a throw-in that TV clearly showed should have gone our way.

Still, at only 1-0 we'd all seen enough football matches to know that even the most dominant of sides can be susceptible to a sucker punch. Therefore, we were kept clinging to the faintest of hopes when MacDonald acrobatically fingertipped a Ledley shot from inside the six-yard box on to the post and away for another corner.

Just how right we were to stay with our side and stay hopeful was evidenced in stoppage time as McGowan flashed a header goalwards from a Smith corner, only to see Commons stoop and head it off the line.

It was clear there and then that the points were gone and Forrest's finish at the death barely registered as we began moving towards the exit.

22

Kilmarnock home,
26 December 2013, 3pm

THIS truly was a Boxing Day horror show from Hearts. A quietly effective Kilmarnock side couldn't believe their luck as Hearts produced a horrendously inept performance, shipping four goals without reply.

Throughout the season Hearts have persisted with this embarrassingly unimaginative ploy from the kick-off that sees the ball laid back for Jamie Hamill to scan the middle distance intently like a pro golfer before skying a delicate hoof in the vague direction of the shambling Callum Paterson, advancing up the far touchline. The hope being, presumably, that a fight over the scraps resulting from Paterson's flick-on will lead to possession being gained further up the pitch. Come to think of it, it's more like rugby than golf.

One of three things usually happens. Firstly, we see Hamill's punt float directly out of play meaning that if it's a Tynecastle game and Hearts have won the toss the ball sails invariably into the arms of a grim-faced Gary Locke, already fearing the worst. Or, since there are as yet undiscovered tribes in the Amazonian rainforest that are aware of Hearts' tendency to start halves this way, Paterson is summarily outjumped by the tallest player in the opposition ranks who'd sprinted over immediately after Hamill had shaped to send over his punt. And, finally, you have probably the best case scenario whereby Paterson does indeed get his head to the ball as planned but seeing as we've just kicked off no Hearts player is within ten feet of him and the opposition are gifted possession.

So not only do we have a resoundingly fruitless yet horribly apt way for us to begin the half it now appears we're increasingly extending this approach to encapsulate our whole footballing ethos. When the onus is on this Hearts side to go out and seek to win games it's as if they can't get rid of the ball quickly enough.

Throughout a desperately disappointing contest Danny Wilson, Brad McKay, Kevin McHattie, Jamie MacDonald, Jamie Hamill (and then Dylan McGowan after Gowser moved from midfield to replace Hamill at full-back) all took it in turns to launch punts in the direction of Paterson, deep into Killie territory, as their team-mates charged forward in the hope of scrapping over a loose ball and regaining possession higher up the pitch.

Who knows, maybe Billy Brown is unable to shake the memory of how effectively this ploy worked back when it was Kevin Kyle receiving the ball but expecting C-Patz to bear the brunt of the attack subtracts massive amounts of credibility from our coaching team.

As Paterson's role in the side regresses week by week, so too does his ability to perform even the most rudimentary of tasks. On the opening day of last season, at home to St Johnstone, Paterson was your quintessential, modern-day, buccaneering right-back, surging up and down the touchline for fun and smashing opposition players into the air like they were skittles.

He even found time to crack a 35-yard free kick off the top of the bar for good measure. You left Tynecastle that day wondering if there was anything this kid couldn't do.

Fast forward 18 months and you're left with a shell of a man, a broken, hulking figure whose role in the side has been distilled down to attempting to get his head on to a succession of hurried hoofs leathered in his direction and haring after lost causes like a fretful Great Dane chasing a stick.

And as the cavalry sprints upfield to compete for his flick-on, the opposition pluck the ball back like school bullies relieving a bespectacled swot of his dinner money. One semi-decent ball over the top is generally all it takes and Hearts are undone. We must be the only side in the SPL that are actually at their most vulnerable when the ball is rolled back to their own goalkeeper or is at the feet of one of the full-backs.

Twitter has been awash with furious debate this week concerning the future or otherwise of Gary Locke. Some are adamant that Lockie needs to be relieved of his duties forthwith and, for the sake of argument, an SOS sent out to Craig Levein who has been seen prowling around in the background.

Yet the fact remains our players are spent. The season is beginning to take its toll on Hearts and the players are visibly running on empty. Would a fresh face in the dugout galvanise a set of players that seem almost broken by events at their club?

I'd love to see where, in the legislation regarding clubs entering administration, it mentions the potential lasting damage incurred by young players as they flog themselves to the bone because their side has been deprived of bringing in any replacements for injuries. It's becoming harder and harder to see how that specific punishment relates in any way whatsoever to a Russian megalomaniac with a penchant for overspending. That it took place in the same building or buildings seems the long and short of it.

Quite frankly it's a bizarre state of affairs that sees a bunch of under-20s carry the can for a doomed Russian's tenure. There's nothing left of Romanov to punish at Tynecastle so those left behind are, in essence, taking the punishment for him.

Of course, no one's disputing that entering administration requires a punishment but it would actually have been less draconian to simply have fast-tracked the newly revised punishment and relegated Hearts straight off, as opposed to forcing them to flog senseless a skeleton staff of under-20s until they stumble bleary-eyed into oblivion.

Increasingly, both are amounting to more or less the same thing. The only thing stopping Hearts being cut adrift and embracing relegation is the intermittently dire form of first Kilmarnock and St Mirren and now Ross County.

Aggravatingly, in games against Hearts, these three sides have risen to the challenge and, with the exception of a paltry point from Ross County, all have taken maximum points from games against us. Kilmarnock continued this trend with a thumping 4-0 victory which could, in truth, have reached seven or eight. As Kris Boyd tucks into his left-over turkey he must still be wondering how on earth he only managed two goals against such a dreadfully poor side. Chris Johnston and Rory McKenzie completed the scoring.

Next up is St Mirren again and it's impossible to see what can stop this trend, especially considering their 4-1 win over Dundee United on Boxing Day. After we lost 2-0 at Celtic Park on 21 December Billy Dodds reckoned it would take a minor miracle to save us as it was just too much to ask.

Replace the word minor with the words ridiculously enormous and you've got where we now are.

23
St Mirren away,
29 December 2013, 3pm

TAKING my seat at New St Mirren Park put me in mind of happier times. The last time I ventured through here it was to see Hearts win a Scottish Cup quarter-final replay en route to that epic 2012 final. That electric March evening, Jamie Hamill made a stunning contribution, blasting home from long range, and on Sunday he emulated that with an even more powerful strike to grab a point for a much-improved Hearts side.

In the sombre aftermath of that Boxing Day debacle at home to Killie, Lockie spoke of his team's need to compete better, to make more tackles, to get closer to the opposition and to want the ball despite confidence being at a low ebb.

For St Mirren, it had been an über-relaxed Danny Lennon who'd entertained the press during the pre-match build-up. On the morning of the game he'd popped up in the *Scotland on Sunday* sounding unnervingly like David Brent as he'd noted sagely, 'If you don't like what you see in the mirror, don't blame the mirror.' You can just see the interviewer taking a moment to properly digest the sheer profundity of this little philosophical nugget and Lennon simply nodding knowingly before whispering to a member of the groundstaff, 'Go and get the guitar.'

The early signs were less than promising for Hearts with more Keystone Cops defending on show. Our infuriating knack of making a complete hash of clearing corner kicks resurfaced for the umpteenth time. Danny Wilson, Callum Paterson and Brad McKay all managed to get in each other's way and, within two minutes, Steven Thompson had tucked the ball away.

This had ominous undertones for Hearts and the worry was we'd again see the players abdicating responsibility and failing to show for the ball. Compelling our defenders to lump it long to no one in particular. We'd lost our last five games, scoring one, conceding 19, and confidence was shot. Yet, in spite of St Mirren having the lead and the lion's share of possession, Hearts stood up to the challenge and made it crystal clear they wouldn't buckle.

Callums Tapping and Paterson both picked up yellow cards for over-zealous tackles as Hearts took Lockie at his word, straining every sinew to close the opposition down. It was a marked improvement from the Killie game where their players always seemed to have ample time to unhurriedly bring the ball down and leisurely pick a pass.

Hearts had Ryan Stevenson back in the side after that partial hamstring tear he'd aggravated up at Tannadice and his return was used as an opportunity to drop Paterson back into midfield. Therefore, Stevo led the line alongside Jamie Walker while Paterson and Hamill steamed around centre-midfield barging into people.

As the first half wore on St Mirren were forced to rush their passes as Hearts really got in their faces and as a result the Edinburgh side saw more of the ball. It's hard not to overstate the role Stevenson played in helping retain possession: his expertise in hold-up play and his unselfish running showed exactly what we'd been lacking in recent weeks.

If St Mirren had shaded the first half despite only forcing Jamie MacDonald into making one genuine save – from Jason Naismith – after scoring, Hearts more or less bossed the entire second and can count themselves unfortunate not to have claimed all three points.

After the break, Paterson was pushed closer to Stevenson as their 4-4-2 was subtly tweaked to be closer to 4-3-3 and the transformation in C-Patz was inescapable. No longer was he a demoralised and lumbering target man, forlornly chasing his own flick-ons. With Stevo by his side he was emboldened and a true colossus, winning everything in the air.

A familiar face from yesteryear, goalkeeper Marian Kello, was in the St Mirren ranks and received a hero's welcome when he strolled over for the start of the second half, even swinging good-naturedly from the crossbar in response to pleas from the Hearts fans. In all honesty he'd looked all over the place in the first half, shanking three clearances into the west stand and seriously under-hitting a fourth.

Like many, I was clinging to the vague hope that all this heartfelt emotion might mess with his head and adversely affect his performance. Not make him doubt where his loyalties lay or anything soppy like that, just perhaps take the edge off his concentration levels. Unfortunately, instead of doing a Skacel, Kello went the other way, seemingly inspired by his rapturous ovation and every cross he came for stuck in those Behält gloves.

Yet, despite impressing, I doubt he even saw Hearts' equaliser. From an unconvincing headed clearance the ball bounced up invitingly into the path of Hamill just outside the box and with desperate howls imploring him to shoot still hanging in the air, he stepped imperiously forward and arrowed a booming right-footed volley unerringly into the top corner.

In the ensuing mayhem of the goal celebration I remember being mildly irritated that Hamill saw fit to shush us. I felt, all things considered, we were all being quite supportive. But, then, Jamie drop-kicked the hoardings and did this pretty sinister, stiff, slow-motion goose-step, his arms pinned rigidly to his sides and his chest puffed out like a bull frog and the shushing was instantly forgotten. Clearly the boy wasn't of sound mind.

The side were feeding off the deafening support from the packed stand behind the goal. St Mirren were hustled and mugged at every turn and only referee Kevin Clancy, taking pity on the Buddies and awarding them a spate of ridiculously soft free kicks, disrupted Hearts' rhythm and kept St Mirren from being overrun completely. In a ten-minute spell Hearts won a string of corners and Stevenson, Scott Robinson and Walker all fired in shots that had Kello scrambling.

The combination of Hearts snapping into St Mirren and the fussiness of Clancy saw Dylan McGowan, Robinson and Stevenson's names join the two Callums in the referee's book and the worry was that in maintaining this high-intensity pressing game we'd lose a player.

St Mirren fought back. Jim Goodwin saw a net-bound effort smash off the raised arm of Brad McKay. The Hearts defender was a matter of inches away and the award would have been incredibly harsh. However, so far this season, referees have been quick to penalise us with these. Our skewed perception of what now constitutes handball made us pathetically grateful for the reprieve.

Visibly irked, St Mirren stepped up the pace and Conor Newton, who'd run Hearts ragged at Tynecastle, dribbled unchallenged from right to left before shooting, mercifully, straight at MacDonald. There has been so much late drama and heartache this season that it was impossible not to watch these late pivotal exchanges without a sick feeling in the pit of your stomach.

On 85 minutes Darren McGregor headed just wide and from the opposite end of the ground it was one of those moments where you quietly hold your breath and grimace, waiting for the net to shimmer like gossamer in the floodlights.

But, from there on in, Hearts just pushed St Mirren further and further back and by the time the board went up they were reduced to jabbering wrecks, tripping over their feet, booting the ball straight up in the air and over-hitting back-passes that the scurrying, over-stretching Kello was helpless to reach to cheers of triumph from an eternally optimistic Hearts support.

From one such corner, in the first minute of stoppage time, Stevo improvised brilliantly and hooked a shot over his shoulder. Kello was caught totally unawares but, unfortunately for Hearts, the ball dropped just the wrong side of the post.

We knew we'd get one more chance, it had been that sort of match, and St Mirren seemed powerless to do anything other than see out stoppage time resolutely defending their 18-yard line. And so it was, right at the death, that substitute David Smith ran clear on the right and swept the ball across the six-yard line and into the path of Paterson who was bombing into the area at breakneck speed.

It had goal written all over it. Paterson slid in, making clean enough contact but somehow Kello, at full stretch, got to the shot, pulling off a quite miraculous save before clutching at the loose ball as it rolled tantalisingly free. Then, a few seconds later, the final whistle sounded and Kello – still clutching the ball – turned and took the acclaim of the whole Hearts end, clearly touched by the sporting and gracious reaction to his last-gasp heroics.

So, as with the last match where we picked up a point, Ross County at home on 23 November, an effort at the death from Paterson came within a whisker of nicking us all three points. Our erstwhile opponents that day lost 1-0 at Aberdeen, pulling us to within 13 points. If we follow today's point with an equally dire run of form, we are, without doubt, doomed.

However, if we can take this form into the next couple of eminently winnable matches, against Hibernian and Partick, and do all we can to keep Ryan Stevenson fit, then the fight goes on and we most certainly keep on believing.

24

Hibernian away,
2 January 2014, 7.45pm

HIBS fans turned up in their droves for this Easter Road showdown convinced it was finally safe enough for them to scuttle out from behind their sofas and snap up their full quota of tickets for an Edinburgh derby. And, although they emerged, full of gloating triumphalism, their narrow 2-1 win against a leg-weary and depleted Hearts side represented the hollowest of victories. The expectation had been that their side would administer a long-overdue thrashing yet the reality proved very different as Hearts made them sweat every inch of the way.

In the eye of the maelstrom, our valiant young side held firm and produced yet another desperately brave performance. That this seismic effort, once again, fell agonisingly short of compensating for the glaring gulf in experience had much to do with the sheer brute force of Hibs and the latest in a never-ending cavalcade of officials hell-bent on showing our side as little mercy as humanly possible. At Easter Road it was the turn of charmless slaphead Bobby Madden. His uncanny resemblance to Howard Webb surely more than simple coincidence and suggestive of more than a few stolen moments perfecting mannerisms in front of the mirror, Sky+ paused and flickering in the background.

Another sell-out Hearts support amassed in the south stand, brought down to Lochend on a wave of blind optimism and resolute defiance. Despite facing insurmountable odds it would have seemed like a dereliction of duty to have abandoned our players now, in their hour of need. Besides, the Hearts fans had no wish to give their smirking counterparts the satisfaction of seeing us divided, scattered in misery and disarray. If we are to go down it'll be with our heads held high and without recrimination.

This match afforded us our first look at this wonderful, new-look Hibs. Certainly, Butcher has got the old Echodome® rocking once again with his affable nature, supercharged work ethic and that weird staring thing he does with his eyes. However, the harsh reality for Hibs is that 'butchball' is about as far removed from the beautiful game as you can get without going the whole hog and switching to an egg-shaped ball.

Throughout these recent decades of maroon domination, the Hibs support have clung to this creepily narcissistic perception of themselves as these anti-establishment warrior poets. To them, the Hibernian way stood for some kind of merrie and twinkling band of romantic bohemians, playing the game the way it was supposed to be played. Happier losing 4-3 than drawing 0-0 just so long as George McCluskey or Derek Riordan or some other misunderstood and flawed genius got to stroll around enigmatically with his shirt outside his shorts, his brow furrowed in existential angst.

Latterly, this was modified to encompass the idea that they were the very antithesis of those amoral Jambos with their Russian overlord and their debt. This gave them a feeling of moral rectitude and empowerment. Their catalogue of derby despair, culminating in the 5-1, didn't make them downtrodden victims. No, *they* were making a principled stance.

That dreamily stylised view of themselves and their beloved side was probably able to withstand 45 minutes, tops, of good, old-fashioned 'butchball' before shrivelling away to nothing. His direct and unapologetically robust route one stylings must have acted as *Clockwork Orange*-esque aversion therapy for any of those sleepwalking Hibbies still fantasising about Latapy, Sauzee, Stanton and Cropley.

At every available opportunity and from quite literally any point on the pitch, the laws of 'butchball' dictate that players are compelled to bombard the opposition goalmouth and the higher you can hoof the ball en route the better. In the first half, from behind Jamie MacDonald's goal, it was like watching the orcs march on Helm's Deep in *Lord of the Rings*.

Ironically, this played right into Hearts' hands. Danny Wilson was a last-minute omission due to a nasty bout of tonsillitis so Brad McKay and Dylan McGowan paired up at centre-back. Being entrenched, facing a barrage of hoofed balls, probably suited them better than Hibs taking the game to Hearts on the deck and trying to pick holes in that makeshift defence.

Certainly, in the League Cup tie between the two sides back in October, the hopelessly derided Pat Fenlon had his side moving the ball swiftly into wide areas and they tore Hearts completely to pieces. It was only a sublime goalkeeping performance from Jamma that night which stopped Hibs going in at the break three or four goals to the good.

Whereas here, the closest Hibs came to scoring in a positively attritional first half were a couple of looping headers. One came off the shoulder of Jordan Forster and bounced off the top of the bar and the other from Jason Cummings saw Jamie tip the ball over. The rest of the time Hearts held firm, flinging themselves in the way of any shots when knock-downs dropped favourably to men in green and white.

In actual fact, the clearest opportunity for a goal came for Hearts. Callum Paterson controlled a Kevin McHattie pass high on his chest, his back to play wide on the left. He swivelled adroitly, nutmegged Michael Nelson and then curled in a superb left-footed cross. It was slightly unfortunate for us that the chance fell to an out-of-sorts Callum Tapping whose unconvincing half-volley was pushed out by Ben Williams.

The second half saw more of the same. The aim seemed to be to get the balls right in on top of Jamie MacDonald who is as proficient a shot-stopper as you'll find anywhere in the league but lacks the physical presence to ever truly command his area. Still, despite being singled out as a weak link, he had big bad Brad McKay to bail him out and the feeling became stronger that if this was all Hibs had in their locker then toughing out the 0-0 may not quite be the daunting prospect we'd all been dreading.

The Hibs fans are backing the Butcher revolution with everything they've got, though and the decibel levels rose as they went through their full repertoire of new songs: they had this badly enunciated one that name-checked both Butcher and, touchingly, his assistant Mo Malpas and another that seemed to ridicule our plight to the tune of Slade's 'Cum on Feel the Noize' but, again, was just too guttural and garbled to properly make out. Sensing the new material wasn't really going down as well as hoped, they wheeled out that favourite old foot-stomper of theirs, 'paedo-, paedo-, paedophile'.

Disappointingly, there appears a time limit on how long Hearts can hold out against sides when being pinned back for longer and longer periods. It's often at or around the hour mark that the pressure eventually tells and the resistance breaks. It was the case last month at Celtic Park and at home to ICT and sadly it was the case here.

Our defenders were present in decent enough numbers when Paul Hanlon knocked down a Liam Craig corner but, as with Stephen Thompson's goal at New St Mirren Park, they were hesitant to the point of being statuesque and, as they dawdled, James Collins pounced and speared the ball high into the roof of the net from inside the six-yard box.

Easter Road simply exploded with a crescendo of noise. There was years' worth of pent-up frustration encapsulated into that deafening and sustained roar and there was nothing to do but stare ahead, unblinking, and wait for the air to stop reverberating. A muted chorus of 'The Hearts Song' was started but faded away to nothing.

The worry was that having breached us once Hibs would be emboldened while our heads would inevitably drop. Needing a goal, David Smith got thrown on for Tapping. This meant he was stationed on the left of midfield, his natural inclination, therefore, leading him to move inside as opposed to his usual touchline hugging.

On 72 minutes this switch proved inspired, resulting directly in a goal for Hearts. Smith's equaliser may have owed something to luck in terms of the ball taking a nick off Ryan McGivern, but it came about as a result of sheer guts from Hearts. Smudger received the ball on halfway and advanced at speed. He danced inside Scott Robertson as if he wasn't there and then nutmegged Nelson as the defender stepped across his path. Miraculously through on goal, his stabbed effort bounced off the chest of Williams. With the Hearts fans desperately craning forward, willing the loose ball to fall favourably, Smith got his toe there first and saw his prodded effort dribble deliriously over the line.

The goal was celebrated with crazed abandon, sparking riotous scenes in both tiers. Supporters tumbled down the steps in unbridled pandemonium, spilling on to the pitch where punches were thrown. With hope reignited the Hearts end sung themselves hoarse, sensing their opponents were shaken and struggling to comprehend how such a threadbare bunch of overplayed kids had somehow managed to tear up the script they were so lovingly envisaging.

In years gone by, derby goals stolen in this fashion have often proved pivotal. You always had a sense that ever-brittle Hibs were on the brink of folding as the Hearts support found their voices and the momentum swung their way. And, unavoidably, we found ourselves sucked into the moment, hoping that the present crop of kids might have enough about them to inflict just such a killer blow. So, when the ball arrived at Jamie Walker's feet midway between the touchline and the edge of the box, he instantly had 4,000 voices screaming at him to commit the defender, get across him and get in the box.

He very quickly achieved the first two but then seemed to doubt himself and his ability to use the ball wisely. Perhaps he was running on empty and felt a penalty represented a better chance of a goal than a tired cut-back into a crowded penalty box. Whatever the reason, he dangled a leg and flopped unconvincingly over McGivern's outstretched limb. It was a terrible decision, borne surely as much out of battle-weary fatigue as malice but an attempt to con the officials all the same.

Petulant shoving and the trading of insults along with Madden's flashed yellow card right away gave Hibs back their voices, even if the tone was one of righteous indignation and they came at us again. Youthful inexperience had killed us in one box and it was soon to repeat the trick in the other. The ball was drifting harmlessly out of play behind Jamma's goal. Lewis Stevenson chased the lost cause and, in time-honoured fashion, Jordan McGhee stepped across his man to shield the ball out of play. Except, he didn't only do that; in his anxiety to see the ball to safety and stop Stevenson he panicked and hung out a leg.

There was no chance of Bobby Madden turning a blind eye to this and with seven to go Liam Craig sent Jamma the wrong way with a sweetly struck penalty. We'd somehow pilfered an equaliser at 1-0 but it was hard to see us going back up the field and getting another, although Kevin McHattie had a great effort palmed away for a corner right at the very death. Hearts had been magnificent in defeat and had nothing to be ashamed of. The better side won.

Sportscene had Kenny Miller and Mikey Stewart in the studio representing, as Jonathan Sutherland called it, both sides of the Edinburgh divide. But surely Stewart could have done that all by himself? Glowering humourlessly, Miller was like a stern off-duty policeman who'd stopped off on his way home to talk to a bunch of schoolkids about road safety or an ex-Marine talking candidly about waterboarding and Gulf War Syndrome. He *was* Tom Berenger in *Born on the Fourth of July*.

With his sleeves rolled up as tightly as they'd go Miller dismissed Hearts' performance out of hand, grumbling that they'd contributed very little to the game. 'Au contraire,' Mikey seemed to say as he launched into a detailed critique of all Hearts' defensive foibles. Certainly, it's a subject close to Mikey's heart and if the call to go on *Celebrity Mastermind* ever comes, he at least won't have too far to look for his chosen specialist subject, 'Okay, Michael Stewart, you have two minutes on "The defensive frailties of Hearts, season 2013/14", starting now: Against St Johnstone in November, who was to blame for Nigel Hasselbaink's opening goal? "Pthwthh! Any one ay them. All gash." Incorrect, the answer we have here is Dylan McGowan. "Aye? Were you at the game likes?"'

25

Partick Thistle home, 5 January 2013, 3pm

WITH this defeat went the last vestiges of hope for our club this season. When arguably the SPL's poorest team (albeit that isn't in administration), a side in freefall that hasn't won since October, comes to your place and makes you look second best in every department then you're left with no option. With a heavy heart I think we're forced to finally admit that a place in the top six probably looks beyond us now.

That pesky little groundhog was snuffling around Tynecastle again. Another must-win match against a side we had tentative hopes of beating and, who knows, perhaps even reeling in: another torturous, laboured 2-0 home defeat. We started play 17 points behind Thistle who had a game in hand over us. A win would have brought it back to 14 with us still due to play them twice more but the loss saw them float away like an unmoored dinghy.

Jamie Hamill was suspended for this clash but any fears we might miss out on our devilishly inventive kick-off routine were allayed by Scott Robinson. Hamill probably shed a private tear of pride, behind those massive specs of his, as he watched Robinson delicately spoon the ball into the air for Paterson to get knocked flat on to his backside and the opposition to win a throw-in. Huzzah!

Ryan McGowan, speaking in the *Sunday Post*, said he could see first-hand how well set up Hearts had been for this game, how the coaching staff couldn't have done any more to drill the players for every possible scenario but inexperience at the back cost them dearly. Twice they switched off momentarily and twice they were punished for it.

A brace of assists from the impressive Kallum Higginbotham were enough to secure the win. On 14 minutes he set up the unmarked Taylor who smashed the ball in off MacDonald from ten yards, then five minutes before half-time it was his cross that Taylor-Sinclair headed home with the freedom of Tynecastle.

Gordon Strachan once famously said, 'You judge how good a side is by the standard of their strikers.' Well that's us fucked then, we don't have any! The result being that any defensive lapses tend almost always to have a direct bearing on the final outcome. This fear has strangled creativity, making the players introverted and reluctant to deviate from the easy option. At times, versus Thistle, we were so deliberate and ponderous in possession, it was like the players were trying to pass a medicine ball around.

Frustratingly, Thistle were no great shakes and I'd take any Hearts side from the last 30 years, even that infamous Laszlo 11 from 2009 that played Adrian Mrowiec as a lone striker, to have seen them off. But here, even when scraggy little half-chances presented themselves, we were toothless in the extreme. Even when Bannigan picked up a second yellow on 81 minutes, we were unable to make any inroads whatsoever.

Other teams have troublesome corner kicks that are zipped in at pace, triggering mayhem in our box. Whereas we have two arms in the air from Kevin McHattie and a big hoof to the back post that clears everyone. Maybe it would be an idea to shelve these pointless signals. All they do is give the fans false hope that something pre-planned may be about to unfold. Something good.

I mean, it's fine to cite nerves and inexperience and fatigue as mitigating factors this season but how do we excuse the frankly dismal standard of our delivery from set pieces? Every week it's the same poor technique and glaringly under-rehearsed routines.

Perhaps unsurprisingly, the thorny issue of underachievement at Tynecastle was flagged up by the *Sportsound* team. Their Monday night offering had Billy Brown and Paul Hartley in the studio discussing Hearts' poor run of form and the appeal to have their transfer embargo lifted.

Brown very quickly lost his cool, perhaps it went during Kenny McIntyre's long-winded intro. His blood was especially angered by the re-hashing of Graeme Spiers's comments immediately following the Celtic 7-0 tie where he'd suggested Locke could be doing a bit better despite those well-documented hardships.

Clearly, he's fiercely protective of his young boss, someone he's known since a nipper, but the whole exchange was fairly unedifying and you were left cringing and just wishing he hadn't bothered. You could feel both his and the club's credibility dwindling away every time the irascible Tom English cut sarcastically across the flustered assistant manager, tying him in knots.

It only got worse for Billy when he went on to try and make the case for having the transfer ban lifted. Quite rightly he was witheringly dismissed for even suggesting such a ludicrous thing and began furiously back-pedalling, to save face, distancing himself from the appeal. You just wish he hadn't put himself in a position to get drawn into such a messy debate. Our punishment was well set out at the start of the season and you could argue we were lucky even to get that as we'd delayed our inevitable implosion just long enough to avoid relegation at the tail end of last season. We knew the penalty. We can't now go crawling back whimpering about leniency. Where's the dignity in that? How did we react when Rangers bleated about being treated harshly and tried to weasel their way out of being punished?

Plus, I'm not sure if it does much for the resolve of the players, him waving the white flag like that and decrying the hopelessness of the cause. That's the next team talk as good as written then, Billy? Way to inspire the players.

You keep your counsel and you keep fighting. Listen, Billy Brown's a great Hearts man who rode to the club's rescue when Lockie needed him most but while he was at Hibernian, a year or so back, part of me felt it was a blessed relief. You'd hear him blustering and farting away to the media before a derby and be relieved it was the opposition he was jinxing and not us with his half-arsed attempts at mind games.

As a *Sportsound* listener you always know you're in for a treat when McIntyre utters the immortal phrase, 'Our listeners have been getting in touch on social media, I'll just give you a flavour of the sorts of things they've been saying.'

Basically, this is a euphemism for, there's material here we haven't the brass neck to address or put *our* name to. It would be confrontational, insulting and perhaps even libellous. However, our subtle ploy of hiding behind these texting trolls means we get to go there after all and it's all in the name of free speech, so, 'Big Drew from Wishaw has tweeted in to say that you have bony girl arms and smell like an elephant's butt, how would you wish to respond to that criticism?'

Time to switch the radio off, methinks.

26
Motherwell home,
11 January 2013, 3pm

FOR many, this fixture will be forever synonymous with the late, lamented Phil O'Donnell, after a Scottish Cup fourth round tie here in January 2008 marked the first game Motherwell played after mourning his passing.

Tam Cowan, erstwhile co-presenter of the excellent *Off the Ball* show and diehard Motherwell fan, is always effusive in his praise of all associated with Hearts for their kindness and sympathy in the lead-up to the game. He talks with great poignancy of how much this meant to him and his fellow supporters and how it's created a lasting bond. That Cowan gave so freely of his time in three separate fundraisers at Tynecastle is undoubted testament to this.

I remember feeling glad at the time it was us they'd come to for their first game back as I knew our supporters would instinctively catch the mood but then feeling a bit deflated when hostilities were renewed so quickly after kick-off. One minute David Clarkson (O'Donnell's nephew) was being warmly applauded as he trudged back to the dressing room after the warm-up, the next the whistle's gone and we're all back to being 'dirty Jambo bastards' again.

Not that that's meant in any way as a criticism of the Motherwell fans and their conduct. They'd been through a horrible, traumatic few weeks and this match afforded them a release for all that pent-up emotion. It must have been almost cathartic and life-affirming. They had laid their hero to rest, grieved for him and now they could lose themselves in a match for 90 minutes. And it's nice to think we were able to do our bit to help with that process.

The present-day Motherwell away support ventured east in fairly decent numbers, scattering shoppers on Gorgie Road with their firecrackers and that infernal drum. The latter was omnipresent throughout the entire game giving the oddly disconcerting impression that at any minute they might be about to break into 'Wild Boys' by Duran Duran.

They've even taken to hijacking the now redundant 'Fernando Torres, Liverpool's number nine' song, adapting the words to pay homage to John Sutton. It meant re-branding him as 'big' John Sutton in order to create enough syllables to make it work but they seemed happy enough in their own little self-contained 'ultra' bubble. In fact they were so wrapped up in it that we never got our customary baiting from the away fans.

The previous Sunday, when Thistle's fans weren't eulogising at length about the myriad delights of Maryhill, they were happily informing us we would 'die with the Rangers'. These songs have such a brief shelf life of accuracy and relevance that having to sit through them most weeks is wearing pretty thin. Opposition fans sing it with such gusto, too, you can tell they really think they're getting to us but it's more tedious than anything else. The Motherwell fans were a refreshing break.

You get a similar thing when away fans visit Anfield and think it's the height of cutting edge humour being the 500th set of supporters to sing 'sign on, sign on' to the tune of YNWA. Fans from Middlesbrough, Bradford and Blackburn ridiculing another city's unemployment stats! You seriously couldn't make it up.

Despite losing 1-0, Hearts were extremely bright in this match and both Keith Lasley and Stephen McManus, along with manager Stuart McCall observed, sportingly, that we'd been well worth a point. That we never took it was probably down to the Motherwell keeper, Gunnar Nielsen, who, despite looking like an accident waiting to happen, did just about enough to keep Hearts at bay in a busy second half.

Hearts took to the pitch in all-white and produced more of an away performance, liberated, perhaps, by the reluctant acceptance that relegation inevitably beckons. Motherwell helped, to a degree, also. Instead of sitting in, forcing Hearts, as the home side, to take the game to them and then hitting us on the break, the Steelmen were more than happy to open up and come at Hearts.

In front of an excellent crowd of 12,888, there was a freedom to Hearts' play, untypical of the stunted, error-strewn mish-mash we've come to expect from home games. Dale Carrick started up front and his willingness to run the channels gave the midfielders a clear out-ball.

At the other end the jet-heeled Lionel Ainsworth was the last thing Kevin McHattie needed. The Hearts left-back had been nursing a tender hamstring all week and the Englishman ran at him repeatedly in the first half. Scott Robinson and then Jamie MacDonald dived to his rescue and the feeling was that if a goal was to come it would be down our left.

However, the goal, when it did come, sprang from our right. On 40 minutes, Iain Vigurs received the ball on the touchline midway inside his own half and played an exquisite pass of slide-rule accuracy into space for Sutton to run on to which completely took out Brad McKay.

MacDonald raced from goal, forcing Sutton wider than he would have preferred, but from an acute angle on the left of the box he found the net courtesy of a helpful clip off the stretching McGowan. The ball may well have been heading in anyway but it was typical of our luck that Gowser's touch made doubly sure.

Sutton turned away in delight, not one iota of sentiment for his old side in that big beaming smile of his. In a way you kind of respect him for that. He was never a favourite son at Tynecastle, we never really played properly to his strengths and as a lone striker he'd often toiled. If Sutts had turned away head bowed as Peter Crouch would do after scoring for

Stoke City against Liverpool the following day, it would have seriously overstated the level of affection with which he was held here.

The build-up to this game had accentuated the tale of woe at Tynecastle. Danny Wilson was still struggling with tonsillitis, McHattie was a late fitness doubt as was Jamie Walker. Ten minutes into the second half Walker came off the bench to replace McHattie with Jordan McGhee going across to left-back and Callum Paterson dropping in at right-back.

However, from adversity, Hearts prospered and the change allowed them to ask more questions of Motherwell. Paterson was supremely comfortable motoring over halfway with the ball, providing width down the whole right side. He appeared to have the beating of Stevie Hammell, too, which caused Carswell and Lasley to scurry across to cover.

For this reason, Walker, Ryan Stevenson and David Smith all seemed to find extra space whenever Paterson joined the attack and a number of presentable chances were created. Stevenson saw a deflected cross clatter off the top of the bar and then Smith had a firm shot beaten away by Nielsen.

After having scored in the corresponding fixture back in October you could see Stevo clearly fancied his chances against the unorthodox Faroese keeper and from 20 yards his rasper was patted away unconvincingly for the corner. This was such a refreshing home performance, it was as if the shackles had been removed. From the corner the ball fell to Walker on the edge of the box who hit as clean a strike as you'll see all season. It flew past the post with only millimetres to spare.

Motherwell's lead was beginning to look increasingly slender and with 15 minutes to go McCall opted to freshen up his attack. Zaine Francis-Angol and Henri Anier replaced Ainsworth and Faddy. This switch led directly to Motherwell having a goal chalked off as they sought to end the match as a contest and claim their sixth league win on the bounce. Anier knocked the ball home after Sutton's initial effort had been brilliantly saved but an uncharacteristically benign Willie Collum ruled it out for a shove.

Right at the end Hearts carved out a wonderful chance to nick a point as the ball ran to Hamill in the box. Frustratingly, he had to adjust his feet slightly and took too long to dig the ball out from between them. In the end all he could muster was a stabbed toe poke which the sliding Nielsen was happy to let bounce away off his chest.

If Hearts went into this game toiling with various bumps and bruises and labouring to fill the subs' bench, they came out of it in an even worse state. Jamie Walker hobbled out of Tynecastle, his foot in a lightweight cast, for a scan on a suspected broken metatarsal. The news that he would be out of action for around ten weeks came as a shattering blow.

Unfortunately, that wasn't the end of it for Lockie when it also emerged that his loyal lieutenant, Billy Brown, was not to have his contract renewed for financial reasons and Saturday's upcoming match in Perth would be his last. At a time when the fragility of the squad became ever more pronounced Lockie needs support, an arm around the shoulder. It seems like all dispensing with Brown does is leave him ever more isolated.

In the midst of this swirling negativity, Twitter suddenly burst to life with the story that Rudi Skacel, Andrew Driver and three other players, one of whom may have been Gary Kenneth, were poised in the wings as Hearts sought to trigger the one out/one in loophole in the transfer embargo. The idea being that five members of staff: John Sutton, Marius Zaliukas, Driver, Mark Keegan and Marcus McMillan left the club in the summer when we entered administration and could, technically, be replaced by these five ringers.

However, these plans were scuppered by the SPFL whose secretary, Iain Blair, informed the club's administrator, Bryan Jackson, that as those players were made redundant they didn't qualify for the one out/one in rule. All we were left with was the point that new players would only be available if further players left, giving Swansea's reported interest in Adam King added resonance.

It was under this cloak of doubt that the players readied themselves for St Johnstone away.

27

St Johnstone away, 18 January 2013, 3pm

BACK under the lights at McDiarmid I was put in mind of another staging post in the 2012 cup run: the fourth round reply. En route to the quarter-finals that cold Valentine's night we snatched a stoppage time equaliser and we did exactly the same here. A towering Danny Wilson header salvaged a point in a fiery and chaotic 3-3 draw.

I parked up a good 50 minutes before kick-off. Skirting around the gathering pools of water in the rutted car park I was stopped in my tracks by loud shouts of 'going down, going down, going down'. I half-turned and on the slip road was a coachload of fans in red and white scarves banging on the windows. 'Aberdeen?' I thought to myself, looking down at my watch, 'who are they playing today?' I found out later they were actually Hamilton Accies supporters who'd stopped off on the way home after their match at Dens Park got called off. And it only seems like yesterday we were humping them 7-0 at Tynecastle: the fifth a sumptuous curling free kick from the incomparable Sandy Jardine. Where do the years go? Well the two or three early arrivals at McDiarmid, sheltering from the pissing rain, really appreciated them stopping by and saying hello.

Muffled in fog, McDiarmid Park had an eerie, almost ghostly quality as kick-off approached. Like the BBC were filming a remake of *The Hound of the Baskervilles* in the far corner of the pitch or something. The floodlights barely pierced through the darkening gloom as the players shuffled through their warm-ups.

Hearts, in all-maroon, made two changes from last weekend with Danny Wilson in for Jordan McGhee and Callum Tapping replacing the suspended Scott Robinson. That meant another start for Dale Carrick and he led the line alongside Ryan Stevenson with Hearts plumping again for 4-4-2.

Play swung from end to end in the early stages, on a greasy, treacherous surface already badly cut up from the warm-up. Then, 20 minutes in, the game burst to life. Gary McDonald was wayward with his ball back to Steven Anderson. Carrick was on to the loose ball in a flash only to be barged to the floor by Anderson. Referee Brian Colvin drew gasps of disbelief, pulling a red card theatrically from his top pocket.

It had been tempting, at the time, to wonder perhaps whether Colvin had simply lost patience with the home side after a series of irksome little niggles. The main culprit being Nigel Hasselbaink who'd got away with catching his studs on the top of Jamie MacDonald's head and then, not long after, he stole the ball off Jamie Hamill from a drop-ball like a Mumbai street urchin.

Then, as the match wore on, it became abundantly clear the only stand Colvin was making today was against rational and sane decision-making. This botched call was merely the precursor to an erratic display of staggering incompetence. It was hard to comprehend how Anderson's foul could be deemed to have denied Carrick a clear goalscoring opportunity but Colvin more than made amends with his aggrieved hosts, recompensing them to the tune of two of the softest penalties you are ever likely to see.

The first award came on 37 minutes after Kevin McHattie was adjudged to have tugged back Hasselbaink on the edge of the box. It was a quite horrendous decision, inexplicably poor. Contact was minimal verging on the non-existent and, even if it had existed, had taken place outside the box. But May wasn't going to linger over the injustices of the award and swept the ball home with a flourish.

On *Sportscene*, Mikey Stewart called the award 'very harsh indeed' and for the first time this season there was an acknowledgement that our side had had more than its fair share of these. On hearing this, Jonathan Sutherland looked like a petrified field mouse that'd just heard the harvester engine start, his eyes nearly popping out of his head. Stewart hadn't finished there, though and even referred back to the joke penalty and red card we'd conceded away at Inverness when the ball had bounced off Jamie Hamill's head.

Erroneous penalties notwithstanding, St Johnstone being a man down meant we were seeing a fairly even contest. However, as had been the case in the two previous meetings this season, the difference was big, scary Stevie May.

The half-man half-bison went stampeding clear two minutes after the restart. Jamma stood tall despite the very real risk of being trampled like a luckless bystander at Pamplona and saved May's shot with his legs. Unluckily for Hearts, though, the St Johnstone number 17's momentum carried him forward, allowing a second bite at the cherry. He slid between Wilson and Brad Mackay and bundled the ball over the line in ungainly fashion. This was seriously tough on Hearts who certainly weren't two goals worse than their counterparts. But, losing a second goal didn't alter their game-plan. At half-time Dylan McGowan had been replaced by Sam Nicholson, with Paterson dropping to right-back. Hamill and Callum Tapping continued to close down play, recycling possession together and feeding the ball wide for either McHattie on one side or Paterson on the other.

Despite the two-goal margin, being a man down was taking its toll on St Johnstone and by the hour mark the traffic was heading noticeably towards Mannus's goal in front of the decent Hearts following.

On 56 minutes, Brad McKay had a shot blocked away for a corner. This came to nothing but the ball found its way back out to McHattie. The left-back dragged the ball on to his left foot and whipped in a dipping ball that was crying out to be finished off. Carrick dutifully did the honours, notching his first goal for Hearts with a close-range, bullet header.

Finally, we'd scored, and St Johnstone looked leggy and vulnerable. Two-nil had definitely felt like a false scoreline and with the Hearts support up on their feet seeking to summon another push, Colvin again pulled the rug from under our feet. He awarded the second of his spurious penalties, a pitiful excuse of a handball against McHattie, and within two minutes of pulling a goal back, Hearts found themselves 3-1 down as May completed his hat-trick.

It would have been quite easy for the Hearts heads to drop. Instead, they threw on little Gary Oliver for Tapping and kept on believing something could still be salvaged from the game. Throughout the opening half of the season a noticeable trend was for Hearts' performance levels to drop off following substitutions. The shape and cohesion would suffer as our flimsy, lightweight youngsters got hounded off the ball. It's a definite sign of how far the side has come that with each switch today we looked better.

The third and final change saw Billy King replace David Smith on 78 minutes and signalled a frenzied spell of intense Hearts pressure. So desperate was their desire to peg St Johnstone back that a number of highly presentable chances were snatched at wildly. Oliver swiped at the ball and missed with the goal at his mercy and then Nicholson had a great chance palmed away by the keeper. But, still, Hearts stuck to their task as St Johnstone seemed almost to shrink in stature on the sodden turf.

Three minutes from time Nicholson got the goal he'd been denied moments earlier, slicing the ball in from close range. We've seen plenty of own goals that wouldn't have looked out of place at the proper end of the pitch. Well this was the polar opposite: a goal at the proper end of the pitch that wouldn't have looked out of place as an own goal.

Defiance and belief were writ large in Hearts' celebrations. In keeping with the season as a whole, there was an almost fevered desire to keep fighting right until the bitter end and Stevo followed the ball into the net with the aim of restarting play as quickly as possible.

Cynically, Frazer Wright blocked his way and things very quickly got messy. Paterson and Carrick also went in search of the ball and Wright ended up on the deck. A stroppy Mannus took exception to this and sent Stevo hurtling into the back of the net. This was the trigger for all hell to break loose. Stevo disentangled himself and got into the tightest of clinches with Mannus, while Tam Scobbie randomly stuck the head on McKay as the bodies piled in.

Colvin had completely lost control of the situation and failed to spot Scobbie's antics. However, the compliance officer was a little more vigilant and Scobbie was given a retrospective two-match ban. On hearing of the punishment McKay took to Twitter to respond witheringly, 'My wee sister is eight and I've been hit harder by her. It wasn't exactly something that was going to put me on the ground. If it was intentional then he deserves the punishment.'

Colvin finally extricated Mannus and Stevo from the melee. Mannus simply had to be a goner and you kind of knew, with a sinking feeling, that we'd lose Stevo. This meant we'd be down to ten men for the four minutes of stoppage time whereas St Johnsone would be reduced to nine. Significantly, however, they'd made all three substitutions, meaning Tam Scobbie was forced to go in goal.

This gave us renewed hope and from the restart Hearts won back possession almost instantaneously and came flying again at St Johnstone. Paterson saw yet another injury-time header hit the woodwork but there was no time to bemoan another hard luck tale as the ball ran for the corner. King scooped the ball up under his arm and sprinted for the flag, roars of encouragement ringing in his ears.

From the young substitute's superb, floated delivery, in the second minute of stoppage time, Wilson hung majestically in the air before thumping a header past the makeshift keeper and into the net. This triggered bedlam in the away end and Wilson raced over to the fans with Paterson in tow, virtually hurdling over the wall in his excitement.

It was a delirious end to the game, given the number of times we've either conceded late goals ourselves or been denied them by the woodwork or exceptional goalkeeping. The point felt all the sweeter given that St Johnstone would have almost certainly won had they not needlessly resorted to such blatant gamesmanship after Nicholson's goal.

Leaving the stadium after our opening day clash here in August there had been many a genial and hearty exchange between the two sets of supporters. I remember even wishing some burly farmhand all the very best against whichever crack unit of part-time Belarusian art students and nuclear physicists it was that were about to dump them out of Europe.

There would be no such pleasantries after this tetchy contest. The gloating St Johnstone fans who'd heaped ridicule on us throughout the match were left choking on their scorn. Ridicule then turned to thoughts of retribution as their obnoxious little ned ultras stole into the Hearts end and tried to snatch a flag. Later, they pulled a knife on a group of young Hearts fans and stole their drum. Pictures of themselves posing with this little kid's drum were then posted all over the internet.

Post-match, Tommy Wright mumped and moaned about the sending off and his side's clear superiority, completely skating over the fact that two of his side's three goals should never have been. You keep it real, big man.

A hoarse Lockie, his eyes still blazing from the intensity of the contest, spoke in hushed tones of the pride he felt in his young side's performance. It emerged that a despairing Locke had been in touch with referees' supervisor John Fleming a number of times, seeking answers to why the officials have got so many big decisions wrong against us. All he got each time was another apology.

It does seems like a number of really poor decisions have gone against Hearts this season. From scandalously misjudged penalties, to the ruling out of perfectly legitimate goals, to glaring inconsistencies that see our players punished while the opposition get off scot free for committing the identical crime.

A rather damning statistic came to light in the aftermath of the game, regarding SPL penalty awards this season. Apparently, so far, 26 per cent of them have gone against Hearts. On hearing that I immediately went back through them all in my head and came up with two out of nine that were straightforward, nailed-on penalties: Partick Thistle away in August when Walker was clumsy and Hibs at Easter Road when McGhee took down Stevenson. And a third, McHattie against Aberdeen, which you could make a case either way for. The remaining six were all highly dubious and had been picked to pieces on *Sportscene*.

After Brian Colvin's one-man horror show at McDiarmid, Tommy Wright took a call from the man himself, offering his sincerest apologies for the wrongful sending off of Steven Anderson. And Lockie? What did the SFA do to pacify him after the opposition was gifted two preposterously soft penalty kicks? An apology? Not so much. He was censured for the aggressive manner in which he'd kicked a water bottle after the second penalty was given.

But what does it all mean? Are we being victimised? Is there a shadowy conspiracy among referees and the SFA top brass to be extra hard on Hearts? The moment those sorts of cases are put forward on internet forums or at the game it makes me recoil to be honest. You talk like that about your team and you're instantly eschewing all credibility. You're echoing the same paranoia that's been the hallmark of the Old Firm for decades.

And, besides, it probably isn't true anyway. It's hard to picture some covert meeting where top of the list is ensuring we get a raw deal whenever and wherever possible. What's more likely, I think, is that subconsciously officials don't perceive there to be any serious repercussions to getting calls wrong against us. We're doomed. We're going down. If the penalty they give against us is a bit harsh it's no biggie: the opposition are bound to score again anyway so what are we all moaning about?

Which is probably why Colvin never bothered to give Lockie a call. There's nothing at stake for Lockie and Hearts, only pride whereas Wright's side are going for the top six and Europe and those two points dropped could prove vital. Unless of course the incompetent chump feels he has nothing to apologise *for* as both of them were legitimate, stick-on penalties, in which case there's seriously no hope for the guy.

28

Ross County away,
25 January 2014, 3pm

HEARTS returned north to the ground where, back in September, many believe that slender hope we'd nurtured of cheating relegation died in the second minute of stoppage time. Barring a turnaround akin to Uma Thurman punching her way out of a coffin buried six feet underground in *Kill Bill II* we will still be relegated in May despite this thrilling 2-1 win. However, on filing out of the stadium at full time, it was hard not to feel massively heartened by a quite devastating display of attacking football from our young side.

Ryan Stevenson was missing through suspension after incurring a two-match ban for his antics up in Perth. Cunningly, though, Hearts managed to inveigle a re-arranged fixture with St Mirren for the following Wednesday, thereby making Stevo eligible for next Sunday's League Cup semi-final with ICT at Easter Road.

Walking over the railway bridge and down to the ground, the stunning Easter Ross hills in the background, I was reminded that County affords you far and away the friendliest welcome of any SPL away ground. Everyone is really cheery and it's like they're genuinely chuffed to see you and have you visit their isolated little outpost. They'd even pinned a couple of plaques to the wall at the away end, thanking us directly for making that 340-mile round trip and telling us football would be nothing without support like this. All that kindness *and* their haggis pies are the best in the land: for my money infinitely better than Killie's.

County came into this match off the back of having taken ten points from their last 12. You kind of got the impression their plethora of new signings probably chuckled to themselves on peering at Hearts' league placing and had visions of coasting to a fairly undemanding victory.

In reality, though, Hearts bossed this game and along the way produced some seriously scintillating football. With David Smith on the right and Sam Nicholson on the left, they repeatedly prised the Staggies wide open throughout a one-sided first half. Hearts' domination began, literally, from the opening seconds. Straight from kick-off Smith found himself in space and pulled the ball back for Nicholson who was sprinting into the box. But the number 28 fired his shot into the seats at the jail end of the ground.

Amazingly, this trend would continue as County seemed almost bemused by their lowly opponents' voracious appetite for the ball. Still inside the opening 60 seconds Smith was again involved, setting up Callum Paterson who, despite having more time than he realised, rushed his effort.

After 12 minutes of attacking keep-ball, Smith drove a daisy-cutter from the edge of the box that pinged off the foot of the post. Being Hearts fans it was impossible not to begin fretting over how many of these gilt-edged chances we were spurning. These chances would surely begin to dwindle and it was hard to imagine County wouldn't sort themselves out at some point in the proceedings.

However, all that followed was even more slick, one-touch passing from Hearts as they switched effortlessly between getting in behind the pedestrian County full-backs with fast wing play and outpassing them through the middle through Robinson and Hamill. Up at Perth, the previous weekend, the boy behind me had shouted, whimsically, at Hamill, 'Go on then, Scholesie.' We'd all had a good laugh yet here he was winning a slide tackle, dribbling round two players and then slotting an inch-perfect ball through for Smith.

Smudger looked up and threaded the ball into the path of Carrick who'd run intelligently across the line but Michael Fraser in the County goal spread himself to good effect and Carrick's strike went for the corner.

This has been the season of the sucker punch so it was with a certain degree of trepidation that County were observed tentatively trying to play their way into the game. On the half-hour mark Jordan Slew rose like a lighthouse and nodded the ball into the side-netting with an underworked Jamie MacDonald shepherding it past with great care.

The attack, despite coming to nothing, had portents of doom for us. We'd monopolised play thus far and absolutely bombarded Fraser's goal with shots from every conceivable range and angle. Yet one ball into the box and County were only the width of the post away from taking the lead. However, on 36 minutes, Hearts belatedly got their reward. A Smith corner from the left was glanced goalwards by Brad McKay and, mirroring our last visit here, Paterson tapped in.

We were braced for a stinging riposte from County but the onslaught never came. Hearts managed to condense the space in midfield, forcing County to seek out Slew and his partner Yann Songo'o with long balls. But the back four coped with the aerial assault and made sure any second balls were quickly snapped up.

In hunting down just such a second ball Dylan McGowan was adjudged to have fouled Slew on the edge of the box. It was a soft free kick, nothing more than that, but given the rough treatment we've been receiving from officialdom of late it was greeted with torrents of SFA-directed vitriol from the Hearts support in the north stand.

Our box resembled *Jurassic Park* as County had a few brachiosaurs bobbing around awaiting Brittain's ball in and you could see MacDonald spit nervously into his gloves and look around worriedly. The delivery was good and inviting and Songo'o got there in front of Jamma, powering his header into the empty net. Our soft underbelly exposed yet again. Going in at half-time all square after far and away our best half of the season was a real sickener.

The second half began in much the same fashion as the first had ended. For the first 15 or so minutes County had a lot of the ball and Hearts were putting in a real shift keeping them at bay.

Largely, they succeeded in this and Jamma was only called into serious action once in this spell, after 54 minutes, flinging himself to his left to tip away a 40-yard rocket from Songo'o. The on-loan Blackburn forward looks the pick of the County new boys and his strike had been arrowing into the top corner like a Scud missile.

Having weathered this mini-storm Hearts then began to pick up where they'd left off before going ahead in the first half and that air of shakiness and uncertainty returned to the County defence.

McGowan loped forward, like an Australasian Cafu, and delivered a rocket of a ball into the path of Nicholson who was tearing into the box at breakneck speed. His header flew agonisingly into the crowd with him virtually under the bar. Slow motion wasn't kind to Nick but in real time the youngster had the keeper bearing down on him, it was a stretch reaching the ball in time and there was a very real chance he'd brain himself on the post as he flung himself at the ball.

At this point, with 15 to go, the heavens opened and shards of freezing rain were splintering earthwards. And through it all Hearts continued to look for the ball and play. Billy King came on for Carrick and was involved immediately, sprinting to catch a ball down Hearts' left and swinging over a dangerous-looking cross. Nicholson got there first, possibly depriving Paterson behind him who may have been better placed. His header spurted away off the ice-sodden turf and was retrieved by the ever-willing Smith on the right of the box. Smudger stood the ball up, asking a question of Fraser in the County goal. Under immense pressure from Paterson he could only weakly pat the ball down and Robinson was on hand to calmly smash the ball home.

Despite having had to wait until the last ten minutes to secure the winning goal it would have been a travesty for Hearts if anything other than all three points hadn't accompanied them back down through the A9 blizzards.

However, we still had ten minutes to see out and the vivid memory of the last time we were defending a lead late on here applied the cruellest mental torture. Unsurprisingly, the Hearts box resembled the Alamo as County launched ball after ball into the area.

The closest they came was when the impressive Slew outmuscled Wilson and, despite being forced wide, fired in a shot that had MacDonald slithering to see away at the far post.

Hearts were well and truly under the cosh but then, with a minute left, Kevin McHattie relieved the pressure in stunning fashion. Not only did he make a crucial interception deep inside his own half but he came surging out of defence with the ball at his feet. He weaved this way and that, crossing halfway and gaining momentum. A drop of the shoulder and he was on the edge of the box. Still he kept going, jinking to the left and connecting with a skidding drive that was blocked away for the corner.

His lung-bursting heroics along with Smith and Paterson playing keep-ball down by the corner flag ensured the ball stayed in front of the 541 frozen but elated Hearts fans for the full two minutes' stoppage time. Finally Kevin Clancy's whistle sounded shrilly and the bedraggled Hearts players took a rain-soaked bow before slipping away, the cheers of the fans ringing out in the freezing air.

A fired-up Allan Preston called out Kenny McIntyre on *Sportsound* after the game. He felt the criticism levelled at Locke by McIntyre after the Thistle game had been needlessly unfair. And now that Hearts had four league wins, equalling Thistle's tally, Preston wondered aloud whether their manager, Alan Archibald, would now come under the same level of scrutiny.

McIntyre's belated response was predictably spiky, the confrontational anchor refusing to back down during *Sportsound Extra*. He had Michael Stewart in his bunker with him and the two of them egged each other on, regarding their negative portrayal of Hearts.

Stewart again voiced his critique of Hearts as a poorly trained side with no discernible shape or obvious playing style: a side that, for him, compared very unfavourably to Thistle. Perhaps if Stewart had actually been at the County game, perhaps if he'd listened a little more intently to the match report, in particular to the fulsome praise the often dour Derek Adams had for a deserving Hearts victory, he might have toned it down a little. Preston wasn't even still on air yet Stewart was back on his soapbox listing the deficiencies of a Hearts side that had just played in-form Ross County off the park. It made him sound argumentative, agenda-driven and more than a little out of touch.

Pat Nevin was far kinder on *Sportscene* the following night, again praising Hearts and their loyal supporters to the hilt for their undying spirit. He was then asked whether there was any chance of us staying up. He paused slightly with a thoughtful expression on his face before responding with a flat no.

And, he's right, of course he is, a flat no is, without doubt, the most appropriate response to that question given that we're 19 points adrift of Partick Thistle. But, then again, 14 more performances like this one…

29

St Mirren home, 29 January 2014, 7.45pm

THE days of routine victories are all but a distant memory. Nowadays, for Hearts to win football matches, it takes heart-stopping drama and palpitations. Here, they just about did enough to continue their recent mini-revival, taking the run to seven points from their last nine. And this came after falling behind on 28 seconds, scoring twice and surviving a late onslaught to move on to the heady heights of five points.

Despite such short notice it was business as usual at Tynecastle. Jamie Hamill, striding through the warm-up in his customary white, extra small, short-sleeved training top, seemingly impervious to the sub-zero temperatures while his team-mates shuttled around in an assortment of hats, gloves and snoods.

Thankfully, our match got the go-ahead despite the protestations of Derek McInnes. The diminutive perma-tanned whinger spat the dummy big style over not having been consulted about this re-scheduled game, visualising potential damage to the pitch impacting on his team's chances in Saturday's League Cup semi-final versus St Johnstone. Difficult to know why he got his knickers in such a twist. Tynecastle was immaculate the last time his Aberdeen side played on it and look what happened to them that day.

Hearts came into this match tentatively confident despite their better judgement. The last two matches up in Perth and Dingwall had been really encouraging but the million dollar question remained whether we'd be capable of recreating that form at home.

For St Mirren's part the advent of the play-offs radically altered the complexion of this game. Historically, this would be the kind of game St Mirren teams of yesteryear wouldn't really fancy.

However, they've found themselves embroiled in a four-way tussle with Ross County, Kilmarnock and Thistle to avoid 11th place and arrived in Edinburgh pumped up, with the intention of snaffling all three points.

Hearts' optimism, stated or otherwise, dissipated within seconds of the kick-off. The scourge of the Edinburgh club this season, Steven Thompson, caught us cold. He rose unchallenged from a Conor Newton cross and found the bottom corner with a header.

Who knows, perhaps if Hearts hadn't struck back almost immediately nerves would've become frayed and we'd have regressed back to the abject home form we'd been subjected to over the festive period. We'll never know, though, as a swift riposte was delivered on four minutes.

David Smith's cross from the right had some of the pace taken off it by a fortuitous nick off a defender and Paterson was able to time his run to perfection and bludgeon home a header with Kello in no-man's land.

Hearts had shrugged off the setback appearing barely to have flinched. The search for an explanation for Hearts' upturn in fortunes has to begin with that three-man strike-force of Smith, Dale Carrick and Sam Nicholson although surely of equal pertinence is that acceptance, however grudging, of our fate in the aftermath of the Thistle home defeat.

After trading two such early goals you could see both sides retreat into their shells for a few minutes to take stock and try and consolidate.

Nicholson was very lively down the left and with 12 minutes on the clock he skipped away from Marc McAusland and clipped in an inch-perfect cross. Paterson timed his run impeccably and hung in the air before crashing a header goalwards. It was a case of waiting for the net to bulge and acclaiming the goal but somehow Kello got across and made a breathtaking save, tipping the ball to safety.

A combination of St Mirren's garish, unfamiliar away kit and the match being played under the lights almost made this feel at times like a European game. The lightning-quick Adam Campbell was wreaking havoc down the Hearts left as the half wore on causing Nicholson to check back and help McHattie, blunting our attacking threat.

Hearts were chasing lime green shadows, keen for the break to come. MacDonald got down well to a Campbell shot from a tight angle as Hearts withstood St Mirren's pressure and just about escaped through to half-time level.

Pantomime villain Jim Goodwin committed a couple of wild indiscretions early in the second half, the second of which – a foul on Carrick – earned him a yellow card, much to the amusement of the home fans.

The fact he was coming under extra pressure was an indication of how brightly Hearts had started the half and from a corner Danny Wilson looped a header on to the bar. The rebound sparked an almighty scramble which ended with Paterson's point-blank header somehow being smuggled away to safety.

On 50 minutes the match swung heavily in Hearts' favour as they took the lead in a home league match for the first time since Aberdeen came calling back in August. From a quick breakaway Hamill found Smith on halfway. The Hearts winger carried the ball to the edge of the Saints box where he looked to play in Hamill, who'd charged upfield in support. Instead, however, the ball found its way to the feet of Carrick who darted purposefully into the box before hitting the deck after cutting across McAusland.

At the time I wasn't alone in leaping off my seat in search of the penalty but, as Steven McLean was reaching into his top pocket, my heart was in my mouth. To widespread sighs of relief he didn't book Speedie for simulation. The card he unearthed was red, signalling the end of the full-back's evening and the award of a penalty.

Danny Lennon wasn't overly impressed with the award but, having since watched numerous replays on BBC Alba, for me the defender brushed against Carrick with sufficient force to knock him off his stride. Lennon can gripe as much as he likes, it was far more of a penalty than two-thirds of the ones given against us this season. A frowning, pensive Hamill stepped forward, looking like a crazed Hells Angel with his shaved head and big bushy beard, and sent Kello the wrong way with a sweet side-footer.

There was too much at stake for the Buddies not to react and on 65 minutes the ten men replaced Adam Campbell with Gregg Wylde. Wylde had been wearing the colours of Aberdeen on his last visit here and created havoc. Tonight was no different: straight away he left both McGowan and McKay for dead to gift wrap a chance for Thompson at the near post. Only the affable, high-pitched summariser knows how he missed, knocking the ball virtually straight up in the air.

That seemed to give Hearts something of a jolt and with 15 minutes left on the clock they won a corner kick and sent the cavalry forward. Smith's ball was headed out but only as far as Nicholson who sent a hopeful lob back into the mix. McKay's back-header played in Carrick and the number 18 saw his shot from ten yards hit the post and run for a goal kick.

As a direct result of that miss the last ten minutes became unspeakably tense and Hearts brought Jordan McGhee on for McGowan in the hope that having his fresh, youthful legs at right-back might help contain the lively Wylde.

Ironically, however, McGhee had only been on the pitch a matter of seconds when he hopelessly misjudged the flight of the ball, allowing Wylde to sneak past him. The ball was once again presented on a silver platter for the in-rushing Thompson and once again he skied it horribly from inside the six-yard box.

It would have been rough on Hearts had they not had the legs to see St Mirren off, although another referee could quite easily have booked Carrick for diving and, of course, it's a different game if Thompson isn't so uncharacteristically profligate in front of goal. All this does is illustrate the fine margins within which we're operating and after losing out so often we pocketed this one unapologetically.

The irony of the match was that it had been re-scheduled with the sole intention of ensuring Ryan Stevenson's eligibility for Sunday's League Cup semi-final but the blossoming triumvirate of Nicholson, Smith and Carrick staked a serious claim to start themselves. Uncharted territory for Lockie: instead of worrying who to pick for the next game, who to leave out?

The only onion in the ointment in the week was the SPFL's decision to veto Hearts' touchingly optimistic request to cancel Alan Combe's playing contract and replace him with Rudi Skacel. How could they not let us swap an ageing goalkeeping coach who's never once played for us with a 34-year-old former Czech Republic international with two Scottish Cup winners' medals under his belt? Bloody killjoys.

30

Inverness Caledonian Thistle, Easter Road, League Cup semi-final, 2 February 2014, 12.15pm

DOWN through the years Hearts have turned spectacular implosion into an art form. Sunday lunchtime's League Cup semi-final versus ICT saw the unveiling of our latest ghastly exhibit as a 2-1 lead against nine men was somehow thrown away with a couple of seconds of injury time to go.

Possession was squandered ever so cheaply and the scrappiest of late equalisers sent the semi-final into extra time. Then, bereft of energy and, seemingly, ideas, the tie stuttered into a penalty shoot-out. All the momentum was with ICT and their 4-2 triumph came as little surprise, leaving Hearts flat out – broken and inconsolable on the bone-hard Easter Road pitch.

Hearts came into this game off the back of two morale-boosting 2-1 wins, the second of which had been hastily re-arranged to allow Ryan Stevenson's two-match ban to expire. It's testament to the esteem with which the Carrick–Smith–Nicholson triumvirate is held, then, that Lockie opted to persist with all three, leaving Stevo on the bench.

Straight after the St Mirren game Stevo had been asked on BBC Alba whether he expected to start on Sunday. His ever so slightly withering 'yes, I would have thought so' suggests Lockie's decision may not have gone down too well. Certainly, Stevo's sullen and jaded performance when eventually coming off the bench did little to dispel that notion.

Joining him on the bench was the new loan signing from West Ham, Paul McCallum (the like-for-like replacement for Swansea-bound Adam King) and his presence brought back happy memories of the same semi-final a year ago and the impact that day of Liverpool's Michael Ngoo.

ICT old boy Terry Butcher had said during the build-up to the game that such was his fervent desire to see Caley go through that turning up to watch would be way too stressful. Funnily enough, he'd coped fine with the stress the previous year. Perhaps I'm being overly cynical but his pronouncement smacked of a cheap attempt to ingratiate himself with the Easter Road faithful. The honeymoon period looks to be well and truly over there, what with Butcher's record after his first ten games inferior to Fenlon's final ten.

Winter sunlight streaked across the pitch at kick-off as a biting gale sliced through the two open corners opposite the chilly East Stand. Hearts took a while to become accustomed to the gusting wind and fiery pitch and could quite easily have conceded a couple of early goals after both Wilson and McHattie got flustered and were caught napping.

The ICT fans had flocked south in their tens and were in cocky, boisterous mood, helpfully informing us all of our club's financial plight as well as our city's reported problems with HIV.

I genuinely can't wait to hear what revelations they'll have in store for us when we travel north in a fortnight. They'd better not give away the ending of *The Sopranos* or (spoiler alert) that Darth Vader is Luke Skywalker's father!

Their fans became noticeably subdued the longer the first half wore on as Hearts gradually imposed themselves on the game. Instead of being rushed into looking for Paterson who was flitting between right-midfield and centre-forward, passes were neatly clipped into the feet of Nicholson and Smith.

Around the half-hour mark, trickery from Nicholson set up Hamill but his shot bounced to safety. This was followed by Hearts going even closer. Again, the slippery Nicholson was involved as his dipping shot from distance was parried away unconvincingly by Dean Brill.

Their big, flat-footed keeper looked an absolute liability. Every so often, with play up the other end, he'd come bounding out of his goal to talk tactics with his centre-halves who you could tell were clearly humouring the guy just in order to get him back in his goal.

The half drew to a close with ICT re-asserting themselves. A noticeable trait in the league match between the sides at Tynecastle in December was that ICT hadn't been afraid to leave the odd boot in here and there to try and intimidate the opposition.

Referee John Beaton seemed content to give ICT the benefit of the doubt with a few questionably wild tackles while, aggravatingly, penalising Hearts for the most minor of offences. He'd allow Warren to come thudding through the back of Paterson, elbows up, sending the Hearts man sprawling yet blow his whistle because the same player used his upper body strength to spin away from an ICT defender.

Against St Mirren and Ross County it had been sheer bliss, we'd almost got used to the luxury of competent officiating but here the status quo looked to have been well and truly restored.

Hearts were beginning to look frail and vulnerable as ICT dominated possession. Gary Warren, in particular, was a one-man wrecking ball, knocking aside Hearts players as if they were skittles. Suddenly, out of nothing, Billy McKay found himself one on one with Jamma but the Hearts keeper kept his side in it with a brilliantly instinctive one-handed save. David Smith limped off gingerly at half-time after coming off second best in a knee-jarring 50-50 with David Raven and Stevo took his place for the second half.

ICT had obviously been fired up by one of Yogi's legendarily inspirational half-time team talks and with the hoarse remit to 'git intae thum fur fuck's sake, thaire jist wee laddies' still fresh in their minds, they came at Hearts with renewed vigour. Gawky Marley Watkins down the right and Aaron Doran on the left ensured an intense examination of both McGowan and McHattie's defensive capabilities. To be honest, neither really impressed, although Gowser made one diving interception that denied ICT a certain goal.

On 53 minutes ICT got the goal that had been on the cards a while, although it had a fair degree of good fortune attached to it as the ball clearly struck the hand of Doran in the build-up. Jamma hot-footed it out of his goal and remonstrated vehemently with the referee, receiving a yellow for his troubles. None of which should take away from the finish by Greg Tansey, though, which was unstoppable.

Having been stung by falling behind, Hearts became more urgent and looked to bring players into play quicker. On the hour mark they were rewarded for their endeavour with a glorious chance for Paterson after Graeme Shinnie and Warren faithfully re-enacted Miller and Hansen's Spain 1982 cock-up against Russia and left him clear on goal. Frustratingly, Brill spread himself to good effect and Paterson was thwarted.

On 63 minutes McCallum came on for Gowser with Paterson dropping to right-back and Stevo to right midfield. Had Hearts prevailed and progressed to the final against Aberdeen, you could have readily pinpointed the subsequent five-minute spell as being pivotal: the moments that defined the ultimate destiny of the contest, swinging the match our way. But, having lost, all looking back does is rub salt in the wounds, reinforcing what a great position we managed to hopelessly screw up.

Nicholson's run at the heart of the ICT defence ended when he was deposited in a crumpled heap by Warren who was shown a second yellow. The offence took place slap bang on the edge of the box and from a well-worked training ground routine Stevo dummied a touch to McHattie but instead fed Hamill who turned and swept the ball into the far corner courtesy of a helpful deflection.

Hearts' tails were up: all square and with a man advantage. With the wind at their backs they continued to attack and three minutes later won another free kick on the edge of the box. This time it was Meekings's turn to up-end Nicholson. Slightly further out than before, Hamill surpassed himself, this time curling the ball high into the top corner as Brill flapped at the post. To have gone from one down to 2-1 up with the opposition down to ten men in five pulsating minutes represented a remarkable turnaround and the Hearts fans in the 12,762 crowd were in dreamland.

For a spell our side was caught between keeping going, pressing home the advantage, perhaps even nicking a third and sitting back seeing out the game on the back foot. An over-reliance on the latter handed ICT the initiative and Jamma was forced to pull off two more wonder-saves from McKay and then Meekings.

ICT's all-out attack left tranches of space at the back and on 85 minutes Paterson came barrelling all the way down the touchline from right-back, cut inside and unleashed a flashing drive that was pushed away for a corner.

Hearts were holding all the aces and, as with the previous two league matches, seemed perfectly well-versed in delaying tactics at the corner flag to help see out another 2-1 win. This point wasn't lost on ICT and a number of their players looked on the verge of losing the plot altogether. Raven had a nibble at McHattie and was clearly spoiling for a fight while Meekings was hit with a straight red for petulantly swiping out at Robinson and sending him spinning to the ground.

Shinnie was next, hurling abuse at the referee and getting booked for dissent. All that served to do was further reinforce the notion that this had to be our day. So when Hearts won a corner, deep into stoppage time, and Stevo failed to win another through lashing the ball against the defender's legs, it barely even registered how much that could end up costing us. But cost us it did.

Gifting possession back to ICT gave them one last throw of the dice and as we stared in uncomprehending disbelief Nick Ross rode a couple of tackles before somehow scoring, the ball spinning agonisingly off Jamma and high into the net. Silence and bewilderment in the Hearts end provided a sharp contrast to the pandemonium among those Caley fans who hadn't left when Meekings walked.

Extra time began and there was a general sense of deflation at having essentially thrown victory away. ICT were more than happy to set up camp inside their own half and frustrate Hearts.

Irrespective of how keen Hamill and Robinson were to get on the ball and look to create an opening they faced a packed penalty area and the only out-ball was often wide to the right for Paterson. The big man had started off the afternoon as a striker, putting in a decent shift up top, before being shifted to the right and then to right-back. He was spent, dead on his feet, with barely sufficient stamina to bring the ball down and run with it let alone co-ordinate his limbs sufficiently to measure a cross into a good area. He lurched forward, clearly operating on autopilot, and shanked a brace of crosses into the fans behind the goal.

Despite only having nine men on the pitch ICT continued to dig in while Hearts increasingly seemed to lack the wherewithal to break Caley down. Right at the death McCallum missed a snip of a chance, his close-range header clearing the bar at an angle that had so much elevation it seemed to defy the laws of geometry.

A number of Hearts fans were unable to conceal their dismay at the manner in which events were unfolding and made their feelings plain when extra time finished. After the rapport that had been built up between fans and players this season it was deeply unpleasant seeing supporters turn on the players. It all added to a building sense that we'd blown our chance and now ICT were in the ascendancy.

During the shoot-out ICT kept their nerve despite Shinnie missing their opening gambit. McCallum, inexplicably Hearts' first taker, also missed and ICT didn't waver again. Carrick and Robinson both scored for Hearts but Hamill missed, giving Draper the chance to put his side into the final. He didn't fail.

Standing, staring, the defeat became imprinted indelibly. Half an hour or so ago we were all contemplating another day out at a final. Idly musing as to whether it would be Ibrox, or Parkhead? Could we mug Aberdeen for a third time? In your mind you're already there, you're wondering which pub to hole up in pre-final and then suddenly it's snatched away in the blink of an eye and the repercussions are a setback even more painful and potentially destructive than the Ross County collapse back in September.

Monday was shaping up to be a dark day with the silence broken only by the continued crowing of jubilant Hibs fans cracking weak jokes about Easter Road and the need for disinfectant. And it's not often you'll find Hibs fans and disinfectant cropping up in the same sentence.

But then along came the announcement that majority shareholder Ubig had agreed to transfer its 78.97 per cent stake in the club to the fans' group. The proposal still needed to be ratified at a Ubig creditors' meeting, scheduled to take place in late March, but this would allow BDO to begin the process of handing over ownership to the Foundation of Hearts.

It was a hugely welcome announcement, helping to put this semi-final defeat in some sort of context. Don't get me wrong, it was a sore one that still hurts but news that possibly the greatest obstacle had been overcome at least gives us something positive to console ourselves with. You can accept losing a battle or two along the way just so long as you win the war.

And anyone still needing cheering up can log on to Hibs.net and laugh at just how many sad, bitter Hibs clowns have emailed the Lithuanian president to try and persuade him to do whatever it takes to liquidate Hearts. The Lithuanian *president*.

Think I'm feeling better already.

31

Inverness Caledonian Thistle away, 15 February 2014, 3pm

THE Thursday before this game it was announced that fan group Foundation of Hearts is being backed by a 66-year-old Edinburgh businesswoman called Ann Budge. Apparently Budge is the sole director of Bidco 1874 which has struck a £2.5m deal with the administrator BDO to get Hearts out of administration. The deal is for the purchase of the shares from Ubig who hold that 78.97 per cent stake in the club.

The statement from the Foundation of Hearts revealed that Budge would become executive chair of the club on a 'no fee' basis and the aim was for Bidco 'to sign a legally binding agreement with the Foundation on behalf of the fans, to transfer majority ownership of the club on satisfaction of their contracted commitments, at the earliest opportunity, but certainly within a period not to exceed five years'.

Bidco, the statement went on, will run the club for at least three years and will not be seeking repayment of the £2.5m for at least two years to allow money raised by fans to be used as working capital.

All of which was massively encouraging, hearing that a definitive plan was in place and with credible individuals. Budge apparently sold her IT company for a reported £40m profit. We still had cause to fret, though, seeing that everything hinged on the deal to take the shares and this still required ratification at the creditors' meeting scheduled for late March.

However, all being well, the Foundation reckoned that we'd hopefully exit administration in April and in raising £6m in five years will be able to 'achieve the objectives of saving the club over the long term and moving into supporter ownership'.

All of which gave plenty of food for thought during the four-hour train journey up to the Highlands. It's hard to know whether the fixtures have been kind to us or not this season. On the plus side we've been spared double doses of Celtic Park, Pittodrie and Tannadice. But this has been offset somewhat by two visits to Dingwall and two to Inverness. The second trip of each being in the depths of winter.

So, here we all were again, back up at the Tulloch Caledonian and the backdrop still resembled one of those under-construction stadia you encounter occasionally on Sky's *The Premier League Years*. But, instead of predatory weasel Ian Rush wreaking mayhem at a half-built Old Trafford or Selhurst Park circa 1994 you've got the world's gawkiest-looking pub team taking to a pitch lined with flimsy, windswept portakabins. It looks like the set of *Auf Wiedersehen, Pet* up there. Which seems pretty apt, given most of the ICT side resemble a bunch of rough-arsed brickies and plasterers.

You just know all it would take would be a suitably fierce gust of wind from the correct direction and all that fibreglass and plasterboard would end up bobbing around with the dolphins in the Moray Firth and snagged around the foot of that infernal Kessock Bridge.

But, depressingly, this shithole is actually considered finished. The builders have long since packed away their hard hats and spirit levels and there's no shiny new stand for these scarcely interested fans to look forward to. Not that they deserve it. Nope, just the same wind-blown building site every other week.

As with our last visit to these parts, in August, Hearts arrived with a couple of notable absentees. Back then our home game with Aberdeen had led to Danny Wilson and Kevin McHattie serving one-match bans while today McHattie (again) and Callum Paterson were missing after accruing too many disciplinary points.

Even without a makeshift defence – Jordan McGhee coming back into the side – ICT were always going to be all about bullying Hearts into submission, after all it's in their DNA.

Back when Jamie Walker was fit and playing every week you could set your watch by the half-chance he'd always eke out and squander within the first couple of minutes, pulling it, disappointingly, into the side-netting. 'Promising start,' you'd say to yourself, knowing full well this was probably as good as it would get. Now, of course, Walker's out injured and his early, scuffed, half-hit shot has been replaced, in kind, by a right-footed Ryan Stevenson curler landing on the roof of the net.

Therefore, once Stevo's cameo role in Inverness was over, it was almost as if the home side set the ball down for the goal kick and said to Hearts, 'You won't be needing **this** anymore.' They took full advantage of a fairly salty sea breeze and pinned Hearts back for the entirety of the first half.

Shaven-headed Scouser David Raven was first up, the wind whisking his cross against the bar. The rebound popped up invitingly for Graeme Shinnie but Jamie MacDonald got down smartly to make the block.

It wasn't long before Jamma was called into action again, this time to thwart Billy McKay. The little Ulsterman had scored a brace in each of the two previous league games against us this season and looked set to add to that tally when put through one on one, but Jamma stood up impressively.

Hearts were retreating further and further back and each attack seemed to inch ICT closer to taking the lead. McKay turned provider and played in Marley Watkins. Resisting the urge to burst the ball with his teeth, lick his balls and then roll on to his back for a doggy treat, Marley made a beeline for the goal. McGhee came sliding in from nowhere to clear with Jamma painfully exposed.

Not long after, Watkins went even closer, Jamma somehow getting a touch to his close-range header and palming it on to the bar. By the time Greg Tansey clunked yet another effort off the woodwork, in first-half stoppage time, it was hard to muster up any more relief, crammed as we were into the crappy zero-leg-room seats behind Jamma's goal. The over-riding feeling was one of numbness as a goal had seemed increasingly inevitable. All these near misses off the woodwork did was delay what seemed utterly unavoidable.

Except, despite being resigned to it, that goal never came and the first-half onslaught was as close as ICT would get as they failed to scale the same heights in the second 45.

The game slotted into its rightful berth in the *Sportscene* graveyard slot. So, instead of a commentator going through the five or so minutes – feigning surprise as events unfolded even though you know none of it is actually new to them and, in the case of Rob MacLean, there's a good chance he also did the radio commentary the previous day – we got Brian McLauchlin talking over the game's meagre pleasures, very much in the style of a man straining to read the bottom line of an eye test.

In the post-match analysis Michael Stewart made the point that once Hearts accepted their fate performances and results improved. His argument being that they were responding positively to being under less pressure. While there is undoubted truth in this assertion, a few weeks back Stewart had laid into Hearts, pegging them as a bunch of shapeless, badly coached, ill-prepared under-achievers, 'lacking any discernible style of play' as he put it.

It must come as a great relief to all at Hearts to know all it took to suddenly give the impression of being coached well was an acceptance of relegation.

32

Celtic home,
22 February 2014, 12.45 pm

DOMESTICALLY, Neil Lennon has more than a hint of 'Competitive Dad' from *The Fast Show* about him, leaving underlings gasping and spluttering in his wake while he powers across to the other side of the swimming pool and then stares back in tearful triumph at his vanquished foes, casting the odd glance of silent gratitude to the heavens. 'Yesss, did it: finished first again!'

Given their crowds and wage bill Celtic dwarf their rivals. But in somehow making out that coming first in a Rangers-less league represents any sort of achievement whatsoever, attention is deflected away from a string of quite catastrophic cup defeats to the likes of Ross County, Kilmarnock, St Mirren, Morton and Aberdeen. Such a portfolio of results would have had anyone other than the impregnable Lennon subject to serious scrutiny from a mutinous support.

In the main they seem more than happy to glibly take what he says. Anyone else managing that club would be repeatedly put on the spot and asked why, in the absence of Rangers, haven't they done back-to-back trebles?

Equally absurd was the fanfare surrounding Fraser Forster and his spurious attempt to surpass Bobby Clark's record of 1,155 minutes without conceding a goal. Forster goes whole games only having to deal with back-passes. The fact this record is viewed as any sort of achievement given the present climate is preposterous.

This lunchtime contest was a prime example. Hearts had, as the focal point of their attack, on-loan West Ham striker Paul McCallum, someone who doesn't even *look* like a footballer. When he chases after loose balls or goes up for flick-ons it's hard to shake the image of one of those plucky DJs or TV presenters running their heart out for SoccerAid.

It's just a shame it wasn't Patrick Kielty or Jamie Theakston in goal for Celtic or a 48-year-old Gary Pallister in central defence. That way, McCallum might have had a slim chance of making the tiniest of impressions on this game. As it was he transcended hopelessness and it made you wonder what made our coaching team sacrifice one of our brightest young starlets in Adam King for this dud.

Yet, despite this, Forster still managed to look uncertain at times, fumbling a perfectly routine Jamie Hamill cross with no one within ten feet of him. This was as close as Hearts got to troubling Celtic in a sterile first half and towards the end Forster waggled his glove in the air to register the record. It made him look like Mickey Mouse at Disney World. At the other end, when Kris Commons wasn't smirking at multitudes of Hearts fans ridiculing his not inconsiderable girth, he was worrying Jamma with a couple of long-range shots that rippled the top of the net.

Leigh Griffiths was featuring for a Celtic side that had won 15 league games on the bounce. Griffiths had been an irascible menace with Hibs so seeing him in a Celtic shirt was definitely a cause for mild concern. That's not to say it was enough to stop the Hearts fans mercilessly ripping into him en masse about the 5-1 and the fact he still really does look like a thumb.

We all knew we'd pay dearly for these years of abuse if he scored but for as long as it was 0-0 and things weren't quite happening for him it seemed perfectly acceptable to tempt fate and ridicule him relentlessly.

All of which meant when he finally did score that inevitable goal only the pettiest, most precious, hypocritical home fan could take issue with Griffiths milking the moment for all it was worth, sprinting to the centre of the Wheatfield and skidding down on to his knees, both thumbs stuck triumphantly into the air.

The goal itself was classic, arch-predator Griffiths. Bouncing away from Nicholson he advanced on Danny Wilson, turning him inside out before returning the ball to his left foot and lacing it into the far corner across MacDonald.

Celtic have got used to winning games and even right at the death when Forster pawed unconvincingly at C-Patz's prodigious throw-in you never truly believed there was anything in the script to suggest a late Hearts equaliser. And like the drumbeats at the end of *EastEnders* we all got the ending we've reluctantly grown used to as Celtic broke upfield and Pukki again found the net against us. So, definitely *not* a complete waste of money then.

Losing 2-0 at home to Celtic is one of those scorelines that is just so depressingly familiar in this fixture. Missing from this version, however, was the usual air of nastiness. To Celtic we'd become beyond parody. In such moments we're usually serenaded with 'aw the wee huns are shiiiite' sung with a combination of gloating contempt and purring patronage. Today, at the end, the whole end simply sung 'We'll meet again'. It was almost poignant.

33
Motherwell away, 1 March 2014, 3pm

HEARTS picked the wrong day to revert back to that one-dimensional long ball game of theirs. Shaun Hutchison and Stephen McManus gobbled up Hearts' lazy lumps forward, dwarfing McCallum and Paterson. Surrendering possession may not have been an issue at ICT but here Hearts were sloppy in defence and paid the price with a 4-1 shellacking.

This was an opportunity lost as Hearts actually started quite brightly and Motherwell were vulnerable down the sides with two relatively inexperienced full-backs in Reid and Leitch.

Yet, in reality, Motherwell probably couldn't have hand-picked a better fixture to get back on the rails on a pitch more sanded than Blackpool beach.

The Steelmen intuitively read every bounce and bobble off their destroyed playing surface. They seemed to know, instinctively, when the ball would fail to bounce naturally and splat sideways.

Iain Vigurs broke the deadlock on 20 minutes, nipping in between static Hearts defenders to prod home in front of the away fans. Not entirely sure what we've done to rattle his cage but he took great delight in shushing us on his way across to thank McFadden for the ball in.

Hearts restarted briskly and attempted to pick up where they'd left off but Fir Park has not been a particularly happy hunting ground for us of late and there was a sense of futility about our doomed attempts to get back in the game.

Stevo saw a free kick from the edge of the box narrowly miss the target before McCallum looped a header on to the roof of the net.

Having comfortably weathered Hearts' paltry flurry of attacks, Motherwell quietly and effectively put the game to bed with a depressingly spectacular second goal. McFadden somehow kept the ball in play by the left touchline and scooped the ball high into the path of Ainsworth who cracked home a stunning volley.

Half-time arrived and big, bad Brad McKay got hooked but only the armband saved Wilson who was slack with pretty much every ball out of defence. The housewives' favourite was replaced by Carrick who started the half in fine style, dribbling down the left, cutting inside and rattling the top of the bar with a powerful drive.

Who knows, maybe starting with Carrick, Nicholson and Stevenson up top might have been the way to go, but for now we seem to have forsaken that brief period of effective strike play in favour of accommodating the execrable McCallum.

Either way, this match was long gone and John Sutton got his customary goal against us on 65 minutes. Faddy was left in a crumpled heap on the edge of the box but Sutton poked home before the referee could blow for the foul and when the slap-headed former Scotland maverick came to it was to news he had a hat-trick of assists to go with his receding hairline.

Fads finally got his name on the scoresheet with 15 to go, knocking in a close-range header from a corner but not before C-Patz had scored with a header of his own, from McHattie's corner.

In the end Hearts were horsed 4-1 and Ross County's point at home to Partick moved them 20 points clear of us and with a far superior goal difference. Bet the relief up in Dingwall was palpable, eh?

At ease, Staggies: you can breathe again.

34

Kilmarnock away,
8 March 2014, 3pm

IT would be tempting to lump this defeat together with the previous week's puny capitulation at Fir Park, given that another four goals were shipped as Hearts lurch unerringly towards pre-split relegation. Except, there was much more to admire in this 4-2 defeat, not least the thrillingly precocious talent of Sam Nicholson and the highly effective Dale Carrick once again staking a decent claim to be the main striker. Yet it was the same old failings that undid Hearts: hesitant, wobbly defending, flimsy, at times non-existent, cover from midfield and a general lack of direction and leadership.

The match was slowly settling into a fairly even contest. Kris Boyd had been skulking around looking barely interested and Hearts had enjoyed decent spells of possession. Then, on the half-hour mark, Killie went ahead thanks to a freakish own goal from Danny Wilson. McKenzie ran clear of McHattie on the right, crossing early, and Wilson's swiped clearance flew back off his boot and past a baffled Jamie MacDonald.

But Hearts raised the hopes of their considerable travelling support with virtually an instantaneous equaliser. Carrick, alert and on his toes, read Ashworth's hesitancy as he dithered shepherding the ball back to his keeper and nipped in to lob the ball over Samson and into the unguarded net.

Therefore, a welcome upgrade on the previous Saturday's debacle at Fir Park saw Hearts go in 1-1 at the break and in fine fettle. All it would take, however, were six painful second-half minutes for normal service to be resumed and for Kris Boyd to continue his one-man crusade against Hearts. By the 51st minute he'd nabbed his third double against us in three games: firstly, robbing a dawdling and criminally sluggish Jamie Hamill to run through and finish and secondly latching on to a McGowan lapse and firing in.

Killie had put the after-burners on and were streaking away from us, 3-1 to the good. Again, we'd failed to heed the lessons of previous encounters with Killie and had no answer whatsoever to the predatory brilliance of Boyd.

Hamill was flagging and soon taken off – struggling as he was to find the relentless energy that was needed to mask his many limitations. The club's predicament has led Jamie – as senior pro – to undergo reinvention as a selfless, box-to-box, midfield dynamo. Everything flows through him as he adopts the mantle of main man, setting the pace and leading by example. Thing is, he's not remotely good enough to take on that level of responsibility. He's a bog-standard, functional midfielder with a decent engine and a penchant for going into tackles slightly recklessly. Under Paulo Sergio, he just about kept the boo-boys at bay by keeping his head down and concentrating purely on his own game. Here, while his efforts are commendable, watching him gamely try to be Roy Keane *circa* 1999 each week you're constantly put in mind of that line in *Top Gun*, 'Your ego is writing cheques your body can't cash.'

Yet, as the season grinds on towards the inevitable plummet, Hamill's floundering taps into a deeper flaw. That the spine of our team is fatally compromised. From goalkeeper to centre-half to central midfield to centre-forward we yield and split like balsa wood.

Jamie MacDonald is a fearsome and agile shot-stopper, surely up there with the best in the land. However, when it comes to crosses, when it comes to asserting himself and commanding his area you'd be as well sticking the guy from the Mr Muscle ads in goal. Centre-half? Danny Wilson did us a massive favour when he agreed to stay with us on reduced wages, yet he's young and isn't a natural leader. The role of main defensive lynchpin appears a stretch for him. And further forward we've spent months flogging the young life out of makeshift striker Callum Paterson.

It's easy to sit here and pontificate but, despite our dire financial state, there's a case for saying we botched our transfer dealings last summer. I don't know, perhaps our hands were tied completely and we were left with no other options. But did we need to keep all of MacDonald, Wilson, Hamill and Stevo or was there any leeway regarding who departed? Hindsight is a wonderful thing but how many more points would we have had with Andy Webster sitting alongside Wilson, nursing him through games, instead of it being the supremely laid-back Wilson as the senior partner in any duo?

And, up front, the much-derided John Sutton simply had to be a better bet than Paterson, especially as C-Patz brings so much more to the party as a swashbuckling full-back. Sutton, as he showed with a double in a 3-3 draw at Easter Road in today's only other game, has flourished at Motherwell with a couple of speedy wingers to either side, feeding him the ball early.

This is especially relevant when you consider that in wide areas we're relatively well furnished. Our central spine may be weak but peripherally we have full-backs, wide midfielders and wingers in abundance. Perhaps the brightest of these prospects, little Sam Nicholson, briefly rekindled our hopes here with a sweet finish from a King run and cross after 70 minutes. But it took only two minutes for these hopes to be extinguished once and for all and the two-goal margin to be re-established – Gardyne firing home after his initial effort had struck the bar. As they'd done on Boxing Day, Killie then tailed off towards the end, leaving Boyd gnashing his teeth once again at a missed opportunity for a hat-trick.

It meant more to him than it did to us. Sitting as we are on six points. Another ten goals from Boyd wouldn't have made the blindest bit of difference.

35
Dundee United home, 21 March 2014, 7.45pm

WHILE Henry Smith mooched around the walkway beneath the Wheatfield Stand, in the vain hope someone might offer to buy him a pie, the rain thudded off the corrugated iron roof and we shivered, more in response to the biting east wind than through anticipation of what footballing joys the evening might have in store.

The best we could hope for was to stave off relegation for a week, ideally removing the possibility of Hibs relegating us at Tynecastle in our next match. Yet, with our closest rivals playing as many as three times before we were next up, it may be that Hibs' job would already be done for them by a week on Sunday.

Either way, Dundee United shrugged off the horrible weather and dispatched a stubborn, spirited yet frustratingly blunt Hearts with a little to spare. That 4-1 reversal at Tannadice back in December may have flattered United but 2-1 here probably flattered Hearts.

The lasting legacy of our League Cup semi-final defeat seems to have been the snuffing out of whatever spark was motivating Ryan Stevenson. Instead of that workaholic Trojan sweatily running opposing defenders into corners and that deadly marksman with dynamite in his boots we now have a morose sulk who squanders possession with an insouciant shrug and lashes the ball goalwards seemingly glad to be rid of the responsibility.

Much like how Robert de Niro now views making a new movie as an opportunity to open another franchised restaurant, Stevo's the same with football games and new tattoos. You can see him jogging disinterestedly after the ball thinking, 'Great, another week and a half and I'll be able to afford that Oriental serpent's head poking out of my arse crack.'

But whatever was lost from Stevenson in that Easter Road collapse was more than made up for in the show of faith in Nicholson and Carrick. Against United, Nicholson seemed at times to glide across the sodden turf, he was like Legolas, his feet barely making contact with the ground.

Teams have gotten into the habit of starting slowly against Hearts and tonight was no exception. Hearts were undeniably busy and inventive from kick-off but it's a trend that may also have something to do with the opposition feeling relaxed enough to let Hearts have plenty of the ball to begin with. We don't have a great scoring record and teams seem quite relaxed to let us have a wee play around with the ball early doors, figuring we won't do much with it and they'll have plenty of chances carved out as the match progresses.

So whether by accident or design, United started tentatively and it was Hearts who played the better football. Kevin McHattie stung Cierzniak's palms before Carrick spun and shot inside the box.

But all season it's been the same, we huff and puff and make it seem like we have the opposition on the ropes, then we blink and we're one down. We are positively porous at the back. After 35 minutes, Ryan Dow flew past two defenders, wide on the left, and picked out the unmarked Robertson who'd drifted unnoticed into the box. The left-back laid the ball into space for Brian Graham who calmly lifted it into the roof of the net for 1-0.

You can't fault Hearts' spirit, though, and they came roaring back through the rain at United, keen to try and get to the break on level terms. Callum Paterson powered a header from a Smith cross marginally too high and then a cute Hamill back-heel teed up Stevo who hit the side-netting.

The tempo increased after the break in increasingly torrential rain and Robertson forced MacDonald into a brilliant one-handed save after sprinting clear down the left. Progressively, the Tangerines found themselves camped in the Hearts half and MacDonald was again called into action, this time keeping out Armstrong.

Hearts were doing all they could to stay in touch with United but were finally breached again on 70 minutes. Nadir Ciftçi skilfully evaded both Robinson and McHattie before holding off Wilson and curling expansively past the helpless MacDonald.

Yet Hearts weren't finished and Wilson got his head to a Nicholson corner and set up a grandstand finish with 12 minutes left. McKay was thrown on for Carrick and stuck up front but it was to no avail. With eight games left we trail our closest competitor, St Mirren, by 21 points having played a game more than them. The end is nigh.

36

Hibernian home,
30 March 2014, 12.45pm

HIBS sold out their full allocation for this fixture weeks in advance, desperately keen to add relegating Hearts to their meagre list of club honours. However, all their pre-match hype and expectation ended up counting for very little as for the second time this season they left Tynecastle empty-handed, with nothing but the jubilant celebrations of a euphoric home support ringing in their ears.

All you'd heard for weeks from Hibernian fans was endless talk of the relegation party they were planning for Tynecastle and, true to their word, they turned up in full revelry mode, bedecked in Hawaiian shirts and brandishing sombreros and inflatable palm trees. St Mirren's 2-2 draw at Inverness the previous afternoon had given them exactly what they'd been craving; the opportunity to be the side to officially send us down. And a victory here would grant them that dearest of wishes.

On one level this carnival atmosphere was quintessentially black Scottish humour, vaguely reminiscent of the Hearts fans who, with second spot already secured, turned up at Ibrox in May 2006 and read the Sunday papers. Yet, on another, what we were seeing went deeper and hinted at something far more sinister.

When viewed in conjunction with the not insignificant numbers of Hibs supporters pestering the authorities in Lithuania, inundating them with reasons to reject the Foundation of Hearts' bid to secure the Ubig shares, it became more. It became a concerted effort to see their oldest, bitterest rivals liquidated out of all existence.

These years of grinding, relentless domination have taken their toll on the Hibs fans. A whole generation have been defined by their subservience. After all the misery inflicted on them many probably felt their actions were justified. Payback time had finally arrived and boy were they going to make the most of their moment.

So, turning up at Tynecastle that dank, clammy, Sunday lunchtime, with the haar swirling in from the North Sea, the very future of Heart of Midlothian FC seemed to hang precariously in the balance. And adding to the sense of foreboding was news of further delays in setting up meetings in Lithuania.

Hibernian's keenness to wipe Hearts off the face of the planet seemed encapsulated perfectly in their delight at the prospect of relegating us. It all merged into one heaving, gloating, smirking mass; licking their lips in anticipation of finishing us off once and for all.

As a support we had no direct control over these wider issues, we were simply placing our faith in events going our way elsewhere. But we did have control over how vehemently and passionately we would stick by our young side. The mood from the Hearts fans packing out three sides of the ground went way beyond defiance. This was about survival; pure and simple. Fighting for the right to exist, to still have a team to call our own. Of staring, unflinching and unblinking into the abyss and showing no fear.

The BT crew of Paul Hartley, Darren Jackson and Stephen Craigan stood at their flimsy little table in the shadow of the Wheatfield as the crescendo of noise steadily built.

Hartley knew he was among friends and grinned up at the home support whenever he thought he was off-camera while a bashful Jackson, mindful of how much of his CV was taken up with the other lot, was slightly more reticent. Craigan, as we've all come to expect, dismissed Hearts out of hand, 'Hibs will win comfortably,' his Ulster accent almost gnawing on the words. 'Hearts are already down and Hibs know exactly what they need to do here.'

By kick-off the clamour was deafening as each set of supporters sought to drown out the other. In an intriguing twist, however, the Hearts support became empowered, reclaiming the 'D' word and using it to cast aspersions on their rival's top-league credentials, 'Down with the Jambos, you're going down with the Jambos.'

We had long become reconciled to our fate and harboured the faintest of hopes that Hibs, in seventh, could yet be pulled into that play-off dogfight. Their horrendous record of one win in 12 had the undoubted whiff of relegation about it but there still remained a six-point cushion between themselves and St Mirren down in 11th spot.

After five minutes of a wildly frenetic opening in which the ball barely touched the ground, Hearts raced ahead. Paterson, found well by Hamill, fired a swerving, dipping ball into the penalty box from wide on the right. It was fizzed in straight at Stevo who was hovering around the penalty spot, and the Hearts number seven did amazingly well to kill the ball, cushioning it down for Carrick with the top of his chest. Speedie took the merest of touches to control the ball before gleefully ramming it high past Williams. Tynecastle, already a bubbling powder-keg, ignited in unchecked pandemonium, maroon-clad supporters celebrating with crazed abandon.

This unscripted start had left the champagne in the Hibs end more than a little flat as 'here for the party, we're only here for the party' rang out, full of defiant swagger and mocking belligerence.

Getting a goal so early in the derby can sometimes be counter-productive. Teams suddenly stop doing what had been so effective thereby handing the initiative back to their opponents. Not here, though. Hearts became emboldened, zipping the ball around with even more verve and gusto.

Smith tested Williams with a decent strike after referee Steven McLean had played a clever advantage while all Hibs had in retaliation were big alehouse punts that repeatedly sailed over big James Collins's big, shaved head.

As the half wore on the mocking refrain 'some fucking party, oh this is some fucking party' became more and more prevalent as the Hibs support sat sullen and dejected in their party gear. Or, in Leigh Griffiths's case, his saggy grey hoodie.

Judging by Hibs' average home attendances this had to be many of their fans' first look at the side since the previous derby back on 2 January (since winning that night they'd only picked up one other league victory) and you got the impression half of them were agog at just how hopeless their side had become. Truly, they were bereft of any spirit whatsoever and were utterly shambolic in that first half.

In the grisly aftermath here Terry Butcher would attach inordinate significance to the injustice of a Jordan Forster goal wrongly ruled out for offside late on. Yet little or nothing was made of the perfectly legitimate goal Hearts were denied when Carrick slotted home after half an hour, the flag going up belatedly to penalise a clearly in-line Sam Nicholson.

Gary McAllister noted sagely, 'Hearts are bossing this,' and their whole first-half performance could be encapsulated in one moment of brilliance in the dying moments. Hibs were harried into losing possession in their own half and Nicholson, a fearless livewire, jinked inside from the left and lashed a sweeping drive goalwards with the outside of his right foot. The ball was flying into the top corner until Ben Williams got across to tip it to safety.

Hibs, for their part, had failed to register even a single shot on target and limped back to the dressing room like chastened dogs when the whistle finally blew. You wondered what Butcher would find to say to his misfiring misfits at half-time that he hadn't already thought of in those 11 previous games they'd failed to win. The big man was morphing, ever so gradually, into a morose waxwork caricature of the effusive colossus it had been impossible not to admire up in the Highlands.

Hibs upped their tempo and work rate in the second half and, as a result, enjoyed a whopping 62 per cent possession. However, much of their time on the ball was fruitless while Hearts and their front three of Smith, Carrick and Nicholson were a genuine threat throughout. Carrick twice set up Smith who narrowly missed the target on each occasion.

Hibs got their first sniff of goal after an hour with McGivern sending a near-post header into his own supporters from a corner. Jamie Mac then got *his* first sniff of *them* seconds later when some lowlife lobbed a bottle-green Adidas Gazelle at him.

Belatedly, Butcher made a switch, swapping Harris and Thomson for Taiwo and Whatmore and their introduction, coupled with an understandable edginess creeping into Hearts' game as the clock ticked down, saw Hibs string a few semi-coherent attacks together.

And, with nine minutes left, they looked to have got the equaliser their possession probably warranted when Forster outjumped Holt at the back post to head home. Inexplicably and hilariously, however, the stand-side linesman had totally missed the prone figure of Dylan McGowan slowly getting back to his feet three feet closer to the goal than Forster and raised his flag.

Now it was Hearts' turn to get out of jail thanks to a wrong call. Although when Nicholson had been adjudged offside for Carrick's goal earlier he'd been level so it wasn't a decision you'd necessarily be surprised to see go against you. This one here? Not so much. It was an absolute howler and the seethe was palpable.

But, then again, Gowser had been due a break from a stand-side linesman. He'd been the victim of a quite horrendous call against Dundee United back in September, having what looked like being the only goal of the game taken off him for a phantom infringement.

As Hibs kept pushing for the equaliser they felt they were worth sizeable gaps were being left at the back. Billy King was brought on for Carrick in a calculated ploy to try and exploit these opportunities and two minutes from time he was upended by Maybury as he raced clear. The former Hearts man had been lucky still to be on the pitch after only receiving a yellow for a crude elbow on Nicholson by the touchline but justice was served as he finally walked.

Going down to ten men barely registered with Hibs, though. With four minutes of stoppage time left it was do or die and they gambled everything on nicking a late equaliser. But Hearts still remained a potent threat on the break and when Robinson intercepted a slack ball from Stanton on the edge of the Hearts box they sprang into action. Robbo quickly fed Nicholson who sped over halfway before finding Stevo who swept the ball on, first time, for King, sending him through one on one with the keeper.

It was breathless viewing. Hearts fans were almost unable to watch as the young substitute calmly notched his first goal of the season, keeping his feet while rounding Williams, before sliding the ball into an empty net and sparking scenes of wild hysteria in the corner of the main and Gorgie stands. Jamie Mac was the Human Torch, a blur of orange, sprinting the length of the pitch to dive into the midst of the celebrating throng.

Derek Rae, commentating for BT Sport, put it far, far better than anyone, 'And the message is clear at Tynecastle: not on this patch of Edinburgh land. Not in a derby. No relegation **today**.'

He was right.

37

Aberdeen home,
2 April 2014, 7.45pm

HAD the scoreline here remained at 1-0 to Aberdeen then defeat would've sent us down and while we've all made our peace with that, it didn't stop us bloody-mindedly delaying the inevitable and grabbing a late equaliser from the penalty spot. That the point was salvaged despite us being down to ten men, after Danny Wilson's second yellow, just goes to illustrate the quite phenomenal spirit bursting through Locke's side.

Whenever Aberdeen come down to Tynecastle I'm always taken aback by just how obnoxious they all are. They chant in spiky, derogatory terms and in doing so you get a sense that they still consider themselves to be this mighty, all-conquering footballing entity. The noise and the force of conviction never fails to startle me because their record at Tynecastle is horrendous. More often than not, they head for the exits at 3-0 with 15 minutes to go, praying it won't be four or five by the time they reach their buses. Newsflash, sheep: it isn't 1985 anymore.

I mean, the likes of Dundee United, Motherwell, Kilmarnock and even St Johnstone and ICT have all caused us many more problems at Tynecastle in recent years. Yet to hear this mob in full voice you'd think they were regularly coming down to the capital and wiping the floor with us.

They boomed out 'Vladimir Romanov' as if this was supposed to be some sort of cruel dagger through our weeping hearts but we greeted his name with nods of recognition and the odd handclap. Of course, we still don't know how that repeatedly delayed creditors' meeting in Lithuania will go and can only cling to the hope that the worst it gets for us is a season or two in the Championship. And were that, incidentally, to be the case would any Hearts fans not have agreed to that trade-off, in return for seven years of Romanov and avoiding that permanent switch to Murrayfield?

Perhaps realising that instead of rubbing salt into open wounds they were merely reminding us that in the past seven years we'd won two more Scottish Cups than them, they dusted down their old 'HIV positive' chant from the 1980s. Bizarre that it's them and ICT that are the only two sets of supporters still persisting with that hoary old chestnut. Has news of the virus only just reached *The Press and Journal* or something? Don't tell me, the cinemas up there are finally done with *Forrest Gump* and now *Trainspotting* is packing out the teuchter multiplexes?

Our side showed one change from Sunday's showdown with Hibernian, Paul McCallum replacing Dale Carrick who never even made the bench. When McCallum signed instant parallels were drawn with another loanee, Michael Ngoo, who'd signed exactly one year previously. Both were tall English strikers who'd made their debuts in League Cup semi-finals against ICT at Easter Road and both took penalties in the subsequent shoot-out. Sadly, that's where the similarities ended. Ngoo was part of a winning team, scoring both in open play and the shoot-out and becoming something of a cult figure. While McCallum lost his semi, missed a sitter in open play, missed in the shoot-out and was most aptly described using a phrase that sounds remarkably similar to cult.

Aberdeen's top scorer, Niall McGinn, had endured something of a lean spell, notching his first goal in three months in the weekend draw with Dundee United. Unsurprisingly, he had a real spring in his step here and gave Jamie MacDonald an early touch with a stinging low drive.

Having suffered the indignity of losing to us twice this season, the Dons were well pumped up for the clash and slowly took control, pinning Hearts back. MacDonald bravely thwarted Adam Rooney from close range before Pawlett saw a shot deflected away for a corner. Rooney looked a real handful. Not for the first time as a Hearts fan I had cause to be grateful for Hibernian's frugality under Rod Petrie. Had he signed Rooney as originally planned, instead of reneging on the deal and seeking a cheaper loan deal, we'd probably already be down. Hibernian fans are so quick to adopt the moral high ground about us living beyond our means under Vlad yet Petrie is repeatedly pilloried for failing to do the same.

But I digress. We were thankful to hear the half-time whistle as our team had been under the cosh for most of the half. Our best effort came from a Stevenson header that never really troubled Langfield.

McCallum got subbed at half-time after he'd been booked for oafishly trying to head the ball out of Langfield's hands. Think Andy Gray versus Steve Sherwood in the 1984 FA Cup Final except Andy Gray is deaf and blind and has had a full frontal lobotomy. Robinson replaced him, meaning Hearts were far nippier in midfield and Robson and Flood no longer had things all their own way. As a result, the second half was far more even a contest, swinging from end to end.

Straight away, Rooney was played in by Ryan Jack and MacDonald had to be sharply off his line to smother the ball. Hearts responded with a Paterson pile-driver that Langfield did well to get his hands to. The match was being played at a furious pace and Rooney again went close, this time with an overhead kick that was fractionally too high.

Hearts under Lockie have always been happier when games open up, allowing them to play more to their strengths and Smith and Nicholson were giving the Aberdeen rearguard a torrid evening. Then, just when it appeared Hearts might be on the verge of making something count, their plans were thrown into disarray when, out of nothing, Wilson was shown a second yellow for an innocuous tug on Rooney.

Hearts would now be forced to play out the final 20-odd minutes a man down but any thoughts of putting up the shutters and toughing out the point, earning a stay of execution, were shredded as Flood drilled the resultant free kick into the bottom corner, sending the away fans into raptures of joy.

'Going down, going down, going down' echoed lustily across the pitch. Having avoided the ignominy of being relegated by Hibs three days previously it hadn't even occurred to me that this shower wouldn't be far behind in the gloating stakes.

The table, as it stood, had us down. Death had placed a clammy hand on our shoulder. Everyone around me was suddenly filled with this desperate, manic desire to clap and urge the side forward, howling for something, anything, to keep us up, mathematically, even if only until Thistle away on Saturday. Now it had come to it I couldn't bear the thought of going down. I didn't feel ready.

It had been such a supremely valiant effort all season, the side had run its heart out and given every last iota of energy for the cause. Their fight to stay in the division deserved a better conclusion than having these lowlifes in the away end revelling raucously in their downfall.

Then, suddenly and inexplicably, Reynolds gifted possession to Stevo and a reprieve was within our grasp. Hopes were instantly raised but Stevo panicked, fluffing his effort and the chance vanished, like it had disappeared in a puff of smoke.

With only a minute or so to go and having no choice but to accept we were down, Paterson muscled his way into the box and was checked by Logan for what was a blatant penalty. The closing minutes on Sunday had been a very tough watch but a penalty kick to stay up, if only until the weekend, was even harder.

The chance to silence those incessantly crowing Aberdeen fans sat with Jamie Hamill. The stand-in skipper took a moment to compose himself before stepping forward and burying the spot-kick to send Tynecastle wild. It felt great to still be alive in the league and we filed out into the cool, crisp night contented.

The point left us 18 behind St Mirren with six games to go. Our SPL heart was still beating, but only just.

38

Partick Thistle away,
5 April 2014, 3pm

AFTER somehow squirming from the grasp of gloating hobos and sheep-botherers, desperate to be the ones to seal our fate, there was an air of calmness verging on serenity at Firhill. All week the sentiments from Thistle had been that they'd take no pleasure from relegating us, should events pan out that way. In the event they didn't. The final blow was dealt by a grizzled old adversary with whom we have history. Someone who came off the bench for one last hurrah. Iain Brines.

Forget St Mirren's part in this, however keen they are to muscle in and take the credit. If it hadn't been for Brines (stepping up from fourth official to replace the ill Euan Norris) and the laughable penalty he awarded the Buddies on 86 minutes, St Mirren, in all eventuality, would have lost this and our 4-2 victory would have taken the fight on into the post-split games.

But, you know what, it was hard to be too downbeat, filing out of the ground at the end. We were down, we'd cheated fate in those matches against arguably the two sides who'd have derived most pleasure from the deed, and no one realistically expected us to win all five post-split matches while St Mirren simultaneously lost all theirs.

Yes, we were resigned to our fate and with the creditors' meeting rescheduled for the following Monday we were all fully engaged with the true battle being waged this season. Would there still be a Hearts to support next season?

The match at Firhill would prove to be Hearts' Mendoza 1978 moment, Ryan Stevenson playing the role of Archie Gemmill with two goals. With the rancour dissipating and the end in sight, Hearts produced an uplifting performance that, despite everything that's happened, had you wondering just what might have been.

Our side had an uncharacteristically shaky start, the players perhaps suffering the effects of those previous two epic encounters. Superman has kryptonite, Sherlock Holmes has Professor Moriarty and our defenders have aimless punts that sail over their heads leaving them flat-footed and exposed. Kris Doolan latched on to just such a ball and rapped the ball home for 1-0, five minutes in.

One should then have become two moments later when Doolan turned provider and set up Lyle Taylor whose shot ended up on the roof of the Farm Foods on Garscube Road.

Hearts slowly felt their way into the match and created a flurry of chances towards the end of the first half. First of all, Paul Gallacher was at full stretch to push away a Robinson header, then King squandered a chance after being put clean through and, finally, McHattie tested Gallacher with a fierce shot.

Then, just when it appeared we had yet another hard-luck tale to endure, on 44 minutes Carrick nodded in from close range after King stood the ball up for him and we went in at the break all-square.

At half-time Denis McQuade was presented on the pitch. Recently inducted into Thistle's Hall of Fame, Denis represents something of a hero to Jags fans what with his heroics in that 1971 League Cup Final against Celtic. But then, as he strode up and down the far touchline, it slowly became apparent we'd been airbrushed out of the festivities. No mention whatsoever was to be made of the 24 appearances he made for us in the late 1970s. We were all left looking at one another in consternation while he waved at the home supporters and seemed oblivious to the massed ranks in maroon calling out to him.

We were Alan Partridge spying his friend Dan across the car park at Choristers, except it was 'Denis' we were shouting and it was a football pitch. 'Denis! Denis! Denis! Denis! No, he's gone, DENNNNIS! No.'

The start of the second half saw all Hearts' near-misses from the season paid back. Everything they touched turned to goals and by the 70-minute mark they were 4-1 to the good. On 50 minutes Billy King, transformed since that derby goal, volleyed a 22-yard rocket into the roof of the net. Ten minutes later King got another assist, this time crossing for Stevo to tuck a header away. And, finally, Stevo got his second, collecting a Robinson pass and firing the ball across Gallacher and into the far corner.

For a few intoxicating moments the day was going better than we could possibly have imagined. We'd won handsomely and taken a chunk out of our goal difference, even though McMillan took the sheen off that a little with a second for Partick, and were aware that St Mirren were trailing 2-1 at home to Motherwell. We couldn't possibly take this fight into another round of fixtures, could we? Into the post-split games?

With radios pressed to ears we heard news of that dramatic late finale in Paisley, and those two late goals, and moments later we were applauding our wonderful players off the pitch, their heads held high.

The creditors' meeting eventually went ahead after more than a few false starts and delivered mixed news. On the one hand, Ubig, the parent company of Ukio Bankas, agreed to sell its 50 per cent holding in Hearts. However, talks over Ukio itself, Hearts' biggest creditor owning 29 per cent of the club's shares as well as security over Tynecastle, stalled leaving Bryan Jackson and the Edinburgh contingent in the dark. This delay was seriously unwelcome, leaving Hearts open to the very real danger of running out of cash and being liquidated.

Further complicating matters you had Edinburgh businessman Pat Munro unhelpfully offering Hearts' major shareholders, Ukio Bankas and Ubig, £15m for their shares. The worry now being that those in Lithuania would want to explore this in more detail, taking time we simply don't have. Additionally there were reports of Hibs fans submitting copious bogus bids in an attempt to sabotage any deal. Bryan Jackson, head of BDO, Hearts administrators, flew back to Lithuania in the hope of gaining approval for a CVA from the Lithuanian creditors. And all of a maroon persuasion held their breath.

39

Ross County home, 19 April 2014, 3pm

THERE was an air of heady optimism in the days running up to this fixture and it would have taken a lot to puncture the mood of joyous celebration pervading Tynecastle. Long reconciled with relegation, the reversal had been more than trumped by the move towards survival and fan ownership. And a massive step had been taken towards exiting administration on the previous Wednesday with creditors in Lithuania finally agreeing to transfer the shares owned by Ukio Bankas.

Ubig, the bank's parent company, had already agreed to sell its 50 per cent holding in Hearts but the delay to the Ukio Bankas deal had made liquidation a very real possibility. But Ukio, Hearts' biggest creditor, finally approved the deal.

MP Ian Murray, who had led the Foundation of Hearts fan group in its efforts to save the club, described it as 'absolutely fantastic news'. Ann Budge, who fronted the cash for Bidco, the company that is now set to take over running of the club also said, 'This is the beginning of a new era for Heart of Midlothian.' The 8,000-plus membership of the Foundation has pledged monthly donations which will pay Hearts' running costs. The relief at Tynecastle was palpable.

The three previous matches against County this season were all pulsating, high-octane encounters in which the lead kept changing hands and the final outcome was in doubt until the last kick of injury time. As both these sides strolled around a balmy Tynecastle, gentle applause rippling down the stands from a mellow, shirt-sleeved support, it seemed highly improbable that this first game after the split would end up nearly as eventful. In the end, however, the match confounded everyone and was packed with drama, with Hearts going on to claim their third win in four games.

County had surpassed their reputation for being the most amicable club in the division by stipulating that the free coaches they'd laid on came with a donation to the Foundation of Hearts and throughout a soporific first half both sets of supporters traded chants ridiculing the predicament of Hibernian. Sure, by close of play, County may have dropped into that dreaded, second from bottom spot but only three points separated them from a Hibernian side in utter freefall. And with the Edinburgh side due up in Dingwall for their penultimate game of the season, you could see the fight to avoid 11th spot going right down to the wire.

The 13,692 supporters basking in the sunshine had little to stir them until the 65th minute when the game seriously caught fire. Kevin McHattie advanced into the box only to be knocked off his feet by

Graham Carey. Jamie Hamill had scored a penalty in that same Gorgie stand goal in the previous home game against Aberdeen and struck his effort home with the minimum of fuss.

This was when events took a turn for the worse for Hamill. Having finished celebrating the goal in fine style he jogged back along the main stand touchline with the ball, for some reason, still plugged under his arm. Songo'o came stomping across to relieve Hamill of it and restart play but instead of doing the sensible thing and dropping it at his feet, Hamill kept on running, insolently taunting Songo'o with the ball as he went. Derek Adams, standing in front of his technical area, suddenly became a reluctant participator in this ridiculous pantomime, when Hamill ran straight into him, sending him tumbling to the deck. Within the blink of an eye the situation escalated from a crass, slightly farcical over-celebration to a melee involving most of the players and coaching staff.

When the dust settled Willie Collum, who else, dished out yellow cards for Songo'o and Hamill and given Hamill had already been booked for catching Michael Tidser it meant he got his marching orders. The yellow would go on to be upgraded to that of excessive misconduct.

We'd had a perfect view of the whole sorry episode from the back of the main stand, having spent pre-match being refreshed in the Bobby Walker Suite celebrating the outcome in Lithuania this week. Being well-oiled it had seemed hilarious at the time, like Hamill was a clown gone wrong or something, but clearly his actions were ridiculous. This was one of the senior pros at the club who needed to be setting a better example.

County piled forward in numbers but could not get the elusive equaliser, Jordan Slew coming closest with a header. And, mirroring the derby three weeks previously, Hearts stole away, deep into injury time, and scored again. Carrick, unmarked, seized on to Robinson's pass and finished in some style past Mark Brown.

Leaving the ground, the sun beaming down on us all, it felt wonderful knowing we'd still have our beloved football team next season. The sale and purchase agreement still needed to be put together but this wasn't considered to be too much of a hurdle by Bryan Jackson and BDO. All that then remained was the 20-day cooling-off period for the Ubig share deal after which point the club could begin exiting administration.

And, in a really odd twist of fate, the 20 days are due to expire on 27 April, the date of our final visit of the season to Easter Road. Did I hear someone say party?

40

Hibernian away,
27 April 2014, 12.45pm

THE only other time I'd turned up at Easter Road feeling bomb proof, feeling that irrespective of what happened on the pitch we'd pretty much be guaranteed to have a monopoly on the bragging rights, was when we played there in the August following the 5-1.

That day, it genuinely wouldn't have mattered what the final score had been, in Edinburgh derby Top Trumps we had a card that couldn't be topped. Yet, today took things a whole stage further. Already having long made our peace with the inevitable drop down, linking it conveniently and inextricably to our ultimate redemption, they literally had nothing to hit us with.

We were impregnable and looked across at the sparsely covered home seats from our vantage point in a crammed, sell-out south stand, the home supporters looking a broken and sorry lot – gutted that despite their best efforts our club hadn't folded and seriously shitting themselves about ending up in that play-off spot.

Their dismal record of one win in 14 league games since beating us in early January alluded to utter stagnation at Easter Road. Butcher appears to be in charge of a side that no longer has any intention of playing for him. It's as if they've lost the will to live.

Usually, when you have a rather blasé approach to a derby you get pumped. Or, at the very least, you get a draw, as was the outcome that hot August day in 2012 when Andy Driver's early prod home was cancelled out by The Thumb. But the Lucozade-liberating street urchin has long since packed away his baggy grey tracky bottoms and his child maintenance forms and headed for pastures new. And without him this Hibernian side has nothing. Hearts were able to nullify them sufficiently to register a fourth derby win of the season courtesy of a brace from C-Patz.

Four Sundays ago Hibs had packed out the Roseburn Stand to savour the delicious spectacle of their oldest rivals finally succumbing to the inevitable. But, in classic Bond villain style, they made that fatal error of not finishing us off when they had the chance. In the run-in to that game they were a gloating Auric Goldfinger, bumptiously telling us they expected us to die. Today, with our curiously unfrozen shares miraculously secured, we were back from the dead to remind them of their place in the world.

They came to dance on our grave, the only problem being we weren't dead yet and another stout tug on their ankles might just bring them tumbling down with us. Both their matches since the relegation party had been lost 2-0 and they had been well and truly dragged into the mire.

So, another Hearts sell-out at Easter Road and a few minor celebrities had also made the trip. Polite and erudite, Skacel and Kello were the very antithesis of Griffiths and Riordan. While the Hibs duo infect cyberspace with chants about Hearts' 'refugees', the only posts from King Rudolph involve endless shots of the ever-patient Czech, posing with a string of starstruck Jambos. Myself included.

After a minute's shared applause for Margo McDonald and Sandy Jardine the game started with Hibernian kicking towards the Hearts support. For the opening quarter of an hour the ball was flogged from one end of the pitch to the other and the pass completion rate had to be in single figures.

Jason Cummings, accustomed more than most to the 5-1 hand gesture, looked like Hibs' liveliest goal threat and roused the home support from their collective stupor with a header that dropped just wide from a Liam Craig cross. Following that he tried his luck from 35 yards but MacDonald gathered at the second attempt.

However, any sense from Hibs that they might attain that one solitary victory required to propel them to SPL safety was blown to smithereens in a breathtaking, four-minute burst, late in the half. Two headers from Paterson on 37 and 41 minutes, the first from a King corner, the second from a McHattie free kick, had the home supporters streaming for the exits in their tens.

However, Hibernian were a different proposition in the second half and on another day might have come back to earn a share of the spoils. Forster had a header cleared off the line and then Thomson hit the side-netting with MacDonald's front post exposed. Jamma was then called into action, saving well from a Craig free kick after Robinson had downed Cummings on the edge of the box.

And, on 69 minutes, Forster got the goal he'd been denied at Tynecastle, sending a flying header into the net. Those home fans that hadn't abandoned their side saw Hibs in the ascendancy as they poured forward in decent numbers.

James Collins, on as a substitute for Cummings, cemented his role as Hibs' latest derby goofball by completely missing his kick three yards from an empty net. His gaffe came in the dying minutes and was the final straw for the fans of the wee team. Clusters of green scarves hit the running track as three sides of the crowd emptied. While, in the south stand, the party was in full swing.

41

Kilmarnock home, 4 May 2014, 3pm

THE previous three league games against Killie this season had seen us ship ten goals which, ironically, is the same number Kris Boyd should have got here on Boxing Day. His total of six is testament to how we've had our youthful naivety punished by those grizzled campaigners who've been around the block a few times (and, in Boydie's case, picked up a smoked sausage supper on the way back).

But there would be no more Boyd-inflicted damage this season, well certainly not on any teams from this side of the city. In fact, the closest he got to a goal all afternoon was in the 11th minute when the first of Hearts' five nudged into the net off his not inconsiderable rump. That stellar contribution aside he was starved of possession as Kilmarnock were snuffed out by a Hearts side seriously starting to enjoy themselves this season.

Hearts, unchanged from the derby, were insatiable and Stevenson in particular was in devastating form. He was at the heart of everything, not only helping himself to three goals but setting up two more and raining in a barrage of shots on the Killie goal throughout.

The Killie fans seemed more committed to singing about how useless their coaching staff were than getting behind their ailing side and by half-time it's fair to say they'd probably accrued enough material to keep them chanting incoherently until kick-off in the St Mirren game the following Wednesday night.

By that point Hearts had put together a scintillating 45 minutes and left the field to a standing ovation; three up, all courtesy of Stevo. His first was a cross/shot from a free kick, for a foul on Nicholson, which evaded Samson. Next, midway through the half, an anaemic clearance dribbled out to him on the 18-yard line and he slammed a low left-footed drive into the bottom corner. Then, in stoppage time, he nabbed his hat-trick with a goal that typified everything that was great about his performance. Grabbing possession just over halfway he swept a glorious pass out to King. The winger swerved and darted down the line before firing the ball across where it was bundled over the line by Stevo, arriving into the box like an express train.

Three up at half-time and Hearts weren't finished crushing sorry Kilmarnock. They were on course for their fifth win in a six-game unbeaten sequence, their best run in three years, and came out buzzing for the start of the second half.

There were many reasons for this recent resurgence in form. Resolution of the ownership issue and seeing an end in sight for administration was one but equally significant was the blossoming of Hearts' young players. This season could seriously have ruined them, shattering their burgeoning confidence. Instead, they've flourished. It's early days but in many cases it looks like it could be the making of them.

Early on in the season you had this generic image of a young Hearts player. A vaguely ineffective, wispy ball-player with spindly legs, waiting to come on for 20 minutes of getting nudged off the ball by the opposition full-back. That's all gone now. These frail little wide players have been replaced by speedy, confident, streetwise powerhouses. None more so than Billy King who smashed home the fourth after being set up by a quite sumptuous first-time, crossfield pass from the right foot of Stevo.

This was one-way traffic and Killie, jittery about what getting annihilated was doing to their mangled goal difference, became more cautious about sending men forward. The combination of their sloppy, half-arsed attempts at keeping possession and Hearts' spring-heeled, lightning-fast breakaways were decimating them.

On the hour Paterson cleared his lines agriculturally from right-back before, several miraculous seconds later, popping up in the box to get on the end of Stevo's cross to score number five. It looked like there simply had to have been two C-Patzes out there on the pitch. Either Ann Budge spent some of her £40m fortune on a secret cloning machine or this kid is super-fast.

This thrashing, coupled with St Mirren's victory over Ross County, put the Buddies safe and marooned Killie one point adrift in 11th. However, a measly two points now separate Kilmarnock, Ross County, Partick and Hibs, with two rounds of games to go. The fight to avoid the play-off now can't fail to go down to the final day.

So while those four teams have to stew until the midweek games, they can't come soon enough for Hearts. Take away the 15-point deficit and Lockie's side would now be sitting in eighth, a point behind St Mirren on 37. Truly commendable and it would lead the Hearts manager to seek clarity over his future in the days to follow.

42

Partick home,
7 May 2014, 7.45pm

KALLUM Higginbotham, looking like a pale, bearded Rivaldo with his bandy legs and fearsome shot, made sure the door was slammed firmly shut on Hearts' hopes of acing all five of these post-split games. Thistle doth ventured east and returned the compliment we'd paid them at Firhill on 5 April with a thumping 4-2 away win. In doing so they guaranteed themselves SPL football for next season and made life somewhat interesting for our city rivals.

Hearts, unbeaten since losing 2-1 here to Dundee United on 21 March, looked to continue their fine run of form and made a couple of changes for what was the final home game of the season. Mark Ridgers started in goal and Jamie Hamill replaced Ryan Stevenson as he'd done in the closing minutes versus Kilmarnock.

Callum Paterson had scored in his two previous outings and repeated the trick here for his 11th goal of the season. Strange quirk that C-Patz presents more of a goal threat from right-back than centre-forward but he was at it again here, marauding forward and firing in a great shot that Gallacher got a hand to but couldn't keep out.

Seconds later it could and should have been two, McHattie and Carrick linking up to good effect and releasing King who blazed over. No one seemed overly fussed, though, as Hearts were well on top and the feeling was more goals would come.

Another goal did come, on the half-hour mark, but did so totally against the run of play with Thistle levelling. The white Rivaldo sent a fine pass through for Taylor who tucked the ball through Ridgers's legs before, inexplicably, shushing the home supporters. On 37 minutes he came close to scoring again but his header drifted wide, this time to howls of derision from the now riled home support.

These same supporters were back on their feet moments later to acclaim Wilson as he restored Hearts' lead. The skipper headed home, unmarked, from McHattie's curling free kick and that was the end of the first-half scoring.

In truth, 2-1 at the break probably flattered Thistle. Sam Nicholson, Billy King and Dale Carrick had led them a merry dance and they'd scored from their one real shot on target. Well, they certainly made the most of their reprieve in the second half, blitzing Hearts and scoring three more times without reply.

Gary Fraser made it 2-2 on 51 minutes with a sensational volley that Ridgers wouldn't have got close to even if he'd had MacDonald in the goal with him. Mair headed home for 3-2 and then Higginbotham put the cherry on the cake five minutes later, finishing stylishly after Ridgers could only push out Taylor's shot.

Thistle's victory here, along with Kilmarnock beating St Mirren and Ross County seeing off Hibs the previous night, meant a rather stark state of affairs for Hibernian down in 11th spot. Anything but a victory against Kilmarnock at Easter Road on the final day and they'd face a two-legged play-off against the second-placed side in the Championship.

43

St Mirren away, 10 May 2014, 12.15pm

DESPITE the pyrotechnics and the stunning Hearts away support, this match was dominated by events elsewhere. If pressed, more than a few Hearts fans would probably admit to misgivings about seeing Hibernian actually drop down a division. There was that nagging worry that a return to the top league, obstructed already by the presence of Rangers, could get a whole lot more complicated by having four derbies tossed into the mix. Yet these sentiments were stuck on the back burner today especially with that laughably misguided relegation party those idiots threw for us back in March still relatively fresh in our minds. No, anything putting the squeeze on these gloating hordes had to be cause for mirth and the name of Kris Boyd provided a constant soundtrack to our 1-1 draw.

Jamie Walker and David Smith came in for Billy King and Jamie Hamill in front of an away support clearly revelling in their fate. 'Que sera sera, whatever will be, will be, we're going to Cowdenbeath, que sera sera', 'When Hearts go up to lift the Ramsden's Cup we'll be there, we'll be there' and 'Bring on the Rangers' were chanted throughout as we embraced the future.

There was a clear sense that this was the end of an era and not simply because Hearts were heading for pastures new. Both managers would be out of contract very shortly. Danny Lennon had looked destined for the chop way back in October and appeared to be living on borrowed time while Lockie had been told he'd learn his fate from Ann Budge on the Monday after the game. Locke had his name sung repeatedly and with genuine affection but it remained to be seen how much of a role sentiment would play in Queen Ann's big decision.

So, while some things change, others remain reassuringly as they've always been. Jim Goodwin looked like he'd been tossed a raw steak minutes before kick-off, squatting, naked on the dressing room floor to gorge it while Lennon did his best to ignore the growling and slurping noises as he put the finishing touches to his team talk. He lurched ferociously around the centre of the pitch, impaling his elbows and studs on any member of the opposition venturing into his vicinity. He was like one of those chained tigers that Russell Crowe fights in *Gladiator*, snarling malevolently and swiping at you should you happen to stray within range.

Luckily for Goodwin, referee Stephen Finnie seemed quite happy to let him career demonically around the midfield. The ambivalent shrugs that followed each assault put you in mind of an ultra-liberal marine biologist putting the case for a shark that had been terrorising bathers,

'Yes, what you've got to realise is that this is the shark's territory, this is what it does.'

St Mirren took the lead on 28 minutes with a goal that started with Callum Paterson switching off and gifting the Buddies possession from a thrown-in. He looked to have gotten away with this lapse when McLean's shot from distance was parried by MacDonald but Conor Newton was quickest to the rebound and Hearts were one down.

Right on half-time there was an instantaneously ecstatic reaction as Paisley was hit by the news that Boyd had put Killie one up at Easter Road. 'Boyd, Boyd, Krissie Krissie Boyd. He gets the ball and he scores a goal, Krissie Krissie Boyd.' There had been the odd rumour that before we'd entered administration last summer Boyd had spoken to Lockie and been amenable to playing for us. So there were dual reasons in singing Boyd's name as more than an element of wish fulfilment existed for next season.

Three minutes into the second half Hearts had even greater reason to cheer as Walker saw his shot blocked by Dilo and Carrick converted the rebound clinically. You got the sense, as the half wore on, that neither side would be that unhappy to sign off with a draw, although Magennis and McGowan both had close-range headers that missed the target.

The whistle had gone at Easter Road, with Hibernian losing 1-0 and consigned to the play-offs. Their last win came on 15 February which is a fairly sad indictment and it seems remarkable, in all that time, they hadn't been able to procure that one measly win needed to save themselves. Seeing them end up in the play-offs, having spent the entire season ridiculing our plight and doing everything within their power to see us liquidated felt, seriously, like the gift that wouldn't stop giving. Yet, if I'm being honest, I found it hard to imagine they wouldn't have enough about themselves to see off which ever one of Hamilton, Falkirk or Queen of the South they'd end up facing.

Back in deepest Paisley the board had gone up signalling three minutes and the season was slowly ebbing away. Deep into stoppage time is C-Patz time and so many times this season he's popped up at the death, looking set to be the hero, only for the woodwork or an inspirational stop from the keeper to deny him. So, in many ways, it was fitting that his was the final say in the last few seconds of the final game of the campaign. His goalbound effort looked in all the way before being tipped away quite brilliantly by the Buddies' keeper. Like I said, some things never change.

44

Locke, Stock And Two Smoking Barrels

ON Monday 12 May 2014, Ann Budge revealed, at long last, her blueprint for Hearts. Her long-term plans for the club would be assigned to ex-player and manager Craig Levein, who would take on an all-encompassing role of director of football. His task, to oversee all footballing matters, had far-reaching repercussions for manager Gary Locke, his backroom staff, and three senior players: Jamie Hamill, Jamie MacDonald and Ryan Stevenson who all departed with immediate effect. The position of head coach would be given to Robbie Neilson who had been helping with Hearts' youths.

Levein had been lingering in the background for a while and rumours had intensified ever since Budge was unmasked as Hearts' benefactor that she had designs on making him responsible for first-team affairs. It would have been hard to have predicted, however, just how big a role he'd be asked to play.

Budge's statement made reference to it being 'an unpopular decision' with some fans but that she felt they needed someone of Levein's experience 'to implement a youth-driven playing policy within the club'. Of Locke and Billy Brown she said, 'They were set an almost impossible task, which they handled with dignity and determination.' Regarding the three senior pros, 'We will have to say goodbye to a number of the fans' current favourites; we will do our best to secure all our excellent young players; and we will welcome a group of new players, who will help us achieve our vision.' Then, perhaps most tellingly of all, she said, 'We have to ensure we live within our means. All of the decisions have been taken with a view to ensuring the future stability of our club.'

When you read that last part it's hard to find any fault with anything she's saying. After the turmoil of administration we do need to live within our means if we are to stave off the threat of liquidation. 'It was clear from my earliest visits to Tynecastle and my earliest meetings with senior staff that the company, Heart of Midlothian plc was, in every sense of the word, "broken". There was no overarching strategy for how the business should be run.' She also went on, 'This, coupled with the sole focus on day-to-day survival, had left the club in a sorry and perilous financial state. This had led to a fundamental disconnect between the various departments and a mountain of issues to be resolved.'

You get an idea of the magnitude of the task facing those involved, and why Budge and Levein are seeking almost to gut the place and start again from scratch.

That all said, seeing Locke go was a sore one. The dignified manner in which he'd guided Hearts through the toughest spell in their history and galvanised the club through his strength of character was truly humbling. For parts of the season it did look as if the task was beyond him and he was subjected to a fair amount of criticism, some of it justified.

At times our football was primitive and infuriatingly one-dimensional. Much of that was down to asking too much of certain players who, under different circumstances, wouldn't have got within a sniff of the first team. For me, most exasperating of all was our over-reliance on Callum Paterson as a striker. Apart from stunting the big man's development, it stopped us trying to play football and lent an air of predictability to our play.

But I don't think this can be blamed for our inability to stay up or that poor coaching was the issue per se. Our big problem was that any slips became magnified out of all proportion because there were simply no goals in the side. If the coaching had been as bad as some suggested you wouldn't have seen that impressive end to the season and Locke getting the manager of the month award in April.

However, more victories were needed and in seeking to dig them out we'd often leave ourselves open at the back, committing men forward in the hope a ball might drop for us. I'd say up until Motherwell came calling on 11 January, almost all our matches had the feel of febrile, do or die cup-ties where defensive solidity went out the window. I never felt criticism of the team's shape and playing style took that properly into account. It didn't address the mental effects of being so far behind the pack and the frenetic, almost rabid desperation to claw back the points.

Thereafter, the unavoidable reality of relegation was a blessed relief and lent greater composure to Hearts, the games became less frantic and the younger players began to blossom. Partly because the games were a bit more relaxed and partly because the players were becoming better, stronger and fitter. These kids had been forced to learn their trade in the glare of first-team football, making those unavoidable mistakes on the big stage instead of in the under-20s and it was truly the making of them. And the fact that that survival would have been achieved were it not for our points deficit was a stunning achievement and a ringing endorsement of the coaching team's ability to nurture young talent.

So, I guess for Locke to read that Hearts will be seeking to make the most of their talented crop of youngsters must have been pretty galling. It left many people curious as to why we couldn't have had Levein as footballing supremo but with Locke retained as first-team coach. Could that not have worked? Well, we'll never know. The fact remains that neither men have ever been particularly close so Levein has gone for Robbie, someone he knows for definite he's on the same wavelength as.

Perhaps he also feels the qualities he's seen in Robbie Neilson make him better suited to the system he envisages for Hearts. For his ideas to have any chance of working Levein needs carte blanche to hire and fire as he sees fit so his ideas for Hearts can be properly constructed and implemented. He was given free reign at Tannadice to rebuild from the bottom up and, judging from Twitter at least, he is clearly still held in extremely high esteem up there.

So both Budge and Levein have a clear vision for Hearts, to consolidate and rise again. You'd wish the same for Lockie and Billy Brown and the players that have left. Not just the three senior pros mentioned, but also Dylan McGowan, Mark Ridgers and Callum Tapping, as well as all the groundstaff released.

Clearly, Jamie Hamill was gutted with the way events panned out, even though he reckoned he'd seen it coming, and it was a shame seeing him fire off a few barbs as he left. His decision last summer to stay with us on reduced wages along with and Stevo and Jamma (and Danny Wilson) won't ever be forgotten.

Incidentally, Hamill did also say, 'Ann Budge has come in and put her money into the club and hopefully they come out of administration as soon as possible and get on the up and back to where they belong,' which was a really fitting sentiment from a wholehearted competitor who never failed to give his all for the club.

The feelgood factor that has pervaded our remarkable club throughout these darkest of days had as much to do with those departing as those staying. So while it's sad to see them go we owe it to our club and ourselves not to lose sight of that undying spirit of unity and togetherness and to give the new regime our full backing and see where it takes us. The support from the fans has been remarkable to behold and be a part of. More than ever before this club feels like a part of us all and it's through the fundraising actions of the supporters and the Foundation of Hearts that it has a future of any kind to look forward to.

But look forward to it we will. A Championship campaign that already looked compelling – what with Hearts going head to head with Rangers – became an even more intriguing prospect thanks to events in the final few days of May.

Despite winning 2-0 away at New Douglas Park in the first leg of the play-off final, Hibernian's bottle crashed spectacularly in the return against Hamilton at Easter Road. Their barely-believable 2-0 home defeat saw the tie decided, ultimately, on penalties, and Jason Cummings missed the vital kick, relegating Hibernian.

In the days following Hibernian's agonising denouement, Terry Butcher paid for the demotion with his job. Their new CEO from Motherwell, Leeann Dempster, sacked the popular Englishman and was linked immediately with both Stuart McCall and Ian Murray. In the end, however, a few weeks elapsed before former Bolton, Celtic and Everton defender Alan Stubbs was eventually appointed.

Meanwhile – between Butcher's sacking and Stubbs's appointment – across the city, on Wednesday 11 June 2014, documents were lodged at the Court of Session in Edinburgh meaning Hearts finally exited administration and had their transfer embargo lifted.

This was the cue for wild euphoria and Ann Budge posted a statement on the Hearts website, 'By now, you will all have heard and, yes, it's true, we have formally exited administration! Everyone associated with the club is ecstatic and now we can really begin to move ahead in implementing our plans for the future. With the greatest respect to Bryan, Trevor, Bob and Duncan from BDO [Hearts' administrators], we are all delighted to see them go! On a serious note, however, we owe them a huge thank-you for putting in the hours to get us out of administration this week, as promised.

'So what now? Well, the first thing is to get season tickets on sale as quickly as possible and the club will be issuing information regarding this tomorrow. Following this, we will shortly be issuing information on new signings and more pre-season friendlies which, I know, is what all the fans are desperate to hear.

'However, for today, let's just celebrate the news!'

Immediately, thoughts turn again to next season. You'd imagine the top three spots will be eagerly contested by ourselves, Rangers and Hibernian, yet only one side is guaranteed promotion from the division. A second team will have the chance to go up assuming they can beat the SPL's second-bottom side in a two-legged play-off. And at least one of the three is guaranteed to spend a minimum of two seasons down in the second tier.

You'd hope the Ann Budge/Craig Levein dream ticket will have us in decent shape for the challenge that awaits at the start of the next season. I'm just utterly ecstatic we still have our club and, for me, those games can't come soon enough.

Part Two:

We Can Aye Go Back Up

45

Annan Athletic home, Petrofac Cup first round, Saturday 26 July 2014, 3pm

A BRAND spanking new era was ushered in to Tynecastle and it was hard not to feel more than a little excited to finally catch a glimpse of the new-look Hearts in action. Our revitalised, reborn side, sporting a fantastic new kit commemorating the centenary of the start of the First World War and refreshingly free of a sponsor's logo, dismantled a dogged Annan Athletic, winning by three goals to one.

Five of Hearts' eight new signings were on show and they all knitted seamlessly with the talent and raw potential we'd seen emerge amid all the tribulations of last season.

A stern-looking Craig Levein surveyed proceedings bookishly from the directors' box like a slightly podgy Clark Kent and must have been mightily impressed by the way his new project was slowly taking shape. The summer's transfer surgery has seen an enhanced, reinforced central spine transplanted into a side already awash with an abundance of riches in wide areas. After last season's transfer embargo it felt a real novelty to see a load of new faces out there and I couldn't imagine ever taking new signings for granted after what our side went through in administration.

Boyhood Jambo Neil Alexander was in goal. The former Livingston keeper was picked up on a free after Crystal Palace opted to let him go. It's way too early to dismiss Jamie Hamill's withering parting shot about the position becoming a 'poisoned chalice' in light of Jamie MacDonald's departure but Neil looked reliable and assertive against admittedly modest opposition. And there was nothing he could've done with Annan's consolation right at the death.

The back four featured three well-kent faces in Paterson, Wilson and McHattie, along with Dutch-born Turk Alim Ozturk who was partnering the skipper at centre-half. Ozturk signed on a three-year deal from Trabzonspor and looked strong and composed as well as comfortable enough in possession to come over halfway and pick out a pass. He also looked a good fit alongside Wilson.

Perhaps the shrewdest summer move was our recruitment of a ready-made central midfield unit in Morgaro Gomis and Prince Buaben. Both had been vital cogs in the Dundee United cup-winning side of 2010 and slotted in supremely well, looking instantly at home.

Up top was another new signing, the Swede Osman Sow who even this early oozes star quality and you could see him going on to emulate the likes of de Vries and Fuller, becoming a real bona fide hero in these parts. Playing slightly off Sow was Dale Carrick and then you had Billy King and Sam Nicholson patrolling either flank.

It was joyous watching the side free from that clanging sense of alarm and doom we'd grown so accustomed to. A side always swimming against the tide. This new-look Hearts were all power, aggression and steely-eyed determination allied to pace, class and, in the first half, clinical finishing.

Annan were speared at will and the opening goal took only eight minutes in coming. Billy King carried the ball with an air of devilment, dancing past two tackles and fizzing the ball past Alex Mitchell in the Annan goal.

Carrick was dropping slightly deeper, acting as a conduit between the two midfield destroyers in Gomis and Buaben and the tall, striding Sow. Hearts were thoroughly in command and their interplay was crisp and inventive. The flawless Tynecastle carpet seemed almost to invite imaginative, expansive football and you couldn't not be an advocate of summer football, sitting in short sleeves as the sun beat down, watching the ball being stroked around.

Our presence in the draw for the next round, even so early in the game, appeared a formality. Of more concern was this daft young seagull that kept waddling up and down the touchline oblivious to the game raging around it and the threat of being trodden on. I thought for a moment, then nudged the guy next to me, 'John Gullquhoun looks not bad on the wing, eh?' Nothing.

Mercifully, the roar from Hearts' second goal, ten minutes after the first, gave it a start and it fluttered away. Carrick cleverly nudged a header into the path of Sow and the big Swede eased forward in an effortless, gliding motion and knocked the ball out of Mitchell's reach.

A real bugbear of last season was how wasteful we were from set pieces. Already, though, we're seeing a marked improvement, most notably via the feet of King who tormented Annan with a succession of wicked deliveries.

And, five minutes from half-time, Hearts went three up from just such a source, Paterson rising majestically to smash home King's corner.

Things were going well, too well, and in first-half stoppage time Paterson went up for a routine header and landed awkwardly, ending up in a crumpled heap. He lay, motionless, clutching his knee which created the instant worry he'd done something untoward to his cruciate and as he was stretchered off all you could do was hope the injury wouldn't end up as bad as it initially looked.

Jordan McGhee came on in C-Patz's place for the start of the second half and calmly picked up where the big man had left off. Hearts under Robbie Neilson seem to favour a careful, almost painstakingly deliberate ploy of playing out from the back. Either or both of Gomis and Buaben tend to be heavily involved as Hearts move the ball precisely and thoughtfully. But then, around halfway, they would often zip into life with a furious bout of swift, high-tempo passing that would leave Annan bamboozled and cut to shreds.

It's not an exaggeration to say another three goals could quite easily have been racked up in the second half but a combination of bad luck, poor finishing and staunch defending kept Hearts at bay. The tempo then began to slowly drop off as the half wore on, meaning Hearts were more reliant on half-chances. Carrick and McHattie both went close as full time beckoned.

Annan had the final say here with Scott Davidson knocking home a sweet 20-yarder with a minute or so to go but all the plaudits went to Hearts for a display that radiated class and hinted at more to come.

46

Rangers away,
10 August 2014, 1.30pm

LIFE in the Championship could not have got off to a better start for Hearts as a jaw-dropping finale saw them emerge with all three points when an injury-time equaliser from Rangers looked to have snatched victory from their grasp.

Last time I frequented Ibrox it was deep in the midst of the Souey era. The Broomhouse hatchet man had cultivated an air of strutting triumphalism as Rangers vanquished all that lay before them in that ruthless pursuit of nine in a row. On that particular occasion I seem to remember Mo Johnston scuffing in the only goal of an untidy game and with a couple of rare exceptions these trips always tended to be dire.

Other than more often than not getting beat I seriously don't know what was worse. Those deferential nods they gave us. Like they were filled with avuncular pride at seeing mini-versions of themselves. 'The part-time proddies ur here, great tae see you boys. Fuck the pope, eh? Aye, youse are jist like us.' Or those inbred gargoyles in the upper Broomloan who'd spend the whole game just tipping pies and Bovril on to our heads.

Every season there'd be ever more obscure and random journeymen from England lining up to boot seven bells out of Robbo and John Colquhoun. From Roberts to Sterland via Hurlock, Gordon and Spackers.

But a lot of Buckfast has passed under the bridge since then. That impregnable Fortress Ibrox of old has long since vanished, along with Craig Whyte, Charles Green and non-payment of taxes. The mood was different now. The supporters still sung the same old prehistoric drivel but with a lot less gusto these days, like they didn't quite believe they were 'the peepul' anymore. Sure, their march up through the leagues had been unhindered but the likes of ICT, Dundee United and even Forfar Athletic had sent them packing in various cup ties without a second's thought. Boyd and Miller were a worrying presence up top but who behind them was going to create the chances for them to score?

When 1,700 boisterous Hearts fans took over a small corner of their ground you could sense the odd uneasy glance coming from the blue hordes as if our blatant lack of anything even approximating trepidation rankled. These looks soon morphed into downright betrayal, once the singing started. They stood, aghast, at the shocking impudence of the Hearts support, mocking their plight with bare-faced cheek despite being vastly outnumbered: 'You let your club die', 'You're not Rangers anymore', 'The Rangers died and the Hearts survived', and 'Ohhh Craig Whyte knewwww' had these grizzled old bears glowering and fuming at us across the vast expanse of Ibrox.

Then, just before kick-off, you had the Sandy Jardine tribute and both sets of supporters were momentarily united, the Gers looking fondly across at their now-forgiven little brothers, redeemed once again in their twinkly blue eyes. The Hearts fans sung loudly and proudly for Sandy until they were hoarse. Sandy was a true legend at Ibrox and will forever be associated with all he achieved as a Rangers player. Of course he will and quite rightly so. But a nice touch in that tear-jerking montage of theirs would've been to share his memory even more and include even a fleeting image of the 1986 SPFA Player of the Year as he'd looked then.

Then, of course, with the tribute over, hostilities were immediately resumed and we picked up exactly where we'd left off, enthusiastically baiting the home support. We didn't even wait for the class of 1972 to shuffle off the pitch. Pleasantries well and truly over. David Templeton, Lee Wallace and Ian Black all received special attention, Wallace, in particular, was repeatedly informed he 'should've stayed with a big club'. The 2012 Scottish Cup-winning captain Marius Zaliukas, on the other hand, was afforded a hero's welcome, much to the bemusement of the locals, and his name was sung for long periods in both halves.

Most of Hearts' problems in the first half were self-inflicted as Alexander had to contend with a number of under-hit back-passes that held up in the longer grass of the early season. The only other narrow squeak came when Ozturk charged down a Miller shot and the deflection sat up kindly for Templeton. But, luckily for us, Temps ducked under his header and popped the ball over the open goal. Jogging back he then had to contend with endless re-runs of his miss on the big screens, each one greeted with sarcastic cheers from the away end.

Then, on 53 minutes, Hearts took the lead. They'd started the second half brightly and King swept another of his skimming corners into space for Wilson to attack. The captain did just that, squeezing between McCulloch and Wallace and heading firmly into the top corner. He was impervious to his overjoyed team-mates jumping all over him and classily refused to celebrate a goal against his old side.

Rangers had no choice but to try and take the game to Hearts but they were muddled in their approach play. Gomis and Buaben didn't help their cause, shuttling in tandem across midfield like a couple of wily velociraptors. As a result of that fearsome barrier, attacks foundered and the ball invariably ended up at the feet of full-backs Foster and Wallace. Out of sheer desperation, they began trying to hit either Boyd or Miller with these forlornly optimistic 60-yard howitzers, much to the obvious irritation of them both.

For Boyd, this manifested itself in him angling looks of disgusted disbelief over his shoulder as these hopeful punts flew past his head at about a gazillion miles an hour. Miller took out his angst on the Hearts defenders and twice went flying in at Wilson with his studs showing. Each time, Wilson raised a quizzical eyebrow at Miller's beetroot-red coupon.

Rangers looked to have been handed a possible lifeline on 65 minutes when Neil Alexander was forced to leave the pitch after accidentally colliding with Ozturk. Not only was there now going to be a whole load of injury time for Rangers to equalise or worse, but substitute keeper Scott Gallacher hadn't inspired a great deal of confidence during pre-season.

A period of resolute defending followed as Hearts charged down a flurry of shots, surviving one fevered goalmouth scramble after another. Their unfaltering dedication to the cause brought them right to the very end of the 90. That highly prized away victory against an old, troublesome adversary and a real morale-booster for the season was within sight.

The board had just gone up, signalling six minutes of injury time, when Rangers struck. Ozturk switched off for a microsecond and left a gap for Nicky Law to advance into and he hit a clever volley that Gallacher got a hand to but could only push down into the corner.

A matter of seconds earlier Law had been announced as man of the match to widespread derision from a disillusioned Ibrox but that was all forgotten in the mayhem that followed. A home support that had been reduced to silence, ridiculed by a cocky travelling contingent, were suddenly given licence to vent all that pent-up frustration. Ibrox was unbearably loud and the roar just seemed never-ending.

It was still resonating as I slumped dejectedly into my seat, head in hands. Only a few feet away the frenzied home support were straining to get across the miserly tarpaulin that offered a semblance of segregation: stewards were sent sprawling as they thrust themselves over no-man's land, their bulging eyes seeking out their tormentors.

They were still on their feet, having not stopped crowing over at us when, ten seconds from the restart, Nicholson fed the tall, rangy Sow who strode into the Rangers box and fired through Zaliukas's legs and into the bottom corner of the net.

The pendulum of fate had swung back Hearts' way. There was the tiniest of delays while events at the opposite goal took a split-second to register and then it was the Hearts supporters' turn to grab each other, to lurch wildly over the tarpaulin and to scream madly. If Law's equaliser had delivered a stab in the ribs akin to Gary Hooper's 87th-minute leveller in the 2012 Scottish Cup semi-final then Sow's winner sparked scenes that were pure Craig Beattie. Utter, manic, unbridled bedlam.

We hadn't yet caught our breath from celebrating when suddenly the ball was being pulled back for Miller and, in an instant, our epic victory was hanging precariously in stasis. In the blink of your mind's eye you could see the headlines forming, bemoaning Hearts for twice letting the win slip through their fingers. And, then, Miller skied it to gasps of relief and we could breathe once more, our precious victory still intact.

Such was the tumult of the second half that we were kept in afterwards. The home support had dispersed pretty much en masse after Sow scored so I'm not sure if it was needed but the upper and lower Broomloan exits were right next to each other and who was going to argue with the Glasgow constabulary?

It's always a bit spooky when you finally emerge and find yourself in streets bereft of any living souls. As I walked back to Asda to get my car I felt like Cillian Murphy in *28 Days Later* furiously scanning the middle distance for any zombies lurking in the shadows. There were a few milling around to be fair but I had no colours on and, mercifully, they left me well alone.

Callum Paterson celebrating a derby winner, August 2013

Jordan McGhee with a memorable late winner for ten-man Hearts against Aberdeen, August 2013

Welcoming Celtic to Tynecastle, September 2013

Stevo's winner in the League Cup at Easter Road, October 2013

Gary Locke and Jamie Walker embrace at full-time, Easter Road, October 2013

Flat-out and dejected after throwing away the League Cup semi-final versus Inverness Caledonian Thistle at Easter Road, February 2014

Leigh Griffiths joins fellow revellers for the 'Relegation' derby, March 2014

Jubilant scenes at full-time against Hibernian, March 2014

Chaos ensues as Jamie Hamill decks Ross County manager Derek Adams as he celebrates scoring the opening goal, April 2014

The dawn of a new era at Tynecastle, May 2014

Opening day joy at Ibrox as Osman Sow downs Rangers with a late winner, August 2014

Sam Nicholson opening the scoring versus Hibernian and celebrating his goal with Jamie Walker, August 2014

Alim Ozturk unleashes a thunderbolt, two minutes into injury time at Easter Road, October 2014

Mark Oxley managed to get a hand to Ozturk's shot – on the way out, Easter Road, October 2014

Alim Ozturk wonders whether he'll ever hit another one that good, Easter Road, October 2014

Rangers' Kenny Miller pleads his innocence after a crude, late tackle on Kevin McHattie, November 2014

Skipper Danny Wilson gets in on the act as Hearts put ten past Cowdenbeath, February 2015

Commemorative programme to mark the passing of the legendary Dave Mackay

Taking the acclaim of the fans after the championship was finally confirmed, March 2015

Celebrating with the silverware after a final day draw with third-placed Rangers, May 2015

47

Hibernian home, 17 August 2014, 12.15pm

LYING low in the Championship I thought we might be spared a season or two of Willie Collum and his pathological addiction for awarding nonsensical penalties against Hearts. But everyone's least favourite weasel-faced assassin found a way to get another fix.

Neither side had properly settled into the game when 20-year-old debutant Jack Hamilton – between the sticks as a result of injuries to Alexander and Gallacher – raced from goal and got his hand to a through ball a split-second before his momentum took him into Handling. The basic laws of physics made contact unavoidable, but to howls of disbelief Collum pointed to the spot and Hamilton was booked. Yet, when you consider Collum's track record through here, instead of complaining, we should probably all have just counted our blessings he never sent the kid off.

Much to the joy of the home support, the task proved too onerous for Liam Craig. Resembling Mikey Stewart with gigantism, the Hibs captain sclaffed his penalty wide, watching slack-jawed as it grazed the post. This was celebrated like a goal by the Hearts fans and the reprieve at last had the old stadium rocking.

For the opening half-hour or so Hearts had been preoccupied with proving to Hibs they could outplay them, sticking rigidly to a game-plan of passing out from the back through Wilson into Gomis and Buaben and beyond. It meant the atmosphere had been slightly flat. You felt it was all a little too methodical and studied when what the occasion really called for was a little old-school blood and thunder.

That said, we may not have been playing the game like a derby but our strategy was still based on guile, high energy and quick thinking as gaps were subtly coaxed open via slick and enterprising interplay. The problem was we were getting nowhere with it, we were like ten bluebottles trapped in a jam jar. The closest we came to a goal in that first half were a couple of long-range skimmers from Nicholson and McGhee.

Throughout the first half the Hibernian support had seemed a little lost. They'd given up communicating via the medium of words and went instead with a variety of farmyard noises, intermittently honking, counting to five and then hooting loudly. All things considered this probably wasn't that surprising. I mean, since their last visit upwards of 80 per cent of their vocal repertoire is now totally obsolete. Their fanatical preoccupation with every subtle intricacy of our club's ownership had been all-consuming. So much so that I think they were toiling to remember any derby songs that weren't to do with us going bust.

I have to say, though, part of me has a grudging admiration for those of them that showed their faces here again. Can't have been easy after last time. They'd thrown the mother of all parties to revel in their rivals' relegation and, with a bit of luck, complete obliteration only, in all the excitement, to take their eye off the ball big style and end up getting relegated themselves. The only thing stopping these incompetent buffoons finishing bottom of the league themselves was our 15-point penalty, otherwise they wouldn't even have had a play-off with which to try and save their sorry skins.

Belatedly, they then sack their manager Terry Butcher and take an eternity to appoint his successor while – in the meantime – those rivals they'd done their utmost to see wiped off the face of the planet implement a sound business model which paves the way for fan ownership and off the back of it a whole raft of astute summer signings arrive. In short, leaving their wretched shambles of a club behind in the slipstream.

If Hibernian didn't exist I think we'd seriously have to invent them ourselves for our own amusement. As Morpheus puts it in *The Matrix*, 'Fate, it appears, has a sense of irony.'

The derby rumbled on into the second half and became increasingly error-strewn. Both teams were doing a first-rate job of cancelling each other out. Walker then replaced King but to no discernible effect and the odd little rumble of doubt began to creep in as to whether our side had a goal in them. Just as it was becoming a case of trying to justify to ourselves that four points from Rangers away and Hibernian at home was pretty decent going, the game fizzed and bubbled into life.

There were 14 minutes left when Nicholson mischievously nutmegged Robertson before racing forward and blazing the ball in off the post from 25 yards. Nick flew across to the fans with Tynecastle in full Krakatoa mode: TV viewers treated to the camera juddering as if the Wheatfield was a giant bouncy castle. Four minutes later we still hadn't stopped enthusing over the quality of the hit when we struck again. Robertson saw red for barging Buaben in the box and the unflappable Ghanaian drilled the ball smoothly down the middle of the goal. Play restarted to that ever-so-familiar backdrop of Hibs fans streaming for the exits in their droves, another derby disaster to try and tune out.

With Hearts moving into a 2-0 lead Hibernian suddenly started to play and the game became more and more charged with each passing second. El Alagui, who I'd never realised was even playing, forced a superb, sprawling save from Hamilton with a downward header as Hibs began attacking with genuine flair.

Hearts needed to take the sting out of the game. You could see the cooler heads, like Wilson and Gomis, desperately seeking to replicate those endless training ground drills; keeping hold of the ball in neat triangles and stifling Hibs of possession.

Their cause wasn't helped by occurrences further upfield. Sow had been at loggerheads with Nelson all afternoon. From the stands it had looked a fairly even contest with both protagonists giving as good as they'd got but, tellingly, Nelson was heavily bandaged after Sow had caught him above the eye. All of which meant when the big Swede caught Nelson again, causing him to squeal like Ned Flanders, he was always going to walk. Last week's hero had now sold his buddies short. You just hoped the price of the lesson wouldn't be our win.

These fears became more fully formed when El Alagui took possession in the dying minutes, after a curiously mistimed Wilson header fell at his feet, and laced the ball home from the edge of the box. It was 2-1 and Hibernian couldn't wait to scamper back to halfway to go again.

Derbies down through the years have been littered with improbable comebacks and defensive implosion right at the death. Suddenly, the possibility of snatching an implausible point worked Hibernian into a frenzied lather and they let their annoyance boil over. Since, exasperatingly for them, they never got to within 50 feet of Hamilton's goal again. Hearts ran down the clock expertly, deep in Hibernian territory, winning a flurry of throw-ins.

As the game was being killed stone dead, Stevenson went in on Walker, raking his studs down the back of the winger's Achilles. Walker sprang to his feet and went eyeball-to-eyeball with the chubby Mike from *Neighbours* lookalike, before Forster and Craig came steaming in and squared up to Wilson and Gomis. There was a lot of posturing and aggressive finger-pointing and you could see dire threats being exchanged. Craig kept pointing at Wilson and then the tunnel, repeatedly mouthing 'see you in there'. Not sure what that was all about. Maybe he'd promised Danny a lift home and didn't want to be left waiting ages for him while he got his hair just *so*.

Walker and Stevenson ended up with retrospective red cards after the compliance office watched *Sportscene* and construed the tiniest forward inclination of Walker's head as violent conduct. If they're seriously handing out two-match bans for violent and aggressive forehead-brushing Walker would've been as well just going for the full Yosser Hughes. After all, you might as well be hanged as a sheep than a lamb.

All in all the win had been achieved at a cost, with Sow and Walker now joining Paterson, Alexander and Gallacher on the sidelines, but none of that mattered as we emerged into blazing sunshine. We'd been handed a daunting double-header with which to kick off our time in the Championship so to be sitting on six points from six felt truly blissful.

48

Livingston away,
Petrofac Cup second round,
20 August 2014, 7.45pm

ONE of my abiding memories of New St Mirren Park on the final day of last season was the gallows humour from the Hearts fans. This was encapsulated in a song about going up to lift the Ramsden's Cup. 'And why not?' I thought, in the manner of Barry Norman, even though he apparently never said that.

Ideally, we'd only be in the damned thing once so why not have a go at winning it: stick it at the back of the trophy cabinet alongside the 1985 Tennent's Soccer Sixes or something. Now, with different sponsors in tow, we'd taken immense pleasure seeing the side demolish Annan in the first round and eagerly awaited the draw for the next stage. Especially with Hibs getting dumped out of the cup at Rangers.

However, in the three and a bit weeks that have elapsed since then the landscape has changed almost immeasurably. The competition has increasingly become more of a hindrance. We'd already lost Paterson, Alexander and Gallacher to injury, not to mention Sow and Walker to suspension. Jack Hamilton was cup-tied meaning not one but two keepers would need to be found: free agents Lee Hollis and Bryn Halliwell. Simply put, our players were dropping like flies and there was the worrying prospect we'd lose someone else for that tricky trip to high-flying Raith Rovers on the Saturday.

Robbie Neilson seems a strong-willed, grounded, sensible sort and made the decision to play what was essentially a reserve side against Livingston. From Sunday's derby, only Jordan McGhee kept his place. Despite his actions being wholly understandable, a number of Hearts fans felt short-changed. Off the back of the derby win, a large travelling support had packed out the Energy Assets Arena in good faith, only to see a bunch of reserves get pumped 4-1.

The match itself was actually pretty even until around 15 minutes to go when Livi streaked away with it although you could see it had been coming. An early Jordan White goal, after new keeper Hollis had flailed at a routine ball into the box, had been all that separated the sides for over an hour.

Following that breakthrough, Hearts had had a few half-decent chances to equalise, David Smith running himself into the ground to try and attain parity for his side.

Things then started to go awry for us when White notched his second on 76 minutes and the game became horribly stretched. In a matter of moments 2-0 became three, then four and it was a case of seeing the defeat for what it was and not dwelling on it any more than was necessary.

Personally, I was more than happy to sacrifice the competition if it meant we'd be fresh for Saturday and incur no more casualties, although part of my ambivalence was down to living within walking distance of the ground and not having needed to knock off work early or anything.

Ally McCoist couldn't resist sticking his beak in, whining, self-pityingly, that at Rangers they don't have the luxury of being able to rest players the way we had. Since, at Rangers, every game is a big game. Ah well, kudos to him for pointing that out to people. No doubt when Raith Rovers pumped them in last year's final it meant so much more to Grant Murray's side knowing they'd done it against a full-strength Rangers side and not a bunch of reserves. Same probably applied to Forfar Athletic in last season's League Cup, too, I'd imagine.

49

Raith Rovers away,
23 August 2014, 3pm

HEARTS continued their fine start to the season, vaporising Raith Rovers 4-0 at Starks Park and moving clear at the top with nine points from three games. All the plaudits go quite rightly to the borderline unplayable James Keatings who put down a serious marker with a blistering hat-trick but, in truth, this was a thrillingly effective team performance.

The side was bristling with attacking intent from the off, obsessed with tempo and well-channelled aggression. The constant pressing high up the pitch, the fizzed movement of the ball and the determination to get forward in numbers as quickly and as often as possible were all major factors in this result.

Much like Livingston it felt like we were among friends in Kirkcaldy. Its official status definitely appears to be Jambo friendly. From manager Grant Murray down through to club captain Jason Thompson and the likes of Calum Elliot and Christian Nade, the staff had copious links to Tynecastle.

That's even before you consider Craig Levein's short spell as manager plus all the established Hearts players who'd spent time here on loan. On the walk up the hill to the ground I chatted with one Rovers fan who enthused at length about Jason Holt and Jamie Walker. David Smith, on the other hand (as Borat would put it), 'Not so much.'

Even the wee seven-year-old mascot wouldn't be swayed from her pre-match prediction of a 3-2 win for Hearts which was greeted by good-natured cheering from the gathering away support trying to code-break their way into the correct seats in the stand behind the goal.

In the absence of the suspended Sow, Keatings made his first start. He formed a three-man strike-force with Nicholson and King and their swift, deft, almost telepathic exchanges brought back memories of the swashbuckling trio of Colquhoun, Crabbe and Robbo.

It took a mere 13 minutes for our busy triumvirate to conjure a goal between them. King streaked clear down the right and keeper Cuthbert made the cavalier decision to come barrelling out of his goal. King skipped around him like he was an oversized traffic cone and then pulled the ball into the middle. From the opposite end Nicholson's impudent flick looked to have crossed the line but Keatings made sure.

Hearts' lead meant Raith had little option but to commit men forward which played into the capital side's hands. The likes of Buaben, Gomis and Holt are all accomplished passers of the ball and having three willing, pacey runners ahead of them gave Raith a monumental headache.

Put simply, Hearts ran over the top of them and the second goal came as little surprise on the half-hour mark. Hearts had a shoot-on-sight policy and Keatings swept home from the edge of the box after an episode of pinball had seen shots from King and Buaben blocked.

A first-half double for Keatings was just the ticket to help endear him to a new set of supporters and he sprinted off to celebrate, his little legs pumping up and down furiously like he was Paul Hartley lacerating Hibernian at Hampden.

A trim Christian Nade was greeted warmly like an old friend as the imminent victory ensured high spirits all round. The mood became even lighter midway through the second half when Keatings secured his hat-trick in fine style. He curled an exquisite 20-yard free kick past Cuthbert with his left foot before skidding down on his knees in front of the delirious fans in the Railway stand.

Right at the death Oliver, who'd come on for a needlessly overheated Gomis, planted home a fourth and Hearts were two points clear of Queen of the South at the top. Three games gone and already we were six clear of promotion rivals Hibernian who'd been beaten 1-0 at home to Falkirk.

50

Stenhousemuir away, League Cup second round, 26 August 2014, 7.30pm

A CROWD of 1,768 squeezed into tiny Ochilview and, squinting into the setting, late summer sun, they saw Hearts down plucky Stenhousemuir with a little more to spare than the 2-1 scoreline might have suggested.

The League Cup is clearly viewed by the management as a step up from the Petrofac Cup as evidenced by Hearts picking a strong side for this second-round tie. The most conspicuous absentees were Buaben and Gomis. Robbie Neilson had come in for heavy criticism from certain quarters for picking what was, in essence, a reserve side against Livingston a week ago, but the sight of Keatings and then McGhee limping off in the first half showed exactly where he'd been coming from with that selection against Livi.

Hollis was back in goal due to Jack Hamilton's ineligibility and was redundant in the early stages as Hearts, wearing their new 'Argentina' away kit, kicked towards their own fans on the covered terracing. The old ground presented something of a paradox. On the one hand it was unapologetically quaint and old school with its terracing and miniature main stand while, on the other, it was quintessentially modern with a synthetic playing surface. Overall, it seemed a benign, kindly and welcoming venue, especially on a warm, mellow, summer's evening such as this.

Oliver's late goal at Starks Park had earned him a starting berth up top alongside Keatings and he took a mere six minutes to repay Robbie's faith, rifling home after David Smith had surged down the line.

Stenny had plenty of spirit and the makeshift midfield fulcrum of Holt and Robinson had their work cut out stemming a series of smart counter-attacks. But, in the main, Hearts were on the front foot and it didn't come as a massive shock to see them go two up, just shy of the half-hour mark. Jamie Walker seemed to come alive on the synthetic surface and his clever pull-back was cracked home by McHattie from 16 yards.

At 2-0 and with 15 minutes to go to half-time, a place in the hat for the next round looked virtually assured. Whether this would be achieved the easy or the hard way remained another matter, though. Walker snatched at a couple of chances before we got our answer: the Warriors breaking upfield and Miller firing home after a nice chest-down by Grehan.

This made for a tense second half as the last thing Hearts needed was the stresses and possible strains of a long, drawn-out evening of extra time and who knows what else. Sow had come on for the limping Keatings and he came closest to providing a second-half goal, heading against the bar from a corner.

With two minutes left we got our first look at new signing Adam Eckersley. The left-back had signed from Danish side Aarhus having begun his career at Manchester United as understudy to Mikael Silvestre. Early days but the ginger Phil Bardsley looked the part.

51
Falkirk home,
30 August 2014, 3pm

A SPARKLING Hearts dismantled Falkirk 4-1 in front of 16,369 fans at a vibrant Tynecastle and, on this showing, will take some displacing from the top of the Championship. A King double along with goals from McGhee and Sow saw Hearts maintain their 100 per cent start with their fourth win on the bounce.

Thankfully, Jordan McGhee had made a full recovery from the knock that caused him to hobble off against Stenhousemuir. He stole forward at a corner and gleefully headed home the opener on 16 minutes.

Hearts were thoroughly in command and went through their full repertoire as the crowd purred in contentment. Like a boxer, intermittently working different parts of an adversary's body, Hearts repeatedly switched the emphasis of their attacks, recycling possession and leaving Falkirk punch-drunk and befuddled.

Gomis and Buaben were ever-willing recipients of the ball and, when the mood grabbed them, quick-stepped through the midfield, playing little, razor-sharp one-twos, shielding the ball and retaining possession expertly. Then, on other occasions, full-backs McGhee and McHattie would glide forward, linking up with either King or Nicholson who were swapping wings for the sheer devilment. Finally, when Wilson or Ozturk felt a mini-breather was in order they'd go long and arrow the ball forward to Sow who'd either bring Keatings or the wingers into play or kill the ball stone dead as if he had Velcro boots on his feet.

Midway through the half Hearts got their second goal and it arose as a result of the latest in a long line of Hearts-related mishaps to befall ex-Jambo Alan Maybury.

Since returning north he's seen red with Hibernian in the comedy classic that was last season's relegation derby and, as a St Johnstone player in 2012, conceded an injury-time spot-kick at McDiarmid Park to help keep alive a maroon Scottish Cup campaign that ended in May on the winners' podium. Here, he simply careered into Nicholson, upending him for an obvious penalty.

Following on from his hat-trick last weekend at Raith, and like all good goalscorers, Keatings was desperate to bump up his numbers. Blocking his way was none another than former Hearts number one Jamie MacDonald. No one in the ground needed reminding of Jamma's prowess from 16 yards but he was happy nonetheless to give yet another demonstration, palming out Keatings's attempt. Unluckily for Jamma his defenders lacked the same cat-like reflexes and King lashed home the rebound for 2-0.

Driven and ruthless, Hearts had no intention of easing up on the Bairns. They ended up going in at the break a healthy three goals to the good as King scored his second on 38 minutes, bulleting home Keatings's cross.

The teams emerged for the second half and MacDonald was afforded a hero's welcome as he jogged across to the Gorgie end. The ovation from the stand was right up there with the Kop welcoming Ray Clemence back to Anfield with Spurs in 1981. Without a shadow of doubt we'd never have got close to that 2012 Scottish Cup without Jamma's saves at New St Mirren Park and then in the semi-final against Celtic at Hampden. So for that, for volunteering to play last season on reduced wages and for a host of other improbably brilliant and heroic saves, he more than deserved his reception.

Figuring he had nothing left to lose, Falkirk boss Peter Houston had made a double switch at the interval, Leahy and Bia-Bi coming on for Dick and Cooper. However, it would have taken more than that to wrest control of this match away from Hearts with them in such irresistible form and they picked up exactly where they'd left off, pinning Falkirk back and starving them of the ball.

With 18 minutes left on the clock Falkirk were afforded perhaps the merest glimpse of a lifeline when Buaben received a straight red for a needlessly over-zealous lunge on Durojaiye. The Prince trudged off dejectedly without a word of complaint.

Hearts may have been a man down but it was them that scored the next goal. Vaulks tripped Sow in the box and the big man dusted himself down and made it 4-0.

Five minutes from time and with supporters beginning to drift contentedly towards the exits, job done, Bia-Bi scored a consolation for Falkirk from close range. Meanwhile, elsewhere, Rangers and Raith had also won which meant our cushion at the top remained at a reassuring three points. Towards the foot of the table, an 85th-minute winner from Alloa's Iain Flannigan consigned Hibernian to their third league defeat from four outings, casting them a pretty sizeable nine adrift of their city rivals.

52

Dumbarton away,
13 September 2014, 3pm

GAME number five and Hearts lost their record of taking maximum points against turgid and resolute Dumbarton at the Bet Butler. However, the point gained from a fairly moribund 0-0 meant they remained unbeaten and were able to take back top spot after Rangers' 4-0 win at Starks Park meant they'd kept it warm for 20 or so hours.

Perhaps having had the previous weekend free due to Livi ending our involvement in the Petrofac Cup was responsible for a slight loss of impetus. Hearts toiled manfully to scale the heights but found Dumbarton awkward adversaries. McHattie limped off after 13 minutes to be replaced by Eckersley and the switch added to the disordered nature of the game.

It took Hearts until ten minutes before half-time to piece together a sustained bout of attacking. Sow had a couple of right-footed shots which had Rogers scurrying across his goal and then Hearts won three corners in quick succession, all of which were snuffed out.

In an attempt to spice up the Hearts attack, Robbie made a double substitution around the hour mark, King and Keatings being withdrawn for Walker and debutant Soufian El Hassnaoui. The Dutch-born Moroccan had signed on a free from Sparta Rotterdam.

As the clock ran down the game became stretched. Chris Kane had a chance to pilfer all three points for the hosts but his shot went straight to Alexander. Then, direct from the restart, Walker saw a right-foot shot well saved by Rogers as it flew unerringly towards the bottom corner.

If Dumbarton felt they'd weathered the worst of the storm with that near miss they were mistaken, though, as deep into stoppage time Nicholson arrived at the corner of the six-yard box and smashed a header against the bar.

The point was enough to at least give us back top spot but our lead now sits at one measly point. For both Edinburgh sides the events of their respective stoppage times had a telling effect on the points gap. While Nicholson was cruelly denied, Cummings had more luck, scoring the winner for Hibernian in the fourth minute of injury time.

At one point they'd been trailing 2-1 and Hearts had been chasing a late winner which would've extended that nine-point gap to 12. Instead, by 4.50pm, Hibernian had successfully whittled it down to a far more manageable seven points.

53

Cowdenbeath home,
20 September 2014, 3pm

THE previous weekend Cowdenbeath had given city rivals Hibernian a pretty serious jolt, succumbing 3-2 with the last kick of stoppage time. Having seen off the obdurate Fifers by the skin of their teeth, Hibernian were probably quite happy to see their city rivals get a taste of that Blue Brazil spunk for themselves.

It was odd seeing Jimmy Nicholl in the technical area. Despite having seemingly been around forever he hasn't really aged. He looks exactly as he did when leading Raith Rovers out in the 1994 League Cup Final even though that whole side have all pretty much retired. Only Berwick manager Colin Cameron is still registered as a player.

I bet seeing that Raith team score in the Olympic Stadium, Munich, seems a lifetime ago for Jimmy. Since then his managerial career has stalled like one of his own interminable anecdotes, 'After the game Zico's come into the dressing room looking for me, so he has, and I've said to big Pat Jennings, right, listen here big man, here's what you need to do...'

There was another hugely impressive near-sell-out crowd rammed into Tynecastle. However, in the main, those 15,594 were mightily subdued as the side began rather tentatively, acting like they'd only just been introduced to one another in the tunnel.

Acing those first four league games had got everyone all aquiver and the thought of that blank at Dumbarton signalling an end to our fun was a bit troubling. We'd need to put that aberration behind us, pronto.

The nerves dissipated after quarter of an hour when Hearts nudged into the lead. Danny Wilson punched a pass into the feet of Billy King who'd located a chink of space around the D of the box. The winger took a feather-light touch and lashed the ball goalwards in one near-seamless action. The ball fizzed unerringly past Thomson before he had a chance to blink.

There were sighs of relief all round. That goal reacquainted us all with those warm, fuzzy feelings from August and the side began picking Cowdenbeath apart with gusto. Keatings set up King and the winger came within a whisker of his and Hearts' second, his effort blocked by Anderson. Gaps were being prised open: the opposition forced out of their shell like a cranky tortoise awoken early from hibernation.

Six minutes later Cowdenbeath snatched a piece of lettuce and promptly retreated back inside that shell of theirs, Tynecastle stunned and once again in near-silence. Within the blink of an eye they'd grabbed an unforeseen equaliser. Higgins had a shot blocked by Alexander and while everyone stood around admiring the keeper's handiwork, Gallagher sprung forward and netted the rebound.

This was when the Neilson effect came truly into force. Hearts basically never batted an eyelid, they stubbornly tuned out that setback and began, almost robotically, constructing their intricate patterns of play.

Sow lashed a shot goalwards only to see it tipped away superbly by Thomson. This was followed by an even better opportunity for Paterson who glanced wide with the goal gaping. The giant right-back was starting his first game since tweaking knee ligaments versus Annan and, although understandably rusty, Cowdenbeath were quaking in their boots each time his massive strides came reaching over halfway.

Any lingering doom and gloom at only drawing 1-1 at half-time were dispelled as the scores from the two key games elsewhere filtered across cyberspace: both Alloa and QotS were a goal to the good at home, respectively, to Rangers and Hibernian.

Whether this buoyed Hearts is hard to know – they seemed fully attuned to the task in hand – but they came out for the second half and turned on the afterburners in a truly scintillating display of powerful, attacking football. Their crushing dominance was total.

Gomis and Robinson were impregnable, never missing a tackle. Gomis, in particular, was giving it the full Claude Makelele, whirring around in perpetual motion, reading and anticipating the game's every nuance. One second he'd be snuffing out an attack with a bone-crunching tackle, the next he was executing a Cruyff turn on a sixpence and wrong-footing three hapless Cowdenbeath midfielders in one go.

It took a paltry three second-half minutes for Hearts to get their lead back. Eckersley swept in a near-post cross from close by the corner flag and Jamie Walker flicked a delightful looping header in off the far post. Having given Cowdenbeath a reprieve in the first half you could see Hearts were in no mood to relinquish their lead a second time.

Two-one quickly became three and again Walker was heavily involved. The little number seven got free in the box and was flattened by Brownlie. Sow sent the keeper the wrong way with a sledgehammer of a spot-kick.

After 72 minutes Carrick took to the field, replacing the excellent King, and the last 20 or so minutes revolved around Speedie tormenting the Blue Brazil keeper. I have this framed photograph on the wall of my study of Temps running to the fans having just scored at Anfield. The reason being that it's the craziest and best goal celebration I've ever been a part of. Anyway, rushing to join in the merriment is a young Dale Carrick. You can't compare that scrawny kid with the beefed-up powerhouse we now have.

For his first involvement in the game he took a pass from Sow – who'd shown almost superhuman strength, shielding the ball from a posse of defenders – and drilled a daisy-cutter into the corner for 4-1.

Then, with four minutes to go, he latched on to a flick-on 30 yards out, took a touch and with the ball out of his feet clobbered an absolute rocket of a shot that rose all the way into the roof of the net.

In the first half it had been King and Keatings who'd carried the main threat and occupied the vexed Cowdenbeath defenders while, as the game drew to a close, Sow, Walker and now Carrick were persecuting them. We seemed to have a thrilling array of options open to us, with players taking it in turns to step up to the plate and take responsibility for hurting the opposition.

By full time our tally after six league games stood at a laudable 17 goals, but even more pleasing was that our three-point lead at the top of the table had been restored. Rangers had come unstuck at Alloa, sneaking a late equaliser through Temps. Meanwhile Hibernian, on the other hand, hadn't had an answer to QotS, losing 1-0 in Dumfries and dropping ten points behind us.

54

Celtic away, League Cup third round, 24 September 2014, 7.15pm

I N a different season going out of the League Cup in this manner would have seriously grated. There's no getting away from the fact that it was an opportunity lost. However, our priorities have been skewed by our need to return to the top division and we're left scraping the barrel to locate the positives from this 3-0 reversal.

The biggest positive has to be the sheer number of chances we created. In years gone by Hearts sides have prevailed here in the League Cup having created a fraction of our tally tonight. One such victory, in 2009, was shown by *Sportscene* during its pre-match build-up. The coup de grâce, a half-hit Mikey Stewart penalty that barely had the legs to cross the line.

The man himself was pitchside alongside Charlie Mulgrew. These exchanges often make for excruciating viewing but Mulgrew was charming and affable, attributing Mikey's poor connection to the clumpy, sandy coloured boots he was wearing, 'Can't believe you took that one with your Timberlands on!'

I love the way at Celtic Park these days it's just a given that as an away support we'll all behave ourselves. Hemmed in there by a couple of strips of luminous gaffer tape. And, at full-time, just turfed out of the ground into multitudes of home supporters on London Road. There you go boys, safe journey home now. I suppose in a way it's quite touching that they trust us not to run amok. Can you imagine what would happen if we tried the same trick with their fans at Tynecastle?

Anyway, a small band of our supporters made the trip over in spite of the unhelpfully early kick-off time. They saw their side start fairly well. Paterson very nearly set up Sow as Hearts won three corners in very quick succession.

Then, midway through the half, Izaguirre sent a testing ball into the box and Wilson failed to deal with it adequately, more or less gifting Guidetti an assist with a wayward header. It was galling seeing all our good work undone like that and you could tell the setback had impacted on self-belief. Eckersley cleared off the line from Guidetti and then Gomis was saved from the ignominy of an own goal thanks to a reflex stop from Alexander.

We rode our luck as the first half ticked away. Then, on the very stroke of half-time, Hearts were presented with a fantastic opportunity. Stokes got his angles all wrong with a pass and succeeded only in playing in Jamie Walker. From the edge of the box the midfielder cracked a shot beyond Gordon only to see it hammer back off the crossbar. If anything he'd got too much behind the ball and tried to force it.

We should have been level at half-time but all that was forgotten early in the second half when Sow toppled under minimal pressure from van Dijk and a peevish-looking Willie Collum pointed to the spot.

Sow had registered a couple of successes from the spot already this season, most recently versus Cowdenbeath last Saturday, and was quickly moving to place the ball down. There's a school of thought that says players who've been fouled shouldn't be allowed anywhere near the resultant spot-kick as they won't be in the right state, mentally or physically. Not sure if that was why Osman missed. It wasn't as if it had been a particularly bad foul on him or anything. But, for whatever reason, the big man botched it, leaning back and ballooning an abysmal effort over the bar. Maybe he should have borrowed Mikey Stewart's Timberlands.

Just in case we were in any doubt that the miss had forfeited any lingering chance we'd had in the tie, the point was reinforced by Celtic breaking upfield and winning a spot-kick of their own from their very next attack. A relieved Collum looked much more his usual self with this award, smiling warmly after Ozturk knocked Guidetti over. And there's no way Commons was ever going to miss.

The game had gone. We needed simply to see out the final 35 minutes and regroup for Sunday's visit of Livingston. The scoring hadn't finished, sadly. Stokes crossed and Eckersley, stretching to try and cushion the ball back to Alexander with his chest, underestimated his pectoral muscle tone and the ball was beyond the keeper before he could react. Happens to the best of us, Eck.

We'd had more than enough chances to win this tie and were let down by a combination of slack defending and profligate finishing. We play in a division where you can make the odd gaffe and still win games. But there's no margin for error here. At this level, everything tends to get punished, and the players found that out to their cost. Moreover, you need to take your chances. In our league, chances are like Edinburgh trams. No sweat if you miss one, just bide your time there'll be another one along in ten minutes. Probably more likely 20, though.

If our focus wasn't fixed on the league campaign the avoidable manner of this defeat would have hurt more. As it was I found it quite easy to shrug off and, like the manager, set my sights on Sunday, agreeing with his verdict, 'Thought the game hinged on the penalty. We went 1-0 down but still stayed strong. We miss the penalty and the game totally changed from there, they go up the park and get a penalty and it's very difficult when the crowd starts getting behind them, the atmosphere changes and they start getting confidence. I'm pleased with the performance overall. Disappointed with the result: at the end of the day the league's the main thing for us and gear up now for Sunday.'

55
Livingston home,
28 September 2014, 4.05pm

HEARTS and Livingston took to the field having had League Cup midweeks to forget, humbled 3-0 at Celtic and 4-0 at Aberdeen, respectively. For the home side, any lasting gloom was purged from the system with an eviscerating 5-0 win while, for Livi, misery was piled upon misery.

Seven games in now and the side not only remains unbeaten but continues to develop into a seriously formidable unit, strong at the back and overloaded with goal threats. However, as Robbie said pre-match on BBC Alba, 'We're six games in, there's still another 30 to go.' The longer we can keep this run of form going, though, the harder it's going to be for teams to stay with us.

Hearts were superior in each and every department. We even won the battle of the fashion faux pas as Callum Paterson's hairband with short hair ensemble trumped John McGlynn's tinted-lenses-at-dusk look.

Hearts have a style and philosophy that Neilson and director of football Craig Levein are keen to see implemented at the club. It prioritises possession and measured football via an exhaustive training regime. Livi simply had no answer to this as Hearts passed them to death: blitzing them off the pitch. The Edinburgh side possessed no weak links whatsoever with every player shrewd and confident in possession.

The only surprise was it took as long as 13 minutes for the first goal to come. Paterson, Sow and Walker had all come close before El Hassnaoui punctured the Livi defence with an angled drive from the corner of the box after Sam Nicholson had found him with his back to goal.

You got the impression Livi's fans probably wished they'd stayed at home and watched the Ryder Cup, flicking nervously over to BBC Alba every now and again to check on the damage. It was one-way traffic and, on 28 minutes, Hearts won a free kick 20 yards out. A permanent fixture around these set pieces, without enjoying much success, has been Ozturk. Who knows, perhaps he's been a real demon in training. Today, we saw why he's so keen to get involved as he hit the sweetest of strikes against the upright. The rebound came at El Hass too quickly for him to react and divert it in.

Never matter, 30 seconds later and Hearts had their second. Buaben found Walker on the left of the box and the little winger took full advantage of the obvious gap Jamieson had left at his near post to roll it in.

In midfield, Morgaro Gomis was dictating the tempo and the thrust of the side's passing, as well as holding its shape alongside Prince Buaben. With these two minders on the case and Alexander barking orders from goal, Hearts were all business and their tenacious pressing brought a third as half-time neared. O'Brien was loose with a pass and Sow gobbled up the chance.

Livi put down a few markers at the start at the second half but staging a comeback involves more than simply running around a bit more and kicking your opponent's best players. Not that this would have come as much consolation to Walker and Paterson, who were both left hobbling around for a few minutes.

Finally, Hippolyte got booked for taking out Sam Nicholson. The winger had already avoided swipes from two other Livi players in a run reminiscent of Claudio Caniggia at Italia 90, hurdling those tackles against Cameroon.

From the free kick, Ozturk was a fraction high with a powerful effort and it was clear he was after a goal today. At the other end, Burchill found himself in space on the right of the box with a chance that surely represented his side's last opportunity to put together a highly improbable comeback. He pulled his shot wide, though.

Gomis then decided he'd had enough of the unselfish donkey work and advanced purposefully with the ball at his feet. He then let fly with a dipping 25-yarder that rattled the bar. Minutes later, on the hour mark, Robbie decided it was time to freshen up the attack. Nicholson and Walker had been lethal adversaries, full of trickery and menace. Livi's relief at seeing the back of them would have been tempered slightly by the sight of Carrick and King ready for action.

The duo were clearly keen to make up for lost time. A sentiment shared by Keatings who then replaced El Hass. Jamieson, in the Livi goal, then spent a rigorous half hour having his goalkeeping credentials examined by a Hearts side seemingly hell-bent on reaching double figures.

The Jam Tarts were in irresistible mood and had no intention of letting up, peppering Jamieson's goal. Minutes after coming on Carrick combined with Wilson to set up Sow. The Swede sent an audacious flick goalwards, only to see it clawed away at the foot of the post. Next up was King after El Hass had swept through midfield and set him up. The substitute's shot was clutched at the second attempt.

If anything, the arrival of Keatings intensified the frantic desire for more goals, he was so pumped up and desperate to stake his claim. Twice in a minute he was denied by Jamieson. On 77, Buaben's cut-back was dummied by Sow and Keats's firm effort was pushed away, then Gomis set him up and from 16 yards he checked inside only to see Jamieson dive full-length and tip his curling effort round the post.

It was an electrifying performance which 3-0 didn't really do justice to. It was gratifying, then, to see Hearts belatedly notch two more in the final three minutes and give the scoreline a far more accurate spin.

For the fourth, King and Carrick linked wide right and when the ball was rolled across for Keats he finally had his first Tynecastle goal.

Then, with the 90 minutes more or less up, Paterson, intrepid and athletic at right-back, hooked a wonderful ball into the box from tight on the touchline. It dropped in front of Sow who cushioned a quite exquisite volley into the far corner before coolly turning to celebrate number five by high-fiving a fan or two in the Gorgie stand.

A raucous home crowd of 14,848 had seen their side pull six points clear at the top, with Rangers entertaining second-bottom Hibernian the following night.

56

Queen of the South away, 4 October 2014, 3pm

C ASTING my eyes across the open terracing on the Terregles Street end of Palmerston Park from high up in the Rosefield Salvage stand it could quite easily have been a game from any point in the last 95-odd years. But, then, a quick glance down at the pitch would give the game away. No mistaking that brushed 3G sheen. The atmosphere before kick-off was absolutely jumping with twirling scarves, swirling maroon smoke and incessant singing. The Hearts fans were in buoyant mood and this match had all the buzz of a crucial Scottish Cup quarter-final.

For me, we're missing a trick by not having a 16-team top division which would be readily accessible to clubs such as Queen of the South. Proper, well-run, well-supported clubs with the stadium exactly where it should be: slap bang in the middle of the community. Give me a ground like this every time; surrounded by houses, within walking distance of pubs and shops and close to the railway station.

You compare this to some of these bland, generic, plastic stadia that keep springing up. Not in the town but stuck along a bypass four miles away. On a roundabout next to a Homebase and an Allied Carpets where you take your life in your hands as you hop across central reservation zones and down grassy embankments. Is that the future of football? I sincerely hope not. These departures out of town are the footballing equivalent of the sorts of destinations usually provided by Ryanair. 'This game we're going to is within walking distance of the station right? Well, yes and no, it's actually three miles out of town but we can get a taxi from the pub next to the station…'

Jim McIntyre had departed for Ross County and this was James Fowler's first official game in charge having impressed as caretaker. QotS had had a steady if unspectacular start to the season, suffering a minor setback last weekend, losing 2-1 away at bottom side Cowdenbeath.

For us, Hibernian had stormed Ibrox the previous Monday and registered a momentous 3-1 victory. As far as the green hordes were concerned the clamour, on their message boards, greeting the win was the equivalent of Boromir's horn of Gondor in *Lord of the Rings*, signalling their intent to hunt us down. Good. Let us know how that goes, won't you?

While all we were fixated on was the six-point leeway we now had over Rangers. We had a nice cushion and while we relished the security of knowing we'd still be top tonight irrespective, it felt crucial that we kept on winning. Kept on pushing. A lead such as this is something to be prized and nurtured and, if possible, built upon.

We'd made a few changes from last week's disassembling job on Livingston. And as the three to stand down were all on the bench it made you think their replacements had perhaps been favoured as they'd shown greater aptitude for synthetic surfaces.

We replaced both of our full-backs: McGhee and Eckersley coming in for C-Patz and McHattie. The other change was King for Nicholson and the formation appeared the same as last week, with Sow and El Hassnaoui leading the line.

The Doonhamers kicked off, playing towards the 3,000 away fans packed together behind the goal and in half of the stand. It was a high-speed start from the hosts. They dominated play from the off and seemed to want to silence the maroon masses as quickly as possible.

Ozturk didn't seem at the races at all, struggling to cope with the lively QotS strikers nipping across his path at breakneck speed. Gavin Reilly left him for dead after six minutes and sent a low shot sweeping past the post with Alexander rooted to the spot.

We were severely under the cosh and struggling to keep our heads above water. Suddenly, this division had gotten serious and those back-to-back, five-goal hauls suddenly seemed a very distant memory. Three minutes later, from Ian McShane's dangerously whipped corner, Andy Dowie planted a header towards the corner. As the home supporters rose, in anticipation of nosing ahead, the ball bounced off the inside of the post and nestled into the arms of a grateful Alexander.

It had been a torrid opening ten minutes. Thankfully, after a brief respite where they caught their breath, Hearts were able to play their way into the game a little more. Queens, however, remained a handful and containment was proving arduous. First Ozturk, and then Buaben picked up ominously early yellow cards.

Twenty-three minutes in and Osman Sow served a notice of intent, powering a header towards the top corner from a King cross. Zander Clark got both hands to the ball. These forays forward were initially tentative for Hearts but given our undoubted talent that was less of a worry than being constantly penned back. We had faith in the goalscoring talent underpinning our +18 goal difference and there was genuine confidence in the ability of our offensive players to eke something out.

That said, it still came as a surprise when we went ahead on 39 minutes. Sow unleashed an absolute thunderbolt from 30 yards for his seventh goal of the season, the ball crashing in off the underside of the bar to wild scenes of joy.

The assistant instantly signalled for the goal and turned back to halfway but the decision was hotly disputed on and off the pitch. Queens surrounded referee Brian Colvin as the home fans howled their displeasure but the assistant on the near side had been adamant and the goal stood.

It was almost like it'd needed something like that to tame Queens. To break them. To shatter their resolve. Two minutes later Hearts had scored again and if their fans were looking for someone to blame for this one they could do a lot worse than look to their own defenders. Buaben rattled through a cluster of insipid challenges and then prodded the ball powerfully into the corner from the edge of the box. To us, that double tap felt like a knockout blow and we warmly applauded our players off at half-time, feeling that a seventh win from eight was within our sights.

The officials returned to the fray to a chorus of booing from the home support. Television pictures weren't conclusive which suggests they may have been justified in airing their grievance. Down south, the Premier League has adopted vanishing spray this season and we're due to follow suit at the turn of the year. Until we also take on board their new goal-line technology there's always the risk of this kind of thing happening. From a purely selfish point of view I was just relieved, if there had been a miscarriage of justice, it had gone in our favour.

Hearts were able to be far more assertive in the second 45. The 2-0 lead meant we were holding all the aces and having weathered that first-half barrage there was a sense Queens had nothing left to throw at us.

The seal was put on the victory on the hour-mark when McGhee ghosted into the box from full-back and was on hand to lash home King's tempting cross. Despite the score, this match had provided us with our toughest test thus far and without that rapid-fire double just before half-time the outcome could have been very different. That said, we possess gifted, highly technical players with an eye for goal and scoring when we did showed a reassuring mental toughness and sharp-eyed opportunism.

With Ozturk and Buaben having been booked early on and still having to make tackles the sensible decision was made to hook them. Paterson came on at right-back and McGhee partnered Wilson. But not before Buaben was replaced by our new Spanish signing, Miguel Pallardó, whose career had begun at Valencia prior to him making his name at Levante. Primarily a defensive midfielder, our new number 14 nearly scored with his first touch, the ball saved low down by Clark.

Clambering aboard the coach back to Tynecastle it was to news that Christian Nade had stalled that Hibernian cavalry charge up the table with a 68th-minute equaliser for Raith at Easter Road. Those 12 points they lagged behind meant, for now at least, they represented as much of a threat to us as Falkirk (also on ten points) or Dumbarton (a point further back).

Our biggest rivals, Rangers, sneaked a 1-0 at Livingston in a game marred by crowd trouble which meant our lead over them at the top remained at six points.

57

Alloa away,
11 October 2014, 3pm

I'D purchased a ticket for the seats at the Indodrill Stadium but on arriving at the ground I realised they were for a flimsy, temporary-looking structure, the sort of thing you'd see next to a marquee at a garden fete. The view it provided was non-existent. I'd have been as well sitting in my Mini in the Morrisons car park, with the game on the radio. At least my knees wouldn't have been crushed.

And there probably would have been commentary, too, given that Scotland had a Euro 2016 qualifier against Georgia at 5pm and, as a result, the SPL card was blank. In an attempt to remind the world they were still a big club, too, Rangers were also idle. Their match away at Cowdenbeath way too hazardous to contemplate without Aird, Peralta, Moshni et al. So not that big a club. Their self-imposed torpor meant our lead at the top could stretch to nine points with a win.

I moved along to the terracing and found a spec standing next to the railing, pitchside, in line with the six-yard box. The low-slung autumn sun made watching the game tricky. Look, if I'm being brutally honest here I wasn't overly enamoured with the surroundings. This was, essentially, a less-charming Ochilview but with a prettier view of the hills.

Instead of following in the footsteps of our main rivals, and mumping and moaning about the state of the synthetic playing surface, Robbie Neilson quietly took ownership of the situation and booked training time on it during the week. Not sure if this was done anonymously over the phone as it handed Hearts a massive advantage in a venue that had managed to ambush both Rangers (who drew) and Hibs (who were beaten).

In the end we pilfered this one, three minutes from time, after Adam Eckersley's speculative free kick into the box skidded into the bottom corner courtesy of the merest deflection. The minuscule margin of victory made it hard to view Robbie's decision as anything other than a genuine masterstroke.

We'd started with a real spring in our step and it was only towards the end of the first half that the state of the surface started to have a discernible effect. Carrick snatched at a chance within the first 30 seconds that could have put us on easy street and then further opportunities were spurned by Sow, King and Buaben.

But by the time the second half got going Hearts seemed to find even the simplest of passes a problem and the ball kept sticking, holding up between players. The effect was the same as you see when puddles of water accumulate and Hearts were clearly getting bogged down.

Kevin Cawley squandered two gilt-edged chances for Alloa and as the sun slowly set behind the main stand it began to look like it might also be about to set on our unbeaten run. This worry was only magnified by the sight of Danny Wilson, flat out, having strained his hamstring. Not only would we be without our skipper for the vital conclusion to the game, but we'd committed all three substitutes (Nicholson, Paterson and El Hass for Carrick, McGhee and Walker) and would need to play the game out with only ten men.

Eckersley's late goal, therefore, felt like we'd got out of jail. Driving back down the M9, with the Scotland game on the radio (another scruffy 1-0) and with Hibernian having drawn 0-0 at home to Dumbarton, it felt like a great time to be a Hearts fan. We'd taken maximum points from two unquestionably tricky away games, we were nine clear at the top, still unbeaten, and next up were Dumbarton at home, then the derby at Easter Road.

58

Dumbarton home,
18 October 2014, 3pm

DUMBARTON arrived in town as the only team in the division to deprive us of a win in the first quarter of fixtures. The two points we dropped in that 0-0 back in September, along with another of their stalemates – at Easter Road last Saturday – suggested we may be in for a frustrating afternoon.

After taking around 20 minutes to fire properly, Hearts blew any lasting apprehension to smithereens with another devastating demonstration of free-flowing, football carnage. Another five goals were blasted in, for the third successive home game, and if you include last season we've now scored five goals in four out of our last seven matches here. By the end, a shell-shocked Ian Murray, relieved his side hadn't shipped eight like Sunderland at Southampton, simply said, 'Anybody who tries to argue they're not the best team in this league at this moment is wrong.'

These massacres are becoming commonplace and in all my years following Hearts I can't remember a more dazzling sequence of games where you simply sat back in wonder and enjoyed the slaughter.

Twenty-six minutes was how long the first goal took. Not that anyone was fretting, worried a breakthrough might not be coming. You wonder what percentage of C-Patz's training schedule is made up of little balls being laid into his path for him to bend invitingly into the box. You sometimes get the impression he could hit these in blindfolded. Fair to say he's got them off pat and from another textbook delivery Sow nodded home.

The show was up and running now and, as with Cowdenbeath and Livi, the first goal tore up Plan A for the opposition. Murray, with his little folded piece of paper and his bookies' pen, would now need to put a line through 'take an age over goal kicks, keep it tight and get Nishie to rough them up'. No longer applicable, Ian. No longer applicable.

The Sons, unbeaten in their previous six games, subsequently committed a few more men forward and from their first attack almost drew level. Graham brought a quite breathtaking save out of Alexander. It's no wonder we currently possess the best defensive record in the country, with only five goals conceded, when you see our keeper make saves like that.

From another aborted Sons attack, Hearts notched their second on 40 minutes via a rapier-like counter-attack. Sow brought the ball out of defence, hurdling large, inanimate objects like he was Ed Moses. And talk about total football: who was sprinting to join the attack over his left shoulder? C-Patz. The right-back was hugging the left touchline and when he took possession from Osman on halfway he knocked the ball, first time, into the box for Billy King who must have been wearing an invisible jet pack to get there that fast. King was then crudely upended for the clearest penalty you'll see all season.

Less clear, it seems, was who would take the thing. Buaben and all the players bar one assumed it was to be the grinning Ghanaian. But, the one exception, El Hass, wanted it and spat the dummy good style when rank was pulled, booting the ball away. His unseemly antics didn't go down too well and, with a few boos lingering in the air, Buaben placed the ball on the spot. On-loan Aberdeen keeper, Danny Rogers, could've thrown his cap on Buaben's powderpuff attempt but somehow the ball squirmed beyond him. In celebrating, Prince booted the corner flag a good degree harder than he'd hit his pen.

A tight hamstring kept Sow in at the break but any doubts we'd lose potency were dispelled on 56 minutes when his replacement, Jason Holt, made it three. Advancing through the middle, Holt just ran and ran and when a gap showed itself he rammed the ball home from 18 yards.

The 15,522 crowd were loving overseeing their rampant side and began ripping it out of Ian Murray with a few rounds of, 'Murray, Murray, what's the score?' This came to a brief halt on 73 minutes when Fleming pulled a goal back for the Sons, hooking home Nish's knock-down for a tidy finish.

Normal service was resumed, though, ten minutes later when C-Patz capped a powerhouse performance with the fourth, a flying header from King's corner. This left us with six minutes plus stoppage time to grab a fifth and have a proper chant to deride Murray with.

With the ex-Hibbie squirming in the opposition dugout and 'we want five, we want five' resonating loudly from all four stands, King swayed in from the right and hit a firm shot that skidded past Rogers's knee and in for the fifth, as requested.

Tynecastle erupted to the refrain '5-1, we only won 5-1!' as Murray sat, tight-lipped, praying for the whistle. To be fair to him, on full time, he was magnanimous in defeat, saying, 'You can't argue with the league table. They're nine points clear and they've scored another five goals at home — it's as simple as that.'

We could never have imagined life outside Scotland's top flight would have been, thus far, so uplifting. Yet there's still a bizarre sense – one endorsed by Neilson himself – that we are yet to truly hit top form for a sustained period.

Hearts' euphoric run of form is increasingly hard for those out-with the club to digest. In Saturday's *Scotsman*, Rangers striker Kenny Miller questioned Hearts' ability to maintain their blistering start to the season, 'You can be miles and miles ahead but to get that last win and get across the line is the hardest thing to do. That pressure does mount. We have got the experience in our dressing room of having to go through it on the final day or having to win an Old Firm game to even claw yourself back into the race. [Then, of Hearts] I don't know any of their lads really so I don't know their attitude or mentality towards the game. I just think if you are ahead by nine points, complacency can maybe creep in. The longer that run goes on, the more other teams are motivated to put an end to that run. They might see teams raising their game more against them, like they have done against us this season. There are a lot of things that come into it when you are trying to win a title [and, most tellingly] that pressure and experience of maybe not being there might start telling, there might be injuries or suspensions to key players, who knows?'

Well, the title-winning experience to which Kenny alluded seems, with their present crop of players, to be limited in the main to the Scottish lower leagues. And as for winning Old Firm games, there hasn't been one for 30 months so good luck drawing from that particular experience. Especially as Rangers were pumped 3-0 in the last one and of the present squad only Wallace and McCulloch featured.

He's right, he doesn't know our players but it doesn't stop him still suggesting they might get complacent or that they lack title-winning experience. Time will tell on both, not to mention whether or not we'll be derailed by injuries and suspensions. But, certainly, there's no evidence yet of the wheels being about to come off the relentless maroon juggernaut.

Neilson, thorough as ever, left immediately after the final whistle in order to get across to Livingston for the visit of Hibernian. No simply taping it on BBC Alba and watching it later for *The Tackle*. Commendable attention to detail. You wonder if he'd have gone to all that bother if the match had been on Sky or BT, though. That infernal Gaelic commentary can be heavy going.

Assistant manager Stevie Crawford was left to take care of media duties and said evenly, 'If the players can't enjoy it at the moment, then they've got a problem.' Let's hope next week is equally as much fun for them.

59

Hibernian away, 26 October 2014, 12.15pm

HIBERNIAN came into the second derby of the season as keen as ever to put a positive sheen on recent results. They'd helped our cause no end with that win at Ibrox but then followed it up with two home draws against Raith Rovers and Dumbarton. Draws which begged the legitimate question: what was the point in beating Rangers if you fail to build on it? Defeat at Ibrox and two home wins would've actually had them a point better off. The Hibernian way, however, would be to ignore this and congratulate themselves on putting together an unbeaten run. Way to go Stubbsy!

Certainly, September's manager of the month would have it no other way. Especially after his side's resounding 4-0 win at Livi the previous weekend.

Filing into Easter Road it was hard not to miss those daft, pimply wee laddies in black hoodies with the drum in the east stand. What were they all about then? Were they part of the deal to bring Leeann in from Motherwell? Was it like when we signed big Dave McPherson and Rangers made us take Shuggie Burns, too? Either way they helped bolster a paltry home crowd.

The game began in the teeth of what felt like a force nine gale and the buffeting wind threw Hearts' short-passing game off-kilter. Instead, they stood firm and flexed their muscles: powerful resilience set against the busy artistry of Allan and McGeouch.

Despite Hearts having won five of the last six derbies and being a commanding presence at the top of the league, Hibernian were bold and self-assured. Their support were curiously brazen and upbeat, wilfully blanking out that 14-point gap. It was almost like they'd somehow had their short-term memories scrubbed.

In between chanting the name of this year's managerial saviour on endless, tedious loops, they tastelessly implied Morgaro Gomis had Ebola virus. In the main, Hearts responded with raucous, mocking good humour, singing, 'When Hearts went up to lift the Scottish Cup **he** was there', and pointing incriminatingly at Jason Cummings. You still had a frustratingly large number of Union Jacks, though, not to mention witless references to 'Fenian blood' so neither set of supporters could assume the moral high ground when it came to unsavoury chanting.

Irrespective of the ebb and flow of derby games, a common trend over the years has been for Hibernian to be unable to capitalise on any ascendancy and for Hearts to get their noses in front. So it came as little surprise to see us shrug off all the delightful patterns Hibernian were weaving and create the game's clearest chance out of absolutely nothing. El Hassnaoui found himself one on one with Mark Oxley but drilled his effort disappointingly into the keeper's midriff.

It was shaping into an intriguing contest but its myriad delights weren't to everyone's taste. An unmoved Fraser Aird had been widely quoted beforehand, 'I have a few mates that play [for Hearts] and I always go and check their results. But if they are playing on TV and there is nothing else on, I'd probably go and watch *Coronation Street* before I do that.'

So, while Aird was watching Carla get upset over the extent of Peter's sentence and Kylie was carrying Gemma into casualty after her seizure in the Rovers, at Easter Road half-time was fast approaching. It felt like it was coming at about the right time for Hearts, but just when it looked like we'd be able to regroup with the game goalless, Hibs stole ahead on 44 minutes. An Allan corner was headed goalwards by Fontaine. A manic scramble ensued after Alexander parried his effort and Malonga fired the ball high into the net.

The Hibernian fans went absolutely berserk, their unhinged, carefree celebrations borne out of the unshakeable belief that Stubbsy's the one to lead them out of the darkness. He's Neo from *The Matrix* but with a Scouse accent and a twitchy eye. Less than a year ago Terry Butcher was their messiah and all these drooling sycophants were piling into New St Mirren Park with pretend bloodstained bandages to pay special tribute to the guy. Prior to that you couldn't hear yourself think at the derby for endless rounds of 'Paddy Fenlon's green and white army'.

This instant deification is understandable as they're all so desperate for an upturn in fortunes. But managers need to earn this level of crazy, intense devotion, otherwise supporters just come across as needy and gullible. Also, when things go wrong, which they've tended to do, these deep feelings of affection readily revert to pure vitriol.

After the win at Ibrox their message boards spoke of two eminently winnable home games and reeling us in at the top. Here, you could see in their eyes that the fightback had just begun for real. These poor deluded souls saw a 14-point gap cut to 11 and Rangers due to visit us.

Who knows, perhaps the potential ramifications of victory made Hibernian lose their nerve, but the second half reduced all their first-half bluster to nothing but hot air. After a couple of early forays forward, in which Allan found the head of Malonga, Hibernian became more and more entrenched in their own half.

Their stance was personified by keeper Oxley who began taking an age over every goal kick. The Edinburgh derby has tended to strip Hibernian of their self-esteem so a growing nervousness with the slenderness of the lead was inevitable. However, to start time-wasting this early in a derby at home suggests a deep psychological flaw in their make-up. Even more so when you consider Danny Wilson's hamstring had popped, causing him to limp off with less than an hour gone. A real chance to down their oldest rivals had landed in Hibernian's lap. Yet no interest whatsoever was shown in seeking to exploit a makeshift central defence now featuring McGhee instead of the skipper.

So the onus rested completely on Hearts to attack and down the sides looked our best bet to prosper. Walker came on for El Hass and looked in the mood. Twice he fired in dangerous crosses but the ball wouldn't run for us. Then, when King mis-kicked in clear sight of goal, it was hard to escape the nagging worry it wasn't to be our day.

Hibernian were still only thinking about seeing the game out and, to sighs of relief all round, Allan trudged off, head bowed, to be replaced by Harris. He'd been Hibernian's brightest player by a country mile but looked to have been sacrificed so they could run the ball into the channels, thus eating up more time. To us, that felt like a huge morale boost, seeing such muddled thinking, lacking ambition or self-belief.

Paterson then went close to getting a toe to the ball and booted the base of the upright in frustration as the opportunity was spurned. He was seriously pumped up and, moments later, let his enthusiasm get the better of him. He was over-zealous in tracking Malonga, catching him high and with his studs for a blatant red card.

Hearts may have been reduced to ten men but the only respite for Hibs came as they caught their breath waiting for C-Patz to leave the field. As soon as he'd gone Hearts regrouped and came again. McGhee went to right-back with Buaben slotting in alongside Ozturk at centre-half.

The board went up signalling four minutes. I looked across at the rejoicing Hibs fans and decided to move towards the exit. I squeezed in right behind the goal and to the right just as Ozturk took a square ball from Buaben and advanced. I remember thinking, 'No, please don't shoot,' as he shaped to strike one from 40-odd yards and then being convinced it was heading straight for the crossbar. Just as I was hoping we'd maybe strike it lucky with the rebound falling kindly, the ball suddenly dropped like a stone, grazing the underside of the bar and thudding back up into the net. The last thing I saw was the net shimmering gloriously in the cold, autumn sunshine before being engulfed by a shrieking mass of humanity.

Oxley sat bemused on his goal line, staring across in disbelief as Ozturk cupped an ear to the main stand. The keeper had been time-wasting for pretty much the entire second half so it was impossible to muster even a grain of sympathy for him. He'd been booked for it, too, so you wondered how many of those four minutes had been down to his antics. Closet Jambos Derek Rae and Gary McAllister were beside themselves with the goal, having repeatedly talked up Hearts during their commentary: Gary Mac sounding like Andy Gray after Steven Gerrard had scored the third against Olympiakos in 2004.

Speaking of the red half of Merseyside, down there Stubbsy was always viewed as your quintessential bitter blue, ungracious and narky in defeat. A few sympathetic interviews, showcasing his vulnerable, softer side mean he's perceived differently north of the border. However, the mask slipped in the aftermath here, leaving only a raw sourness, 'We've played the so-called champions that everyone is calling them and we've more than matched them […] we were by far the better team.' While of Ozturk's thunder-bastard, 'The lad will hit another 999 shots and none of them will be on target.' He finished up by saying, 'There were a few celebrations at the end today as if something was won. I noticed that. We'll see in March, April…'

That last comment suggests those scenes at the end put Stubbsy's nose out of joint. If not that then something certainly has. But, come on now, a 40-yard equaliser in the second minute of stoppage time in an Easter Road derby that helps preserve an 11-game unbeaten run is a seriously big deal and, despite Stubbsy's carping, our delirious celebrations were entirely in keeping with the occasion.

And as for talk of us being champions, clearly it's ridiculously early for anything of that ilk. That said, singing 'we are unbeatable', as we all piled over the Bridge of Doom and back to civilisation felt absolutely magic.

60

Raith Rovers home,
8 November 2014, 3pm

IN the deathly gloom before kick-off with the floodlights piercing the teeming rain, a lone piper played 'Flowers of the Forest', a lament for fallen soldiers. It was unspeakably sad and poignant and followed by a minute's silence impeccably observed by a more or less capacity crowd of 16,373. The only sound was the steady drumming of rain on the stadium roof.

The emotions run close to the surface at this time of year in Gorgie but especially so this year, with it being 100 years since the outbreak of the Great War and the raising of McCrae's Battalion.

Hearts had this season's commemorative kit emblazoned with the poppy while Raith were kitted out in green and black, the colours of the Hunting Stewart tartan worn by the Royal Scots Regiment and had 'Remember' where other clubs have a sponsor.

These two teams were remembering those who died, including their own players. Seven from Hearts (John Allan, James Boyd, Duncan Currie, Ernest Ellis, Alexander Lyon, James Speedie and Henry Wattie) and three from Raith (Jimmy Todd, Jimmy Scott and George McLay) never returned with McCrae's Battalion.

It surely was no coincidence that these sides were picked to play one another on Remembrance weekend. The one drawback of referee Crawford Allan's touching decision to allow Raith to play in green was that the dark and gloomy evening made it increasingly hard to tell the rain-sodden tops apart.

More than once, players were seen executing incredulous double-takes as the pass they'd thought was perfectly engineered for a team-mate ended up at the feet of a rival. Thankfully, these misplaced passes had no bearing on the overall outcome of the game.

The early moments of the match were notable for the crowd beseeching Alim Ozturk to shoot and four minutes in he was more than happy to take them at their word. The big man steamed forward and unleashed another long-range howitzer that was hit with enough venom and swerve to deceive Davie McGurn in the Raith goal.

Seeing Ozturk score with his very first attempt following on from the previous week's late equaliser at Easter Road was sumptuous, heaping even more scorn upon Stubbs's sour tirade.

This season, games at Tynecastle have tended to catch fire once Hearts have scored their first goal. Teams which have arrived with a dedicated game-plan of working their socks off to deny Hearts space and run down the clock are forced out of their trenches a little. While they may not exactly abandon their stifling, containing tactics, you often see a lessening in intensity and cracks inevitably open up.

This wasn't the case today. Raith seemed almost to forget that Ozturk's goal had ever happened. At one point, midway through the first half, their keeper ran the risk of making history and becoming surely the first player ever to get booked for time-wasting while his side were losing. Perhaps, as with Liverpool at Real Madrid on the preceding Tuesday, their aim had been to bide their time before wheeling out the big guns with 15 to go. Raith may have had no Coutinhos, Sterlings or Gerrards bunched up together on that away bench but they did have big Christian Nade lurking in the shadows.

In the face of Raith's defensive diligence and the referee's reluctance to punish a series of visceral, sliding tackles, Hearts began to look blunted and toothless. El Hassnaoui, in for the injured Sow, spearheaded the attack with the trio of King, Walker and Nicholson all interchanging behind him. Disappointingly, none of those three were able to make any headway and El Hassnaoui cut an increasingly isolated figure, reduced to chasing down his own clumsy attempts at trapping the ball.

Raith took encouragement from Hearts' unexpected and welcome shortcomings and Watson saw a header from an Anderson cross land on top of the net. The Fifers took this gritty obstinacy into the second half and tested the resolve of the Hearts back-line. A semi-makeshift defence which featured one-for-the-ladies, big, bearded Brad McKay at centre-half replacing the injured Wilson and McGhee in for a suspended C-Patz.

Hearts did everything within their power to put the game beyond Raith with that all-important second goal and all three substitutes had been committed to the fray with 15 minutes still left to play: Keatings replaced El Hass, Holt replaced Nicholson and then Buchanan came on for Walker. This could easily have backfired horribly, though, as Eckersley then took a sore one on the base of his spine and was forced to hobble off.

So, a defence already not quite at its best took a further hit. Ajax alumnus Buaben showed his total football heritage by filling in expertly at left-back and McKay was a colossus heading away everything that came into the box.

When a man down at Alloa and Hibs, Hearts had been suitably galvanised to carve out late, crucial goals but, here, the side were clinging on to those three points for grim death. Oddly, and to our unabashed relief, Nade was left stewing on the bench, much to the clearly audible disapproval of the sizeable away support.

The striker they did bring off the bench, Mark Stewart, was presented with a gilt-edged chance with a minute or so left but his effort lacked punch. The howls of panic from the Hearts support had barely subsided, though, when Raith went even closer. Neil Alexander's botched clearance fell at the feet of Liam Fox who was confronted with an empty goal.

Fox took a swing but the Hearts keeper was able to recover, gratefully clutching the ball as it flew in.

In the end all you could hear at full time were sighs of relief. As Neilson said after the match, 'I hoped we would [repeat that four-goal showing at Starks Park] but it's not always going to be like that. Raith are a good team. With all the Remembrance stuff before the game, it can be difficult for the players to focus, but it's three points.'

Amen, brother. And Hearts are still clear at the top. Rangers' midweek victory in their game in hand at Cowdenbeath coupled with their win today at home to Falkirk brought them to within four points.

61
Falkirk away,
15 November 2014, 5.30pm

BACK in olden times, away trips to Falkirk meant Brockville and were synonymous with a guaranteed near-death experience at full time trying to negotiate that perilous bottleneck at the exit by the corner. Thankfully, all that's now left of that poky deathtrap is one remaining turnstile in the Morrisons car park. Forget my earlier eulogies about old-fashioned grounds, I'd make an exception for Brockville and was delighted when it got bulldozed. Give me The Falkirk Stadium every time.

This was my first visit here and despite it being completely open down one side, affording all of us in the main stand an uninterrupted view of the panoramic splendour of the A904, it was a neat, nicely proportioned ground.

A special ceremony marking the 100th anniversary of the gathering of McCrae's Battalion took place before kick-off. All who fell were remembered, including the seven Falkirk footballers who never returned (Alexander Johnston, Andrew McCrae, James Laing, James Sharp, Harry Taylor, John Ramsay and James Conlin).

Back when first confronted with a nominal fixture list, Falkirk away always stood out as being a tricky hurdle to negotiate. Now here, it's come at a time when Hearts are showing the first hint of faltering. If you discount our 5-1 romp at home to Dumbarton, we've stuttered over the line in three of our last four fixtures (Alloa and Hibs away, Raith at home). Factor in that Rangers were kicking off before us – with the chance to pull to within a point with victory at home to Alloa – and you were left with a potentially fraught visit to The Falkirk Stadium.

The point was not lost on big-talking Rangers beefcake Darren McGregor who sought to crank up the pressure on the morning of the game, 'We are on a good run and need to keep the momentum going. We need to take three points and apply pressure. People tell you they don't look at papers or their closest contenders – but the first thing you do after a game is look to see how the opposition's done. Hearts will be no different. This will be the first time in the last couple of months where they will really feel that pressure if we get it to a point. We'll see how they deal with it.' He finished off by saying, 'I really do think they've done superbly – my question would be when the pressure starts tightening and the points deficit gets down, can they handle it?'

Their bullishness was understandable up to a point. Rangers had won their last five on the bounce yet still trailed us by four points. Something surely had to give, restoring them to their rightful berth, leading from the front. And, where better for Hearts to come a cropper than at a venue where their recent record is patchy at best, with only two wins from their last eight trips.

Rangers fans are imbued with this unshakeable sense of their team's inherent superiority and you'd imagine many will have turned up for Alloa's visit already drooling over the prospect of winning at Tynecastle next Saturday to go two points clear.

So far this season, however, Rangers' anticipated domination has been yet to materialise. And, not only was the hope Falkirk might do them a turn dashed – as the maroon juggernaut eventually rolled over the belatedly obdurate Bairns – but their own side failed to come up with the goods, allowing Alloa to grab a point. So Rangers could forget all about cutting Hearts' lead at the top to a point and, by the closing credits of *Strictly Come Dancing* on Saturday evening, our team had quick-stepped six points clear.

From the outset, Hearts took the game to Falkirk and raced quite quickly into a two-goal lead. There were no indications of how tense the closing stages would end up as the home side seemed only to want to swamp Hearts with sheer weight of numbers.

Pallardó came in for his first start and slotted in alongside Gomis releasing Mr Total Football, Prince Buaben, to play further forward. Last week, the Prince was filling in at left-back for Eckersley, in the derby the week prior to that he played at centre-half and here he was as a number ten, supporting the attack.

And it was Buaben who started the move for Hearts' first goal, on 26 minutes, feeding Billy King who feigned and darted his way along the 18-yard line. It was too crowded for him to get a shot away so he fed Kevin McHattie who was in for the injured Eckersley. The pass was a little behind him but McHattie improvised brilliantly, spinning and sending an angled shot high into the net.

'We shall not be moved' rang out in the freezing air. The side just seems unbeatable at the moment. Even when not playing well, goals are conjured out of thin air and slip-ups punished with cold-hearted efficiency.

Five minutes from half-time Hearts doubled their lead. Walker tormented and then destroyed Shaughnessy down the left and crossed for El Hassnaoui to finish smartly. It was a typical number nine's goal and Souf has looked better as a main striker. In fact he looked so good that Jonathan Sutherland, in the BBC online highlights package, credited his goal to Osman Sow. Hell of a stretch that was, all the way from the bench on halfway!

Half-time saw Falkirk wheel out a couple of legends, one of whom was a rather sheepish-looking Scott Crabbe who waved furtively in the direction of the 3,251 Hearts fans who'd swelled the attendance to a little over 7,000. The links between the two sides, of course, are manifold and two former Jambos – Jamie MacDonald and David Smith – featured in the Falkirk starting 11. But the sentiment wasn't exactly overflowing. Smudger got subbed at half-time and couldn't get away down the tunnel fast enough while Jamma was all business when he came out for the second half, refusing to swing from the bar or even properly acknowledge the away fans. Either Houstie felt August's love-in took the edge off his keeper's performance or he's got the hump because we never sing his name and misses working with his old boss.

Falkirk's best bet had appeared to be to dig in, get men behind the ball and disrupt Hearts' rhythm by needling them. But, then, a double substitution a few minutes into the second half provided a little more cut and thrust from the hosts. Botti Bia-Bi and Cooper replaced Grant and Smith and Falkirk became a different proposition altogether.

Hearts had given the impression all they felt was needed would be to see the game out, weathering whatever weedy backlash Falkirk would inevitably muster before nicking another goal or two late on when they'd given up the ghost. Who knows, perhaps, earlier in the season that's what would have happened and we'd have seen a 4-0 or a 4-1. Here, without the cool, unflappable Danny Wilson reading the play, making astute interceptions and retaining possession with crisp, immaculate passing we looked a sorry state at the back.

The triumvirate of Wilson, Gomis and Buaben have come into their own in moments such as these. QotS away was a prime example, where our 2-0 half-time lead was preserved through slick passing movements as the trio played their way out of dangerous situations. But, here, with Gomis not yet entirely attuned to Pallardó's game and Brad McKay lacking finesse on the ball, possession kept ending up back with Falkirk.

Clearly, Hearts hadn't expected to be needing to stretch themselves and were being made to look nervy and a little threadbare. On 70 minutes they couldn't clear their lines and Botti Bia-Bi finished well.

Then, to the anguish of the Hearts fans, Walker and Keatings missed excellent chances which would have spared us the anxious, panicky conclusion we all dreaded was coming. In the dying seconds Shaughnessy blazed over from inside the six-yard box after a free kick had carried through to him. A major let-off. It had looked easier to score.

We were left puffing out great sighs of relief at this glaring miss. Our unbeaten start now stands at 12 wins from 13 matches. Meanwhile, our main rivals, Rangers, lurch from one catastrophe to another. On the Wednesday following this game Dave King issued a statement urging Rangers fans to stop supporting the club financially. He said, 'The future of the club depends on every fan now taking a stand.' King was responding to having been told he had shown insufficient proof of funding in his bid to buy the club earlier in the year.

In many ways disillusioned Rangers fans seem already to be heeding his advice as attendances and season ticket sales are well down on previous years. The suggestion to take things further, though, has to be a massive worry, especially after it was widely reported that Mike Ashley's recent loan of £3m staved off administration.

King's comments came on the back of Graham Wallace, the chief executive, being made redundant to cut costs and was then followed with the news that further, radical, cost-cutting measures at the club had led to ten more people losing their jobs.

For so many years you'd be fearful it'd be us melting down, handing the initiative to our opponents just when things looked to be going too well. I mean, were Romanov still at the helm you just know that it'd be around about now that Neilson would be getting handed his jotters. Sacked for not fielding enough Sagittarians or for looking at Romanov's wife a bit funny down the pub or something else equally barking.

As a support we're so dyed in the wool of disappointment that it's hard not to be slightly fearful going into the Rangers game, steeling ourselves for a sting in the tail that must surely be due.

62

Rangers home,
22 November 2014, 12.45pm

RANGERS arrived at a rammed, expectant Tynecastle and delivered a brutal, bludgeoning performance which was designed to knock free-flowing Hearts out of their stride and eat into that six-point lead at the top of the table.

Having repeatedly called into question Hearts' nerve and staying power they probably felt the time had come to assert their perceived authority and put these brash young upstarts back in their box. This rabid physicality, however, would prove their ultimate undoing as the outcome of this attritional six-pointer spun on the 21st-minute sending off of Stevie Smith for a crude lunge on Paterson and then the early, enforced substitution of Kenny Miller. A tactically astute, unflinching Hearts, missing both Ibrox scorers (Wilson and Sow) as well as Prince Buaben, held their nerve and triumphed 2-0.

Prior to the sending off and, in truth, for a short period after it, Rangers' rugged energy had Hearts penned in; unable to pick a path through the forest of flailing elbows and niggly tugs. McCulloch, Black and Daly might have been barely recognisable in those unnecessarily tight, white, Lycra, cost-price tops but there was no hiding their spiteful belligerence.

Encouraged by a gratifyingly diminished away support still peddling the same archaic sectarian drivel, Sally's army waged a series of mini-battles all over the pitch: Wallace v Paterson, McLeod v McHattie, Black v Holt. Enlivened, the Rangers fans became a bit light-headed and forgot which team was leading the way at the top, informing us we 'were only here to see the Rangers' and then adding, for good measure, that we could shove our independence up our arse!

Throughout these tussles you could see Hearts doggedly seeking the thread of their passing rhythm: the ingrained game-plan that has served them so well this season. And, for all Rangers' bustle and bluster Alexander was only really called into serious action once, and it was a save you'd have expected him to make from a Law free kick.

Then, from around the 30-minute mark, the match slowly began to turn the way of Hearts. They were diligent and fastidious in possession and began to impose a vice-like grip on the tempo of the game. They were like a boa constrictor, imperceptibly but insistently squeezing the life out of Rangers and, for the final ten minutes of the first half, Hearts' possession peaked at 75 per cent.

During this period of ascendancy, Hearts created three highly presentable chances. Ozturk boomed his now customary free kick a little too close to Simonsen, Gomis wrapped his foot around a 20-yarder which skidded a few inches wide and then big, bearded Brad McKay guided a clever header goalwards only to see Simonsen tip it on to the bar.

Davie Weir, alongside Stuart McCall and Mikey Stewart for BT, felt that despite only having 39 per cent possession, Rangers had looked well on top in the first half. I guess it's hard for that significant portion of players who've graced both clubs to know how to play it sometimes. What with corporate hospitality gigs and the like they'd be quite literally biting the hand that fed them. Big Slim McPherson's another who comes into that category. He came on to the pitch at half-time and chirped merrily that the game could easily go either way. For me, the biggest worry was that Paterson or Gomis would over-stretch or mis-time a tackle and Craig Thompson would be more than happy to even up the red card count.

Having made a brief, initial stand against Rangers' cynical bully-boy tactics with the sending off of Smith, Thompson had then rather worryingly spent the rest of the half furiously back-pedalling. Jon Daly, Ian Black and Lewis McLeod were all being allowed free reign to commit multiple fouls while the tiniest indiscretions from Hearts players were being penalised.

Thompson would continue his shamelessly benevolent officiating into the second half and Miller somehow only saw yellow for viciously scything across McHattie, flying into him, studs flashing. The Hearts left-back was left beating the turf in anguish, his worst fears later confirmed with a scan on his knee showing medial ligament damage and a minimum six-week lay-off. It was hard to argue with Davie Weir, post-match, and his assertion that the tackle was probably worse than Smith's.

All of which subtracted even more credibility from big, daft Jon Daly's comments about Hearts seeking to con the referee by squealing and going down like they'd been hit by a sniper. Six weeks out for a dive? Would someone, please, show Kevin McHattie how to fall properly, he's clearly not doing it right.

Daly, his skin-tight top making him look like a weightlifter who'd yanked his belt a little too tight, had left the imprint of his elbow on a succession of Hearts players. When Thompson belatedly lost patience and reached for his top pocket you could see him pointing all over the pitch, totting up the fouls. The sheer number alone begged the question why he'd taken so long to produce a card. What, was each elbow only worth 0.25 of a foul?

McCoist then felt compelled to sub the visibly enraged Miller, presumably as he didn't fancy his side's chances with only nine men. The shovel-faced marksman petulantly dragged his heels as he came off before remonstrating with his manager. Derek Rae jokily attributed the deafening crescendo of booing to Miller's previous affiliation with Hibernian. Yes and no, Derek.

Yet, amid all the horrendous tackling and bare-faced attempts at intimidation, Hearts refused to buckle. They continued to be brave on the ball. Pallardó and Gomis had ice in their veins and didn't baulk as the tackles flew in, while at the back Ozturk and McKay were rocks; patient and assured, circulating possession with calm authority. In the continued absence of Wilson, Ozturk has grown in stature by the week, taking over the skipper's mantle and playing out from the back.

As Tynecastle simmered, Hearts continued to build passes and Rangers were forced to scurry furiously after the ball. And, on 56 minutes, Hearts surged gloriously into the lead. Paterson, like a leggy bison, gobbled up the yards running on to a Gomis ball and hit one of those speciality early bending balls into the box. His cross deflected off McCulloch and then hit McGregor before rolling perfectly into the path of the in-rushing Jason Holt. Tynecastle held its breath, willing him to find a finish and he did just that with a quite exquisite swipe of the right boot.

Suddenly, after barely daring even to contemplate it, our lead at the top, as it stood, moved to nine points. However, falling behind ignited Rangers and they came surging back at Hearts. Wallace somehow engineered a cross when he looked crowded out in the corner and Daly knocked the ball back for Nicky Law who caught the ball full on the volley. Alexander got down, making a barely believable parry and the rebound spun up for Foster who saw his effort deflected on to the bar courtesy of a flying block from Eckersley. Undoubtedly a colossal let-off and you couldn't help but glance over at Miller, glowering on the Rangers bench, and wonder what he'd have done with that rebound off the keeper.

Rangers weren't finished and lurched forward at Hearts once again. Nicky Law sped into the box and went down with Paterson in close attendance. Replays showed, categorically, it had been an attempt to con the referee as C-Patz made zero contact. Mikey Stewart downplayed the fact it was cheating, plain and simple, and ignored the inexplicable lack of a yellow card, delivering that classic old chestnut, 'He went down anticipating the touch.' Well, who knows, perhaps if he'd stayed on his feet he could have anticipated scoring the equaliser.

The great white hype, Lewis McLeod, was sacrificed as Kris Boyd was summoned for one final push. This was greeted by half-hearted chants of 'Ally, Ally get tae fuck' by the two sections of Rangers fans, which was then drowned out by an almighty chorus of 'Super Ally' from the Hearts supporters. That has to be about the biggest indignity one set of fans can inflict upon another, mockingly singing the name of their manager. We've done it to so many honking Hibernian managers I think I may, genuinely, have lost count. I've got vague memories of first singing it to John Blackley circa 1985. Unquestionably, it felt superb singing it to this rabble.

The closing stages became undeniably edgy. You only needed to think back to last season to be aware of the havoc Boyd is capable of. But the sullen hitman never got a sniff and it was Hearts who scored again, putting the game beyond Rangers, from the penalty spot, with a few minutes left.

Jamie Walker had had a fairly erratic match but redeemed himself at the death, firstly winning the penalty after controlling a high ball from Pallardó and being toppled by a clumsy Ian Black tackle and then assuming responsibility himself and sweeping the ball right down the middle. This, despite unseemly attempts at gamesmanship from Rangers as he prepared himself, Black repeatedly yelling 'Walker' at him and McCulloch standing in front of the ball after he'd placed it on the spot and then vigorously ruffling Walker's hair. Black, incidentally, escaped a second yellow for his foul as Thompson continued his policy of over-leniency towards the visitors.

All that was left was for Rangers to unravel completely and Boyd took out his simmering discontent on Brad McKay, leaving him writhing in agony on the floor after a tackle every bit as bad as Smith's and Miller's. Fair play to Boydie, though, who at least came out later in the week and acknowledged his offence had been worthy of a red.

In the aftermath, Neilson was sanguine and understated, saying simply, 'They put some challenges in and we put some in,' and then, when asked about the possibility of more sending offs, he replied, 'The ref makes his own decision, I thought he had a decent game.' Clearly, this new Hearts regime will not be actively courting negative publicity, steering well clear of unedifying headlines. It would far rather keep its counsel and be dignified. Perhaps Craig Levein's previous brushes with authority have taught him that you've more chance of being treated fairly if you avoid ruffling any feathers. It's worked up to a point so far, although you could argue Rangers got off extremely lightly in this game and were only denied an equaliser and possible share of the spoils by the width of the bar. You'd hope Hearts' aura of calmness and serenity isn't put to the test more fully in the coming weeks.

The delusional sense of entitlement from former Rangers players on behalf of their side continued well into the following week with Charlie Miller and then Stuart McCall stating they both had every faith Rangers would still be champions come May.

This was a point debated at the end of *Sportscene* after every last ounce of interest had been wrung out of the uninspiring top division. Steven Thompson suggested the gap would be too great to bridge while a vaguely simian-looking Calum Davidson reckoned Hearts weren't playing very well and nerves could possibly afflict them in the run-in.

So, played 14, won 12, drawn two, lost none, goals for 37, goals against seven and Davidson's still not impressed? Jeez, tough crowd! When pressed for an answer, he knitted his brows in puzzlement before emitting a monosyllabic grunt, 'Dunno, I'm no' sure.' Tough *and* stupid.

63
Celtic home,
30 November 2014, 3.15pm

LIKE a lot of people I found it hard to get too worked up about the Scottish Cup this season, even before we were paired yet again with Celtic. This year the league has been all-consuming. In fact, results have been going so well the last thing I think we needed was the distraction of this cup tie with Celtic and all the baggage and animosity that invariably comes with it. Celtic won, with a bit to spare, but once again the fixture was blighted by the unacceptable face of Scottish football rearing its ugly head, and I'm not just referring to Willie Collum.

At the identical stage of last season Celtic came through here and were victorious. Their expensively assembled team of internationals and Champions League regulars won 7-0 against a bunch of under-20s wilting under the ravages of administration. A spectacle described, bewilderingly, as 'football utopia' by the now-departed Neil Lennon. His replacement, pretend Dutchman Ronnie Deila, quipped about perhaps watching the game from a steel cage but he was basing this on the assumption that people were even vaguely interested in anything he had to say. Maybe, next season, to stop our ground getting trashed by his team's supporters we try out Ronny's plan on the Celtic support.

In a really thoughtful tribute to the recently departed Arthur Montford, the *Scotsport* theme rang out just before kick-off. Shame we couldn't just nod off and wait for the English game to come on. Instead, we had to sit through this steaming pile of predictable dross.

Our challenge, however much it would have amounted to, disintegrated within seven minutes as Morgaro Gomis saw red for a two-footed lunge on Scott Brown. It's hard to argue against the award, although Brown was able to spring straight back to his feet and get right in Collum's face, unlike, say, McHattie or McKay had been the previous week.

This has been coming with Gomis, though. He seems to play every match on the edge, on the very cusp of losing it altogether. His six bookings already had him ruled him out of next week's clash with QotS and he was booked early on against Raith, Falkirk and Rangers, relying on the discretion of the referee in the latter stages of all three games.

If you're associated with Hearts the words 'discretion' and 'Willie Collum' don't really go hand-in-hand. Johansen and Brown both had little nibbles at Gomis's ankles and his anger was clearly visible as he waved his arms at the referee. The red mist then descended and Brown was cleaned out along with the ball.

While reluctantly agreeing he had to go, Mikey Stewart on *Sportscene* enthused about those sorts of tackles, even though the last time he'd hurtled through the air like that was when he got sent off at Hamilton and lost his footing kicking a water bottle on his way up the tunnel.

Hearts kept the same personnel on the pitch but, instead of marauding forward, full-backs Paterson and Eckersley barely crossed halfway. Celtic didn't extend themselves, it was like they'd wounded a stag and were quite happy to bide their time, tracking it from a safe distance through the forest, knowing sooner or later they'd be feasting on its flesh.

Hearts' strategy of containment limited the score at half-time to 1-0. Anthony Stokes, proudly sporting the most preposterous weave this side of Greater Manchester, smashed a ball across the face of goal and van Dijk cleverly used the pace to guide it in.

Falkirk's Jamie Mac got a fond homecoming in August when he ran towards the Hearts end at the start of the second half. Craig Gordon, our other cup-winning keeper still playing, surely deserved at least as big a cheer. Not only was he a seriously brilliant player for us, he left for big bucks and has done nothing but speak well of us since leaving. You'd even extend that to the build-up to this game where he said nothing could happen that would change his opinion about the club and its support. He added, however, that he was hopeful of a warm reception. Unfortunately, this fixture brings out the worst in a lot of people and the response to him running over was mixed, a few around us even booed which just seemed mindless to me.

With Collum in town it's not a case of if but when Celtic get that barely believable penalty. So it was hard not to just burst out laughing when he pointed to the spot early into the second half after Guidetti lost his footing with no one near him.

Brad McKay was adjudged to have taken him down and got a yellow card for remonstrating with the Manchester City dud. TV footage would later exonerate McKay completely. Stewart was livid, accusing Guidetti of diving to con the referee while Pat Nevin argued there was no intent to cheat and he'd merely slipped. Stewart then went on to bemoan the referee's aberration, labelling it a game-changer since, at only one down, Hearts were still very much in the tie. I'm not sure we were to be honest. By this point it looked like many of our players' thoughts had already turned to next weekend.

Guidetti rammed home the penalty and Stokes made it three not long after, with a daisy-cutter from outside the box. You could see Celtic beginning to sniff a rout and the worry was we'd get a real hiding and our confidence might take a dent. Griffiths and Commons couldn't wait to come off the bench and for a short period it looked like Celtic might be trying to top last year's tally. Thankfully, they only found the net once more through van Dijk as our defenders switched off at a corner. The closest they came to more goals was when a fifth was mysteriously chalked off as Commons looked to have capitalised on a fumble from Alexander.

This game was supposed to allow us to gauge our progress against an SPL side but thanks to the Gomis sending off and, to a lesser extent,

Sow and Wilson sitting in the stand, we didn't learn very much at all. We already knew that Willie Collum is an inconsistent snide who needs little or no encouragement to shaft us and Scott Brown has carte blanche to do whatever he likes against us. He's untouchable. He's the school bully who knows where the weedy headmaster lives.

We are also very well versed in the fan rhetoric of these occasions. The Celtic support probably couldn't believe their good fortune when they saw a few daft wee laddies goading them with Union Jacks and unleashed their full putrid repertoire. 'Ooh aah up the Ra' rung out followed, horribly, by 'Glasgow Celtic IRA'.

But, then, a lot of the time, it was impossible to decipher what it was they were actually singing. Have they all got really bad teeth or something? An order of service might be the way forward so we can at least know exactly how bilious they are being. At one point they sung 'SPL: you're having a laugh' which just seemed poorly thought out and, if I'm being honest, a bit lazy. I mean, we're sitting nine clear at the top of the Championship so you'd have to say the campaign for promotion is, undeniably, on track.

By the end, however, it all became drearily familiar with the Celtic fans, singing 'so fucking easy'. They're playing a side from the division below who've been forced to make do with ten men for pretty much the whole game. What exactly did they think was going to happen? The Celtic players seemed equally hell-bent on milking the victory for all it was worth and ran like conquering heroes to their warm, loving support giving it big fist pumps. All but one. Craig Gordon took no part in the vainglorious showboating and, classy as ever, just ran down the tunnel.

The bitter enmity between both sets of supporters has been festering away for years. The only difference here was that instead of quietly repairing the devastation to the away end and sending the bill to Peter Lawwell, Ann Budge decided Hearts would meet the problem head-on and went public.

The Celtic support had displayed their usual classless, loutish behaviour and destroyed more than 100 seats, spraying graffiti everywhere and smashing up the toilets. While acknowledging that Hearts have a minor problem themselves with sectarianism – announcing that any supporters found to be engaging in this behaviour would be banned – she went on to denounce the Celtic support for the damage caused, for compelling families to flee their spitting and coin-throwing and their intimidation of staff.

It was hard-hitting and entirely typical of the woman. She has responded to every single challenge with a refreshing and unflinching honesty. Predictably, Celtic bristled at the criticism. They value this mythical reputation of theirs around the world and anything besmirching the good name of the so-called Celtic family is swiftly batted back. Celtic replied that their players had been subjected to sectarian abuse and pelted with coins but they too would be happy to enter into discussions as to how this might best be addressed moving forward.

No direct mention was made of the damage to Tynecastle but the inference seemed to be that if these poor wee sensitive souls suffered that much provocation then it's probably no wonder they got a bit worked up and took out their frustrations on a few fixtures and fittings. At some point you'd hope someone somewhere will have reminded Peter Lawwell that Tynecastle isn't the only away ground these wonderful supporters have trashed. Did I hear someone say Fir Park? Dens Park? Griffin Park, Brentford?

One particular Celtic player, a man known to be partial to partying with IRA sympathisers, then weighed in with his tuppence worth, tweeting that he'd never seen sectarian abuse as bad. Poor baby! I guess those IRA parties just aren't what they used to be.

Later in the week *The Sunday Post* was sent images of the graffiti in the Roseburn Stand which mocked the Ibrox disaster. Clearly, The Best Supporters in the World™ would never stoop so low as to spray the words '66 dead huns' everywhere and Celtic responded as you'd expect with a terse riposte, 'These people aren't Celtic fans.'

Right words, wrong order: these Celtic fans aren't people.

64

Queen of the South home, 6 December 2014, 3pm

QUEENS arrived at Tynecastle in the middle of a decent run of form. In the six league matches following our 3-0 win at Palmerston, they'd notched up four victories and two draws and done so playing a brand of attacking, entertaining football.

A few days before this clash, Rangers had been dumped unceremoniously out of the Petrofac Cup, squandering a two-goal lead away to Alloa. Hapless chubster McCoist had aimed a verbal swipe at Hearts for picking the understrength side that succumbed at Livingston in August yet here was his first 11 getting binned in the semi. Statesmanlike as ever.

His club, though, are nothing if not consistent, and the setback prompted them, once more, to turn their attention to Hearts and how that pressure at the top is bound to take its toll.

After Darren McGregor had questioned Hearts' nerve immediately before his own side's bottle crashed at home to Alloa and then, a week later, were dumped 2-0 at Tynecastle, you'd have thought they'd have chosen to lay off the cod psychology, at least for a week or two.

Alas, no, and Kenny Miller had something he needed to get off his chest, 'We've got 22 games left, though, to claw it back – and we will… you'd like to think they're going to get beat at some point. Whether that's tomorrow or in a month's time, who knows. I know the hardest thing in a league is getting over that finishing line. So come March, April, May time – that's when it will really tell. And if we are closer, which we will be, to them and applying that pressure, then it's a different kind of mental attitude you've got going into a game when you know you're getting so close to that finishing line and you need to win…there's no doubt every team has slip-ups in them. We've just got to make sure if they do we're there to capitalise.'

Well, for a 15-minute spell at the start of the second half here, it looked like Kenny's hopeful prophecy might be about to come true as a slip-up definitely looked on the cards. At the precise moment Queens drew level at Tynecastle, Rangers were going ahead versus Cowdenbeath and, on such pivotal moments, the destiny of league titles has spun. Queens had our side exactly where they wanted them and, in seasons gone by, previous Hearts teams may well have wilted.

But this year's vintage is made of stern stuff and in the marriage between Neilson and his players an unshakeable resolution is born. Alexander pulled off a spellbinding save to keep the match level and slowly but surely – thanks to a couple of tactical masterstrokes and the players digging deep – Hearts regained the initiative, finally drubbing Queens 4-1.

The game had begun with Danny Wilson being welcomed back into the fray. Those at Ibrox with hopes pinned on a Hearts blip seem not to have considered that we may already have had it. For me, the absence of Wilson has had a profound effect and five of our last six league games (Alloa, Hibs, Raith, Falkirk and Rangers) have all gone right down to the wire. Football matches often hinge on the slimmest of margins and we could quite easily have dropped more than those two measly points during that exacting run of games.

Queens had clearly done their homework and were keen to disrupt Hearts' inclination to build play from the back. Seeing this, Wilson began bypassing the heavily marked Buaben and Pallardó, to try his luck picking out Keatings and Buchanan, directly. Understandably, given he was a tad ring rusty, the skipper took a little time to find his range but stuck to the task and 20 minutes in the ploy paid dividends. His long ball glanced off the head of a Queens defender and Keatings sped clear before clattering home a stupendous left-foot volley.

This goal was the catalyst for Hearts to start playing some wonderful, free-flowing football. You could see they were doing their utmost to ruthlessly finish Queens off and make the second half a dead rubber. As the temperature plummeted on a bitter, blustery afternoon Hearts turned the heat up, swarming all over their uneasy opponents.

Minutes after the goal Paterson sprang forward and hit a low, bobbling drive that the keeper scrambled wide. Then, from one of a number of corner-kicks, Dowie was adjudged to have bundled into C-Patz and referee Craig Charleston pointed to the spot. At the time the award looked on the soft side but it was a cast-iron cert compared to the one he'd later gift Queens.

Buaben sent the keeper the wrong way but his effort slammed back off the base of the left-hand upright. Various papers described his attempt as 'lazy' but, as far as I was concerned, that did the Prince and his deceptively languid style a huge disservice, he'd simply been out by the narrowest of margins.

Our visitors knew they'd earned a reprieve and their resurgent start to the second half was foretold at half-time by Robbo who reckoned Queens weren't beaten yet and given half a chance would take control. Kerr was replaced by Lyle as they set about doing just that. Their extra striking options gave them fresh impetus and Alexander twice had to save from the excellent McShane. The game had barely restarted and already we were ruing all those first-half near misses.

The equaliser was coming, you could sense it. However, when it arrived it was via another dubious penalty after McShane hit the deck with Walker loitering nearby. The offence, if it even was one, looked to have taken place outside the box but it made no odds to Russell who made no mistake.

Neilson looked unmoved and calmly instigated a tactical reshuffle with Robinson coming on for the debutant Buchanan, freeing up Buaben to move closer to Keats. The switch was truly inspired. Firstly, Robinson was on hand to clear off the line after Alexander got down superbly to Higgins's header then, as the half wore on, his astute pass found Buaben on the edge of the Queens box and the Ghanaian escaped the clutches of the defender before toe-poking the ball into the far corner.

In between those two moments Wilson had edged Hearts 2-1 in front from a corner, the ball more or less slapping against his face and ending up in the net after glancing off the upright.

Trailing 3-1 with 15 minutes to go, Queens still posed a threat and pushed up even more on Hearts' side. Spotting this, Neilson switched Walker for McGhee and shunted Paterson up on to the right of midfield. It was a change that allowed Alexander to hit long balls out of defence and C-Patz's aerial prowess meant, more often than not, possession was retained.

With just over ten minutes remaining Hearts put the seal on the win with yet another classy strike. Paterson released King for a clear run in on goal. The winger flew across the turf like a prize-winning greyhound before veering inside and setting up Eckersley with a sharp back-heel. The left-back stylishly guided the ball home.

The victory, coupled with Chelsea coming unstuck at St James' Park, meant Hearts were now officially the only unbeaten side in British professional football, except in the eyes of a few Twitter pedants who cited the case of TNS in Wales. And, later in the week, Robbie received the manager of the month award for November. Historically, these types of awards are viewed as something of a kiss of death, like a vote of confidence from the chairman or Willie Collum covering your home match with Celtic, but we appear to have moved way beyond that this season, especially with this being Robbie's third award out of four.

65

Alloa home,
20 December 2014, 3pm

HEAVY frost put paid to Hearts' clash at Cowdenbeath the previous Saturday, meaning our side were fully refreshed for the visit of Alloa. Results this season pointed to the Clackmannanshire side being a stubborn nut to crack but 41 goals in 15 league games showed Hearts were fully equipped to breach even the most obstinate of sides. And so it proved as two first-half goals were enough to maintain our nine-point lead at the summit.

On the eve of that Central Park postponement, Rangers lost 2-0 to QotS in a Friday night horror show at Palmerston: the prelude to which was farcical even by their massively dysfunctional standards.

Our ever-promising push towards automatic promotion received a major boost with the barely believable news from Ibrox that the very man who'd coined the phrase 'we don't do walking away' looked set to do just that, albeit very very slowly. Don't get me wrong, for around an hour or so this news was mildly disconcerting as suddenly we were faced with the worrying prospect of Rangers appointing someone who knew where the cones, whiteboards and big marker pens were kept.

Our worst fears were quickly allayed however when it emerged none of Messrs Davies, Butcher, McCall or (seriously?) Gattuso would be arriving any time soon and the hugely gratifying absurdity showed no signs of abating. In a nutshell, the perilous financial state of the club meant they were unable to pay up McCoist's one-year rolling deal in full.

McCoist then went from 'absholutely, mosht definitely, yesh I am' seeing out that time as the manager to being asked instead to spend it on so-called 'gardening leave'. Perhaps the board were fearful of what an uninhibited Coisty might blurt out at the upcoming AGM and felt, on balance, he'd be safer eyeing the hardy perennials in Dobbie's Garden Centre. Kenny McDowell was charged with succeeding where McCoist had failed and finding, not only those cones, boards and marker pens but, in an ideal world, that elusive cupboard with all the bibs, whistles and spare balls, too. Durranty was demoted to the under-20s and the job of assistant manager went to Gordon Durie.

A poignant tale had emerged, penned almost certainly by sympathetic media lackeys, of a deeply troubled Coisty penning his resignation after a series of cost-cutting measures had seen his most favourite members of staff leave. Gushing personal tributes to his lamented secretary sat somewhat incongruously with the big man getting that humungous salary of his hiked back up to full whack for the duration of his notice period.

Ibrox was around half empty for what proved to be McCoist's swansong; a sketchy 2-0 win over Livingston. A state of affairs you can see only getting worse before it gets better. Especially should Hearts' lead at the top stretch to 12 points with a win at Central Park in three days' time and then Rangers stumble at Easter Road the following Saturday.

A rambunctious AGM saw these and various other frustrations boil over in unseemly fashion. This inescapably hilarious discord at Ibrox meant that from a Hearts perspective the whole week leading up to the Alloa game felt like Christmas had come a week early. As we were sitting nine points clear at the top and with a game in hand, Rangers would need to put a pretty tasty run together and hope we'd falter to make serious inroads. While you'd hope we wouldn't stutter, any chance of Rangers being in a position to capitalise on any slip looks ever more unlikely the longer they remain in turmoil.

Irrespective of the opposition and events elsewhere, though, there is a nerveless, grinding resolve to Hearts so far this season. The players appear phenomenally well-drilled and, allied to inexhaustible fitness levels, ooze drive and focus. Part of this fearlessness is a result of bringing in the right sorts of players. Pallardó, for example, delivered a peerless midfield display. This, despite the 28-year-old being named along with 42 others in connection with allegedly receiving money to fix a Spanish league fixture between former club Levante and Real Zaragoza in May 2011. If Miguel was troubled it didn't show and he glided economically across the turf, his superlative ability buying him time on the ball.

Another reason why there's such an assuredness on the pitch lies in the benevolence emanating down from the stands. Hamill and Robinson may beg to differ but last season there was almost an unspoken moratorium on getting on the players' backs. A trait which has carried on into this season. Aided and abetted in no small measure by the ever-burgeoning, ever-Budgeoning, feelgood factor immersing our club.

The early stages against Alloa required a little of that learned patience from the vast majority of the 15,224 crowd as Hearts pioneered a slightly altered playing style. Aware that Alloa would more than likely sit in and seek to frustrate, Neilson had his troops sit off, allowing Alloa the ball in their own half, the intention being to then hit them hard and fast on the counter.

Teams visiting Tynecastle undergo a rigorous examination of their credentials and, in that sense, whether Hearts sat off or played a high pressing game felt almost irrelevant. If this set of players spend a week training together, becoming accustomed to a tactical plan, whichever it may be, you'd be surprised if they weren't able to link to good effect and hurt the opposition. Increasingly, this is a set of players you feel you can trust. But, certainly, in terms of the result, the tactics worked a treat, with Hearts recording their ninth win out of nine at home.

Alloa were only saved from a proper pasting by the woodwork, some careless finishing and a subconscious drop off in intensity as the clock ran down and thoughts turned to Tuesday night's challenge over in Fife.

A brace of first-half goals saw Hearts home. The first was a snappy, clipped finish from Keatings after he'd executed a Robbo-esque drop of the shoulder to nip through on goal. The second had more than a hint of last season about it, Paterson linking up with Walker and then getting in front of his man to fire home adroitly. Of course, last season, we probably wouldn't have scored it. Either the linesman would've flagged for something only he'd seen or Paterson would have been taken out by a stray elbow and been left prostrate on the edge of the six-yard box as play raged on around his inert frame.

At times, these last two seasons often appear like mirror images of each other. Most weeks we're winning and stretching our lead at the top, as opposed to last season when we were losing and being cut adrift. Moreover, it's like we're being recompensed for all those instances of bad luck. At 1-0, Alloa hit the post and the ball stayed out. As it did at 1-0 home to Rangers and 0-0 away to Queen of the South. Then there were those late, near misses from Falkirk and Raith when we were only one goal up, not to mention crucial late/injury-time strikes from Eckersley at Alloa, Sow at Ibrox and Ozturk at Easter Road.

Last season it often felt as if we were jinxed. Spurious penalties and sending offs, the concession of late goals while last-minute chances for us invariably came back off the woodwork or were thwarted by goalkeeping heroics. People speak of these things evening themselves up; I've never been a great advocate of that but there's no denying things are going for us at the moment. What was it Gary Player said, 'The more I practice the luckier I get?' That could apply just as readily to Neilson and Hearts. Their triple training sessions, their attitude and application are grabbing this league by the scruff of the neck and they're making their own luck.

Hibs won, 3-1 at Raith, giving them their first back-to-back league wins of 2014. This risible 'achievement' caused Liam Craig to have a funny turn and proclaim that his side haven't yet given up on the title, 'We have always been looking up the table rather than over our shoulder. We're seven points behind Rangers and know how big next week's game [against Rangers] is. If we can win that one it closes the gap again. That's what we need to keep doing, keep looking in front, looking at both Rangers and Hearts. There's a lot of games left but we need to go on a run of six, seven, eight wins in a row if we're going to have any chance of winning the league.'

His words immediately put me in mind of a tweet by Liverpool owner John W. Henry after Arsenal had put in a bid for Luis Suarez, 'What d'you think they're smoking over there at the Emirates?' In fact, just replace 'Emirates' with 'Echodome' and you're there.

66

Cowdenbeath away, 23 December 2014, 7.45pm

HEARTS had pushed hard for this postponed fixture to be re-scheduled as quickly as possible. The team were clearly pumped up and raring to press home that advantage at the top and this élan was reflected in a 3,000-plus travelling support cramming, uncomfortably, into Cowdenbeath's ramshackle, decrepit fleapit of a ground.

In there, it felt like being transported back to mid-1980s Belgrade or Bratislava or some other equally distant and obscure eastern European footballing outpost. All that was missing, as the players trudged out on to that marshy bog of a pitch, were the air-horns, monkey noises and a cluster of riot police waiting by the side of the running track, batons poised.

Ever one to tweak the system, Robbie went full-on alehouse at Central Park. His 4-3-1-2 had C-Patz leading the line alongside Keats with Jamie Walker playing just off them as a nominal number ten. Pallardó, Gomis and Buaben were stationed across the midfield and McGhee and McKay came into the defence. Ozturk had a knock and missed out.

Hearts started at a furious pace, fizzing passes at each other across the spongy turf and could have gone ahead within three minutes. Walker, revelling in his free role, clumped a shot goalwards and saw it deflected on to the post.

Hearts had all the possession and it was a case of peering through the murk and chicken wire at their endeavour and hoping their reward would come. Twenty-four minutes in the breakthrough looked inevitable. McGhee cleverly evaded a defender by flicking the ball over his head and then picked out Walker at the back post. The number seven killed the ball on his chest and then hit a blurring volley that Thomson did well to get to.

You could see Hearts were building up a head of steam and this side in full flow is an irresistible sight. A minute later they'd plundered the first goal. Pallardó, who'd been a magnet for the ball, found Eckersley motoring beyond him from left-back. He shuttled past the flat-footed defender and crossed early for Keats who'd timed his run cleverly and prodded the ball home. It was no more than Hearts deserved and any fretfulness in their approach play was soothed away by the goal.

Moments later, Keatings slammed a 25-yard free kick against the base of the post and you could see Hearts' fervent intention to put the game to bed before half-time. From the resultant corner McKay outjumped his marker but his header was too straight. A second goal would have been a nice insurance policy in the improbable event of the Blue Brazil sparking to life and Hearts passed up two more glorious opportunities as the half drew to a close. Wedderburn passed straight to Paterson in the box but C-Patz's attempted cutback to Keats was intercepted and then Keats returned the compliment, putting C-Patz through on goal but the big man was spoilt for choice and tugged his effort wide.

At the onset of the second half you felt our slender lead only told half the story and a quick start was warranted, to give the scoreline a fairer slant. Worryingly, the opposite happened and we appeared sluggish and heavy-legged on that sodden gluepot of a pitch.

Cowdenbeath stuck Sutherland on for Callaghan and the striker became Eckersley's new best mate. He nullified the left-back's forward thrusts while also dominating him in the air when his side attacked. This tweak, coupled with a tendency for Hearts' passing to be a little tentative, meant possession was being surrendered very cheaply. At this point, Alexander came to the fore and bailed his side out. Higgins found himself free in the box but saw his effort brilliantly smothered.

This felt slightly reminiscent of the recent home game with Queen of the South in which we'd totally bossed the first half but only had the one goal to show for it. Like then, the opposition had been forced into becoming more attack-minded and we'd lost the initiative. Any doubts regarding the destiny of the points, however, were blown away by a quite breathtaking C-Patz volley just past the hour mark. The big man took a cross-field ball from Pallardó on his head and, as it dropped back to him, cushioned the ball on his chest, wheeled, and thudded home an unstoppable volley from outside the box. Later that night Craig Levein's tweet summed the mood up perfectly, 'Didn't think Alim's goal at ER could be beaten, but this sure runs it close.'

Two goals up and the demons vanished in the dank Fife gloom. Cowdenbeath still called upon Alexander to earn his corn and he produced a handful of saves: one in particular to deny Sutherland was top-drawer. But that two-goal cushion saw the swagger return to Hearts. With their tails up, passes once again crisply found their mark. Buaben ghosted passed two defenders and then rocketed a drive inches wide.

The time slowly ebbed away and it became apparent we were going to negotiate this potential banana skin. The whistle went and the players skirted around the giant tyres and across the wide racing track, back to the dressing room. Virtually half the campaign has elapsed and we're still unbeaten, sitting pretty 12 points clear.

This genuinely feels too good to be true.

67

Livingston away,
27 December 2014, 3pm

'WE WON'T allow our focus to drift beyond what's directly in front of us. We have a huge game with Livingston now, and we're extremely keen to right the wrongs of the cup game we played there.' Some managers trade in 'manager speak', mumbling platitudes and speaking in semi-delusional terms of their side's achievements and capabilities. Robbie Neilson seems the very antithesis of this; placid and undemonstrative, he remains unflinchingly honest. Talk of retaining focus became even more prescient as kick-off approached, in light of Hibernian having Rangers on toast for lunch. Their 4-0 win at Easter Road offered Hearts the tantalising chance to extend that lead at the top to a whopping 15 points.

Last Boxing Day, a four-goal annihilation from Kilmarnock saw our brittle young side's glaring inadequacies exposed in a season forever characterised by that 15-point deficit. To be in a position now where a win away at Livingston would see us 15 clear represented a 12-month turnaround on a scale no one could have foreseen.

By and large the side produced another savvy, driven performance which resulted in all three points accompanying Hearts back along the M8, although a combination of second-half jitters and the first real signs of fatigue meant the goalscoring was limited to just the one. And, as the match wore on, we saw less and less of the free-flowing, triumphant style to which we've all become accustomed and you felt a better side than Livi might have punished us.

Away games these days seem more and more like pilgrimages. These are unquestionably the hottest tickets in town. The building momentum of this phenomenal unbeaten sequence has made each sell-out match an event to behold: to be savoured and celebrated. Reportedly, the largest travelling support in British football over the festive period – over 7,500 – descended upon Livingston, jostling for parking spaces alongside bargain hunters in the Almondvale Centre.

By kick-off, three sides of the dinky Energy Assets Arena were crammed full of eager Hearts fans desperate to see their beloved maroon juggernaut power onwards and hopefully upwards.

Hearts began with their customary swift tempo; Wilson, quick to try and find the feet of Keatings, Nicholson and King as Livi diligently blocked off all his short-range options. After Tuesday night's slug-fest at Cowdenbeath, Hearts looked in a hurry to put themselves out of sight so they could get the cigars out and do a little internet shopping for the last half hour.

After 12 minutes it looked like the side had got their reward for starting so keenly. Holt was sent flying in the box by Kyle Jacobs and Keatings was first to get his mitts on the loose ball. However, Jamieson in the Livi goal had saved five of his last eight spot-kicks and, frustratingly, this became six from nine as he dangled a leg and kept out Keats's tame effort.

Our second successive miss from the spot was exasperating but, after a slightly ragged start, we'd built up a decent head of steam and, without wishing to be blasé, felt confident more chances would come our way.

Three games in a week, with only really one proper, fit, recognised striker was probably, in hindsight, something of a gamble for Neilson to take. But you have to admire that bullish attitude; his faith in the players more than paying off. And, on 25 minutes, Keatings atoned for that penalty miss by notching his fourth goal in as many games. Eckersley and King initially made to go for the same ball, as it sped towards them on the left touchline. King spun forward, darting up the line as Eckersley scooped the ball into his path as it looked to veer out of play. King then faced up the full-back before presenting Keatings with a routine finish at the back post. The prolific little number 19 dashed behind the goal to celebrate with the fans only to be booked rather uncharitably by referee John McKendrick.

The trend, since the derby at the end of October, has been for the side to start at a furious pace, blitzing the opposition, and then to lose their way a little in the second half once the opposition is forced to stick on an extra attacker and really go for it. Leaving aside the Rangers game which was a law unto itself, the matches against Raith at home, Falkirk away, QotS and Alloa at home and then Cowdenbeath away have all followed this pattern to some degree.

Thus far we've either had enough of a first-half cushion to see us home or we've been let off the hook by a combination of poor finishing and heroic goalkeeping from Alexander. Additionally, Neilson has orchestrated subtle yet masterful tactical tweaks and we've had enough in the locker to see each game home. It's a process which has been dynamically effective with six (soon to become seven) straight wins since Ozturk took centre-stage at Easter Road. Who know, perhaps better sides would have punished us, instigating comebacks. All we can do is play who we're asked to and give it our best shot.

Here, when we started to flag after an hour, Pallardó came off the bench for Holt with the express aim of keeping the ball better. The tempo had slowed right down, almost to walking pace, and as a result our options on the ball suffered.

Hard to believe a midfield containing Pallardó, Prince and Gomis could struggle to keep possession but being starved of outlets further ahead of them didn't help matters. Keatings looked dead on his feet and was lucky to last as long as 70 minutes. His replacement, Oliver, was sprightly and keen but lacked his predecessor's touch and ball-retention skills so the change had little effect on the flow of the game.

We looked a tad cumbersome. Last season, as supporters, we'd have been quite happy to see the clock down and tough it out for all three points. However, this year, we've been spoilt by the seriously high standards on show. We're used to seeing our free-flowing side sweep forward, carving the opposition apart at will.

The mood was summed up perfectly in the final few minutes when Nicholson had cause to turn and grin at a shout from the stands, 'C'mon Sam, I've got 3-0 here!' Yet, despite the inelegant second half, it was still a precious win and meant that the scorching form of the first quarter had been replicated in the second: another eight wins and a draw. Certainly, interim Livi manager Mark Burchill was left in no doubt whatsoever about Hearts' title credentials, 'Undoubtedly, Hearts are going to win the league. They have the best team, the best manager and the best tactics. They are going to win the league.'

As someone who sat and wept in the enclosure at Dens Park on 3 May 1986, showboating and singing 'championees' just feels plain wrong and until simple mathematics render the evidence irrefutable, we can't allow ourselves to get too carried away. And, besides, January is shaping up to be one hell of a month for Hearts, what with Hibernian at home, Dumbarton and Rangers away, Falkirk at home and then Alloa away.

There's much talk of a striker arriving in January and if we can't guarantee Sow's fitness the outlay would seem a no-brainer, especially when measured against the riches his goals would surely move us towards.

68

Hibernian home,
3 January 2015, 12.45pm

BOTH sides' personae in the run-up to this compelling 1-1 draw were telling. Hibernian were buoyant. Their mood was typified by Fontaine who said, 'We can go through the rest of the season undefeated. The fact Hearts have done it proves it can be done, so why can't another team do it? Why can't that team be us? If we can hand Hearts their first defeat it might start to sow the seeds of doubt in their head. Hopefully there will be more twists and turns in the Championship this season.' Hearts, on the other hand, were subdued and understated, keen not to be seen to be underestimating Hibs and coming across as cocky champions-elect.

The Hibernian stance was based on them having no option but to muster every ounce of self-belief in a do-or-die attempt to keep alive their tenuous hopes of reeling us in. Whereas Hearts were loath to show Hibernian anything other than complete respect lest they seized upon some perceived slight or implied air of triumphalism with which to motivate themselves.

However, you'd hardly need hypnosis or a lie detector test to see how transparent and delusional Hibs' bluster was. For all the talk of being our equal, there was no mistaking a clear inferiority complex.

After going ahead just past the 20-minute mark, Oxley in the Hibernian goal began time-wasting. Again. I'm sorry, but football teams that believe in their own worth simply don't do that. And, for it to have happened twice now suggests it comes directly from Alan 'we've nothing to fear from them, you know' Stubbs. At least in the Easter Road derby, Oxley waited until the second half before starting with that shit but midway through the first half? As Gary Lineker once famously mouthed, 'Have a word with him.'

As expected, his Hibernian side were well up for the contest and made an impressive start in which they pressed Hearts back. In Scott Allan they have a player who puts the chavvy in Xavi. The midfielder cranked up the enmity with a few little winks and sly smirks to the home fans before swerving a wonderful ball into the area which Cummings stuck away for 1-0. Ozturk and Alexander exchanged a little glance which seemed to suggest the keeper had expected more help from his centre-half.

Having been released by his boyhood heroes, Cummings took immense delight in gesticulating at the unimpressed occupants of the main stand as he milked the celebration for all it was worth. The yellow card he received from referee Steven McLean looked, at one point, like being upgraded to a red by the compliance officer who'd spotted an extra, previously undetected, arm movement after pausing Sky+ and then watching it, frame-by-frame, with a giant magnifying glass. But, thankfully, common sense prevailed: it's bad enough seeing yellows dished out for offences such as these. The day supporters stop giving players utter dogs' abuse is the day they or anyone acting on their behalf has the right to get on their moral high horse when players give a tiny little bit back.

Hearts were yet to concede more than one goal in any league game this season and you could see Hibernian visibly sag when Cummings then missed a snip of a chance for 2-0. He pulled his header, disappointingly, wide. Given the way Hearts have been playing this season it was almost as if they knew that miss would come back to haunt them.

And, sure enough, within a matter of minutes Hearts were level. Jamie Walker spun off Allan and unleashed a thunderbolt of a drive with his right foot. Oxley never had an earthly and the ball was billowing the back of his net before the bearded time-waster could twitch a muscle. And from the restart he was observed, most amusingly, operating at normal pace again.

Having carded Cummings for his actions at Hibs' goal, McLean clearly felt Walker would also need to go into the book, even though his celebration had consisted of little more than running across the pitch and looking quite happy with himself. Really? This warrants the same punishment as Miller's tackle on McHattie, who is still out injured?

Hearts kept the ball better in the second half and subsequently showed a greater inclination to take the game to Hibernian, although not to the extent that they might allow the game to become too stretched. The result being that they played very much within themselves. From the stands you felt this was probably all very sensible but it still felt mildly aggravating. It *was* a derby after all. We were the home team, the league table wasn't lying – we knew our side was superior – but our players were tentative and unprepared to gamble sufficiently to go out and prove it on the day.

You could see, as the match drew to a close, Hearts becoming more and more reluctant to commit men forward. They became noticeably wary. There was this moment, late on, when Paterson had the ball wide right and when he looked up we had one player, Gary Oliver, in the box. The rest were all stationed in a straight line 40 yards out. Just in case. Any other home game poised at 1-1 (unless maybe if it's Rangers on the last day and a point wins us the league) with the board about to go up and it'd be like the Alamo. We'd have been piling bodies in there but here you could see the players clearly had their orders.

A few people, unkindly I felt, made the point that Ozturk may have won us a point in the previous derby but he cost us two here in losing Cummings for Hibernian's opener. While it's fair to say he didn't exactly have his greatest ever game in a maroon shirt, pinning the draw on him does the big man a huge disservice. Apart from anything else it completely overlooks the wonderful last-ditch tackle he made, with five minutes left, to deny substitute Boyle what would have almost certainly been a late winner.

Hibs fans took to social media after the game claiming the draw as a moral victory since Hearts had sat back at the end and were happy with their point. They'd been severely wound up by Prince Buaben and the time it had taken him to stroll off with a minute or so of normal time left to go. Sift through all the bile and they had a valid point, Hearts had seemed slightly fearful of their Edinburgh rivals. But, then again, at least Buaben had waited until late on in the game to drag his heels, how do you even begin to justify Oxley's antics over the last two derbies?

But, then, it emerged that a sizeable number of these deeply troubled souls had inundated the offices of the SFA, urging them to dock us points for supposedly contravening the terms of Gary Oliver's loan deal at Stenhousemuir. It served as a reminder, were it needed, that decades of maroon domination have ravaged a generation, leaving behind bitter and empty husks of people.

For me, it was abundantly clear Robbie Neilson was cautious about the threat Hibernian posed. Arguably, they represent the most talented side we've faced this season. Yet, as far as they're concerned, the title's long gone and I can't help feeling that our coach's primary concern was simply not surrendering too much ground to Rangers. Hibernian, languishing 19 points off the pace, have become fundamentally irrelevant.

Single-minded as ever, Robbie knew a point here would ensure we kept ticking along nicely. The third derby of the season successfully negotiated and Rangers' 3-1 victory against Dumbarton meant our 15-point lead at the top only got cut back to 13.

69

Dumbarton away,
10 January 2015, 3pm

SHIVERING under the rock in Dumbarton, it was tempting to rename The Bet Butler Stadium as the Rhett Butler since, if Ian Murray had got his way, the fixture could quite easily have gone with the wind.

The boy at the turnstile passed on morose instructions for me to retain my stub 'just in case' which was pretty disheartening, given that my train had taken 95 minutes to wheeze asthmatically from east to west and I had little to no inclination to repeat the jaunt anytime soon.

I then spotted a windblown Craig Levein, fruitlessly attempting to adjust his hair as he paced around the centre circle, a pinched and concerned expression etched across his face. The snows were coming, storm clouds gathering and it was bone-crushingly cold in that desperately exposed stadium which was rattling and juddering in the wind.

As it was, the only blemish on Levein's afternoon was getting mud on his nice, shiny black shoes as he slithered across Dumbarton's unenticing cow-field of a pitch. After weathering a literal and metaphorical storm, his Hearts side delivered a devastatingly masterful performance. Five-one sounds like a hammering but in the words of the song, 'You lucky bastards, it should have been ten!'

The wind was being funnelled in from the Clyde, rendering the entire playing area nothing more than a wind tunnel at times. Yet, despite playing into this fearsome tumult, by the break Hearts had still managed to secure a healthy 2-0 lead.

They'd had to ride their luck at times as the Sons put Alexander under severe pressure with a spate of nasty, swirling crosses. Turner hit the bar with a header that bounced down worryingly close to the line, then Ozturk coolly cleared another effort as Alexander lay prone outside his goal. Those two scares aside, Hearts simply had too much in their locker for Murray's boys.

Hearts' ultra-assertive, early-season swagger was back and the key to its return lay in the presence of a second striker, in the shape of their burly new loanee from FC Groningen, Genero Zeefuik.

There's no getting away from the fact that our bulked-up new boy was carrying a fair bit of timber but despite the *Sportscene* sniggers and the *Daily Record*'s jibes he more than looked the part. His presence, alongside Keatings, brought out the best in the whole side. It meant, instead of a third midfielder, a Pallardó or a Holt, trying their utmost to thread eye-of-the-needle passes through to the lone figure of Keatings – outnumbered three to one – we now had a strong, effective target man up top. Someone capable of hold-up play, laying the ball off and, most significantly of all, a serious goal threat who would occupy defenders and cause no end of anxious moments.

Here, Keatings and Zeefuik were a restless handful which meant Nicholson and Walker – both singled out for special praise by Neilson – were able to buzz around, subject to far less attention than they'd been used to of late. The two wingers positively revelled in the extra space and fed voraciously off Zeefuik's skilful flicks and knock-downs. Nicholson scored the first of his double after only eight minutes as he skimmed forward and unleashed a skidding, bouncing 35-yarder, into the wind, that nestled gloriously in the far corner.

Arguably, even greater beneficiaries of Zeefuik's inclusion were Buaben and Gomis. They seemed far more comfortable as a double-act, anchoring the side between them instead of adapting their partnership to accommodate Pallardó or Holt.

Zeefuik had a hand in Hearts' second goal on 26 minutes, pulling the ball down expertly, juggling it and playing it into the feet of Jamie Walker. There was still a little work for Jamie to do as he evaded the attentions of a defender before cracking the ball home off Rogers.

The wind came sweeping across from the Clyde with even greater ferocity at the start of the second half. To such an extent that for a short spell Dumbarton were struggling to get close to halfway with their clearances. In the midst of this blinding maelstrom of wind and sleet Zeefuik made it 3-0, knocking in a Walker cross.

This led a delegation of Dumbarton players to petition referee John Beaton, whimpering at him to abandon the match. Hadn't noticed any complaints from Murray's shower of pansies when the wind had been at their backs throughout the first half. Thankfully, the official gave their sappy hypocrisy short shrift and 3-0 soon became four, Nicholson rifling home his second after a vicious Paterson cross had been missed by Mair.

Hearts had a suffocating stranglehold on the game and with the driving sleet at their backs ruthlessly pinned their opponents back. If it wasn't Nicholson or Walker skinning the full-backs it was Eckersley or Paterson thundering past them up the touchline and delivering wickedly swerving balls into the box for Keatings and Zeefuik.

The game only stayed at 4-0 for three minutes. Walker, reportedly catching the eye of Spanish second-tier side Real Betis, was on fire throughout and his square ball allowed Zeefuik to slide in his second.

This was an afternoon in which the so-called 'big three' were all playing what amounted to their bogey teams. In Hearts' case, all that really meant was playing the only side bar Hibs to take a point off us, a fact Ian Murray couldn't bring himself to omit from his ever-so-erudite programme notes. Murray's former club were entertaining a Falkirk side they were yet to take a single point from while Rangers were at Alloa, opponents they'd drawn twice against in the league and been humbled by in the Petrofac Cup.

We were all reminded that Dumbarton still had attackers on the field 60 seconds after Hearts' fifth went in when Kane fired home through a forest of legs following a bout of head tennis. This, hilariously, provoked the loudest cheers of the afternoon from the 900 or so Hearts fans as, for the second time this season, it gave us licence to bait a pursed-looking Murray with another resplendent rendition of 'Five-one! We only won 5-1!'

Hearts stomped straight upfield, in this freakishly entertaining contest, and Walker went over a defender's outstretched leg in the box. Jamie generously tossed the ball to Zeefuik who hadn't exactly been lurking shyly in the background and suddenly we had the sensational prospect of our debutant notching a hat-trick.

Moira Gordon, writing in *Scotland on Sunday*, noted that the Hearts fans weren't really fussed when the big man's effort was saved as it meant we still had our 5-1 scoreline to cherish. Not me. I freely admit, goading Ian Murray is never anything other than hugely gratifying but, personally, I'd have derived a good deal more pleasure from seeing the match ball stuffed under Zeefuik's arm at the end of the game.

The final 15 to 20 minutes was like a shooting gallery as Hearts peppered Rogers's goal with shots from every conceivable angle and range, but to no avail. Keats was the worst offender. The little striker missed a bucketload of chances but given that his four goals sustained the side during December – when he was our only fit striker – you'd gladly forgive the wee man the rarest of off-days.

Elsewhere, that corner Hibernian had supposedly turned ended up leading them back to the start again and a fifth home draw from ten. Their game ended 3-3 after a 3-1 half-time lead had been squandered. At least, on the plus side for them, the result will have provided Liam Fontaine with an answer to that open-ended question he left us to ponder last week, 'The fact Hearts have done it proves it can be done, so why can't another team do it? Why can't that team be us?' Hibernian may still view us as their equals but now trail 21 points in our wake with 16 games to go.

Rangers, on the other hand, survived a late onslaught at Alloa to pocket a 1-0 and stay 13 points behind us. The ink was barely dry on the match reports before Fraser Aird was putting down a marker for Hearts' impending visit, 'There is a confidence in their squad, and they have a good squad. But I still think we have a better squad than them and better individual players...It is easy saying that sitting here. We need to prove that on Friday and hopefully we can.'

70

Rangers away,
16 January 2015, 7.45pm,
match abandoned

WHILE the Hearts fans were on *Kickback* debating which chants would wind up the blue hordes the most, the Ibrox fans themselves had far weightier issues on their minds. The previous Thursday it had emerged that their board was considering mortgaging off Ibrox and Murray Park in return for a £10m loan from Sports Direct and Newcastle United owner Mike Ashley.

Several hundred supporters amassed in the steadily falling snow and gave full vent to their anger, wrestling with stewards and chanting 'sack the board' outside the main entrance. The air was toxic and combustible.

As these events were being played out I was sitting, fretting, on one of two Dunfermline Hearts buses as it sloshed at a snail's pace along a snowbound M8. There was absolutely no chance we'd make kick-off and the motion to cut our losses and find a pub that was showing the game was finding more converts by the minute.

By kick-off we'd ground to a halt at a gridlocked, ice-bound roundabout just past Coatbridge and were making do with Liam McLeod, Derek Ferguson and Willie Miller as they tried to make some sense of the unfolding splish-splash show.

From home, mates were texting to say the game was unwatchable, the yellow ball almost indistinguishable from the snow as players slipped and skidded in pursuit of it. However, you figured that having deemed the pitch playable at kick-off they'd be bound to persevere, even more so given that you had the BT cameras there, beaming the game live to the nation.

It was hard to follow proceedings on the radio for a couple of reasons. Partly, because a few guys at the back of the bus insisted on singing 'Since I Was Young' over and over and you couldn't really hear the commentator, but mainly it was down to conditions underfoot rendering it a complete and utter farce.

The groundstaff had very thoughtfully cleared the lines for the players but the pitch itself had been left covered in a layer of slowly melting snow and ice. Additionally, the undersoil heating appeared to have had zero effect, leading you to question whether the cash-strapped club had even bothered plugging the thing in. Later, I heard via a Rangers fan mate who'd been in hospitality that Richard Gough was adamant it couldn't have been on. His rationale was that in all his years at the club he couldn't remember a single home game ever falling foul of the weather.

According to Ferguson, Robbie Neilson was constantly bending the ear of the referee and fourth official, complaining about the safety of his players but TV images showed Deek was being slightly disingenuous there. McDowell looked equally pensive and later it emerged that both medical teams had grave misgivings when they saw the game had got the go-ahead. However, the general assumption was that the snow would melt away and conditions had to improve.

You could just about make out snippets of songs over the radio as it crackled and hissed. Loud renditions of 'Glasgow Rangers: you let your club die', seriously antagonising the wound-up home support who howled their derision.

Texts from those inside Ibrox were painting a growing picture of a nasty, vitriolic home support, spitting and hurling down anything they could lay their hands on at the fans cowering in the exposed lower Broomloan Stand. Police and stewards, they reported, were showing little or no inclination to intervene.

The coach slowly started to build a little momentum, the snow gradually turning to freezing rain. Allowing ourselves the merest glimmer of hope about catching the second half, the commentator cut quickly to Chick Young, trackside. Referee Bobby Madden wanted to give the playing surface five minutes to show any improvement before abandoning the match. Later, when interviewed by Mark Guidi for BT, he'd say this was simply a ploy to allow police and stewards the time to make adequate preparations. You'd have to say he was incredibly fortunate neither side scored during this period. There would be serious disorder in the moments to follow but can you imagine how much worse the outpouring of fury from Rangers would've been if they'd scored during those five minutes and been ahead in the game?

When the final whistle eventually did go, after 24 goalless minutes, it was to a crescendo of whistling and booing and, almost straight away, a flashpoint erupted in the Sandy Jardine Stand. Enraged Rangers fans, baying for blood and revenge, surged towards their rivals who took even greater delight in goading them.

Back in August, there had been this sense of their supporters being caught almost unawares by the extent to which the Hearts fans ripped the absolute pish out of them. It had been unexpected and the sheer scale of the taunting caught them a little off-guard. There had been this frantic, incident-laden finale with two stoppage-time goals and, in a flash, the game was over. Suddenly, the police were shepherding them away from the ground before it had had a chance to properly register. Hang oan a minute Tam, did you hear what they cheeky bastirts were singing?

Not only were they thoroughly prepared this time, having had another bout of open ridicule to contend with at Tynecastle (those of them who'd been able to get hold of the significantly reduced numbers of tickets), but circumstances on and off the pitch had taken a drastic turn for the worse since August. In the present climate of protestation and in light of their deluded and spurious sense of entitlement regarding the winning of football matches, there was simply no way that level of sustained mockery was ever going to be left unpunished. The scenes at the end therefore became increasingly fraught and febrile.

Hearts fans were spat on and assaulted as they headed back to their buses. Bobby Madden's five-minute warning had not given the police enough time and large numbers were seen rushing to the ground where trouble had already broken out. Also, greater priority had been given to the cordon protecting the board members in the main stand meaning that in the vicinity of the coaches all hell was breaking loose. A 15-year-old Hearts fan slipped and fell on the ice and was immediately set upon by ten to 12 Rangers fans who kicked him senseless.

By this point our bus had turned around and we were heading for home. The guy across the aisle from me began trying to contact his wife and two daughters who'd been on the second bus to depart from Fife and the news was pretty disturbing. A band of around 20 or 30 hooded Rangers fans had apparently tried to storm on to their bus and the door had been smashed in. We stopped off in Livingston and more and more stories were emerging via text and social media, of widespread bricking of buses and of Hearts fans being physically attacked.

Later that night Craig Levein tweeted, 'Hope everyone got home safe from the match tonight. Not a good night for Scottish football for a number of reasons.' Yep, master of the understatement, our Craig.

71

Falkirk home,
24 January 2015, 3pm

JUST over a week ago the Hearts fans got ambushed at Ibrox and today it was the players' turn for a rude awakening. Our proud, long-standing unbeaten run was finally brought to a halt by a well-drilled Falkirk side, 21 games into the season. I seriously never saw this one coming and pre-match we were all happily predicting scores of 3-0 and 4-0. Fair play to Falkirk, though, they caught us below par and took full advantage thanks to an excellent performance. Their 3-2 victory was thoroughly merited.

It was as if all the planets had aligned at once and each and every department of our side chose today to malfunction. I'd even go as far as including Robbie in that. Harsh as it seems, as *The Tackle* hasn't put a foot wrong all season, but leaving Pallardó on the bench all game was a mistake and Keats needed to be unleashed long before the 65th minute.

But Neilson was also unfortunate. Hard for him to have predicted the extent to which choosing McGhee over McKay to replace the suspended Ozturk would backfire. But backfire it did as McGhee produced a trembling and unconvincing performance, unsure whether to drop off or go and meet the ball and frequently doing neither and getting caught in no-man's land.

Hindsight's a wonderful thing. McKay would've come in on a high after his match-winning exploits in the midweek under-20s derby and, more significantly, has considerable experience partnering the skipper, last month's 2-0 win at Cowdenbeath being a prime example. Whereas, other than the last 15 minutes at Palmerston in October – when we were already three up – I'm struggling to recall many opportunities McGhee has had there.

It's fair to say we were porous and jittery at the back throughout. But our destabilised defence wasn't helped by our usually reliable central-midfield duo being all at sea. Both Gomis and Buaben spent the match scurrying around, chasing shadows, as Alston and Sibbald ran the show. Both our boys were booked, caught out for pace, as eager Falkirk players nipped away from them.

Yet these two have been the lynchpins all season, they've been our buffers, cushioning the defence, and they've also set up attacks, combining almost telepathically. They've been classy and consistent. So it's impossible to be too hard on them. Emblematic of the team as a whole, they've surpassed all expectations and it would be unrealistic to expect those unremittingly stellar standards not to drop off at some point.

Oddly enough, though, we got off to an absolute flier, with Zeefuik scoring after 83 seconds. His link-up play with the returning Sow was fearsome. The two of them inter-changed like Ruud Gullit and Marco van Basten destroying England at Euro 88.

Perhaps such an early goal duped the players into believing yet another routine win was in the bag. They seemed to coast a little in the immediate aftermath, as if they assumed they'd get the win without needing to go at it full tilt.

That said, our idea of what constitutes a bad Hearts performance has been distorted this season as the side has set the bar extraordinarily high. Even the slightest drop-off becomes exaggerated out of all context. And, against another side, we may well have escaped punishment but we picked the wrong day to be this casual and slipshod.

After our goal, the first half became one-way traffic with Falkirk bossing proceedings. We've become so used to it being our players imposing their will on the opposition. Our game-plan tends to be the one that sets the agenda in matches.

The equaliser, when it came, was from the spot. Personally, I felt at the time McGhee had got something on the ball when Loy went down but I seemed to be in the minority. It would have been churlish to baulk at the decision, though. Falkirk were well worth their goal, stuck away by Baird, and the overriding feeling at half-time was that we were lucky not to be behind.

The break was spent deliberating over what Robbie needed to do to pep things up. Our strike-force required tweaking – Keatings needed to come on, either for Sow or Zeefuik – but, more pressing, was our midfield. The thought was that we needed to get Pallardó on to the pitch pronto and a case could be made for taking off either one of Gomis or Buaben.

Robbie, as he's done a few times this season (to extremely good effect, to be fair), put faith in his original starting 11 and gave them the chance to make amends, to implement the strategy they'd spent the week perfecting. He clearly felt there was nothing fundamentally wrong with the tactics or formation per se, the players simply needed to give more, show greater impetus.

The players let him down big style, though, continuing to produce a stuttering, lacklustre performance. These massive sell-out home crowds have been a big plus this season, creating a real sense of occasion, especially when teams were getting swatted aside by fours and fives. However, when things start to unravel – as they did here – it can be counter-productive and from the steep stands the silence, punctuated by the odd catcall and rumble of dissent, was deafening.

It was no surprise when Falkirk took the lead on 52 minutes, Loy spearing the ball into the postage stamp from 18 yards as McGhee stood off. We were still pedestrian in midfield and our attempts at stepping up the pace succeeded only in passes being rushed. All the loose balls were landing at the feet of players in blue and white. But that was no accident, they were on their toes, they were alert to every possibility, quick, nimble and supremely well-organised. After a slow start this season, Peter Houston has really got them playing.

At 2-1 Sow was hooked. The big man had done fairly well in his comeback game but by drifting out wide to receive the ball his effectiveness became blunted and Falkirk crowded him out to good effect. Keats replaced him and, you'd have to say instantaneously, the spring returned to our step.

The yellow cards were fluttering like Argentina 78 ticker tape as Falkirk were forced to try any means at their disposal to keep Hearts at bay. Nicholson nodded what had to be a certain goal straight at MacDonald from a brilliant Paterson cross, then Buaben stepped through a few tackles before also leathering the ball against Jamma's chest.

The noise levels were upped. This wasn't the true Hearts of old, they were still labouring, but Falkirk more than had their hands full. To scenes bordering on mild hysteria, Keatings lashed home the equaliser on 73 minutes, after Zeefuik set him up, and suddenly that iffy performance mattered not a jot. Despite being some way short of our best we'd got it back to 2-2 and we willed our side on, to stick another win on the board. With Rangers' game at Cowdenbeath falling victim to frost, our lead at the top would then have stretched to 16 points.

The cavalry charge never came, though. We weren't camped in the Falkirk half, watching them manically hoof the ball clear with crazed expressions on their faces. In fact it was they who came back at us. Gomis put the seal on a stinking performance by getting caught dallying on the edge of his own box. Sibbald dumped McGhee on the seat of his pants and then stuck it into the bottom corner for 3-2.

In the aftermath there were concerted pleas for a degree of perspective to come into play. Maybe a performance like this has been on the cards for a while and we were all placing unrealistic expectations on our 'Unbeatables'. One defeat in 21 is still spectacularly consistent. As things stand Rangers' maximum points' haul is 89. Twelve wins from our 15 remaining fixtures would put us on 90, so we remain firmly ensconced in the driving seat.

The key now, though, is to ensure that in the annals of footballing history this result registers as a mere blip and not the onset of a side slowly wilting under the twin pillars of fatigue and expectation.

Seeing whether the players can hold their nerve next weekend at Alloa will go a long way to revealing which one it's going to be.

72

Alloa away,
31 January 2015, 5.30pm

'TAKE a game like tonight in Alloa,' smirked an impish John Colquhoun, beginning to warm to his task, 'any Hearts player in that dressing room that says he's looking forward to it is lying! This isn't a game you look forward to. We've all been there,' he waggled his microphone in the vague direction of Robbo, Henry Smith and Jimmy Sandison, seated in a line next to him.

'All you care about is doing whatever it takes to get the points, you're not even remotely interested in how well you play. D'you think Robbie Neilson is? With that wind, on a freezing night like tonight? No. In, job done, out. Apart from anything else that pitch of theirs is an absolute disgrace. Seriously,' he thought for a second and then pointed vigorously at the floor of the Gorgie Suite, 'they'd be better off playing the game on that.'

At the last minute I'd decided to forego my planned Saturday tea-time jaunt up the M9 to the horribly unappealing Indodrill Stadium, Alloa. John Colquhoun had been announced as guest of honour at Gorgie Live and seeing my all-time favourite Hearts player interviewed by Scott Wilson about his time at the club was an opportunity I didn't want to miss.

I arrived early and got my picture taken with JC before taking my seat at a table next to the stage. Arch-predator, Robbo, was bounding around the place, larger than life. I watched him snaffle a few chips off this little kid's plate when he'd looked away, fatally, for a split-second. 'The wee man's still got it,' I observed to my mate Graeme.

Colquhoun, as he'd done on the pitch during his two spells at the club spanning 345 league games, dazzled and captivated the audience. A self-confessed Celtic fanatic as a young man, he spoke candidly about how his dream move to Parkhead turned sour. His manager informing him, after his first full season, that he could forget all about challenging Davie Provan and should prepare instead for life in the reserves. However, seeing as the club had high hopes for Owen Archdeacon, he could expect to be on the bench more often than not.

Flukily, JC's career jolt coincided with Hearts making a cheeky enquiry about Provan. This was rebuffed but in the ensuing dialogue JC's name cropped up and before long he was reluctantly packing his bags.

Personally, I never understood why he never flourished at Parkhead. Maybe Hearts put in a bid for Provan because they'd automatically assumed JC was set to take his place. Certainly, we were all fully aware how good he was, particularly as Celtic seemed to save him for games against us and he always terrorised Hearts. I remember him scoring in a 3-1 win for Celtic at Tynecastle in December 1983, tying Walter Kidd in knots on the way.

Yet, despite not wanting to leave Parkhead, JC was at pains to point out how quickly he settled into life at Tynecastle, producing far and away the best football of his career and enjoying his happiest times as a player. He bubbled enthusiastically about the warmth of the support, how he felt like he belonged here and how much of a joy it had been getting to play in front of a packed-out Tynecastle.

Of that dark day at Dens he was philosophical, laughing that he was well over it, 'It was in our own hands and on the day we never delivered.' Robbo shot his former strike buddy a pained glance of incredulity, whereby JC offered him the services of a really good psychologist!

He was positive and upbeat about his time at Hearts, citing the home game with Bayern Munich as the best atmosphere he has played in (although the 3-2 Scottish Cup win over Rangers in January 1986 ran it close, a game in which he was convinced there had to be at least 40,000 in the ground).

Then, his famous 30-yarder against Celtic in November 1987 flashed up on the screens and he bitched good-naturedly about how Billy McNeill had deigned to call it a 'freak' goal. The interview was slowly drawing to a close and the issue of fitness was raised, JC revealing that under Alex MacDonald Hearts had to have been the fittest team in Europe. This may or may not have been slightly tongue-in-cheek given that minutes earlier he'd been reminiscing about all-day drinking sessions in The Rutland before hitting the casino.

But then, quite aptly as it happens, Scott Wilson butted in to notify us all that the self-proclaimed 'fittest team in the league' had just lost an injury-time equaliser to Raith Rovers' Christian Nade at Easter Road and it had finished 1-1.

Not for the first time these super-fit dynamos had succumbed to a late equaliser at home and this was their sixth home draw from ten. Once the cheering had died down JC shook his head with laughter, 'Aye, we always won the derby. Didn't matter how the game was going, they could be absolutely battering us, but we'd always win…I'd see Robbo going through one on one and I'd turn and run back to halfway…the wee man never missed.'

The air resonated with positivity and the panel all predicted a Hearts victory, ranging from a tight 1-0 from Robbo to 3-1 from Henry Smith. Then the screens all around the Gorgie Suite came back on to reveal the players taking to a chilly, windswept Indodrill.

Pallardó replaced Nicholson as Hearts plumped for three midfield destroyers and up front Keatings teamed up with Sow and Zeefuik was benched. The team had a nice look to it. Jamie Walker reprised the number ten role he'd played in a 4-3-1-2 at Cowdenbeath. The final switch saw Ozturk restored to the starting line-up after his one-match ban.

Back in October the artificial surface here had played havoc with Hearts' short, passing game, the ball repeatedly sticking as if it were made of Velcro. Since then the pitch had apparently been boosted with 3G implants. This meant the ball was prone to these hugely exaggerated bounces that put you in mind of Neil Armstrong playing golf on the moon, the ball booming away into the dark stratosphere.

None of this mattered to Hearts. Whenever all three midfield amigos take to the field together you get a sense that the side really means business. With them all out there it's a grown-up, man's midfield and a very reassuring presence. Especially with two front men to hit as was the case here. Five minutes in, Pallardó took a square ball from Gomis and scythed home a 30-yard screamer with the outside of his right foot to put Hearts in front. It was just the sort of start you dream of in such a tricky fixture and you could see the relief at the table beside us, Ann Budge celebrating warmly with JC and Robbo.

The rubberiness of the pitch and the wind whistling down from the Ochils made monopolising possession tricky. Both sides tried quick passing movements but kept gifting possession back to each other. Alloa very nearly profited from this slackness with their first genuine attack, two minutes later.

Buchanan dragged Paterson out of position and played a smart ball through for Simmons. The ex-Hearts man hit the inside of the post with a scruffy effort and thankfully Paterson was able to redeem himself, horsing the ball to safety as it rolled dangerously along the line.

Five minutes later we were all up off our seats again punching the air in delight. Keatings took a pass with back to goal, swivelled, then twisted and turned Ben Gordon into the ground. The ball hadn't stopped moving when, lightning fast, he rasped a 25-yarder into the bottom corner. Twelve minutes in, two up, and both goals had come from players we'd felt we'd missed last weekend. After that reversal this start felt like manna from heaven and with the wind at their backs Hearts looked liable to vent all the week's frustrations on luckless Alloa.

Benedictus took out Sow, leaving him in a heap like a discarded, wind-blown deckchair. Ozturk once again sought to emulate Messrs Bale and Ronaldo, hitting the ball right on the valve from the free kick. It moved in the air but not sufficiently to fool McDowall who took no chances, palming it over.

The keeper didn't look quite so bright from another free kick as the half drew to a close. After a bright opening Simmons's game was coming apart at the seams and he committed a bad foul on Walker on the edge of the box. Keats decided this one was his and hit a carbon copy of his effort at Cowdenbeath, thudding the ball against the bar with the keeper helpless.

At half-time JC was first on the mic, suggesting Robbo would have struggled in the current Hearts side seeing as they don't score any rubbish goals. Robbo replied that he'd have loved to have been part of the present crop as the presence of Zeefuik would mean he wasn't the fattest!

Scott gave the panel the chance to revise their original predictions in light of what they'd seen in the first half. Henry stuck with 3-1 which wasn't really surprising and Robbo stuck with 1-0 which was. Then JC, when asked, cryptically replied, 'One-one Chelsea Man City' and moments later he was gone, his second mug of Lapsang Souchong barely even touched.

I only hoped we wouldn't take our foot off the gas in the second half. It's been a bit of a trait this season, especially after decent first halves. Falkirk away came into my head, perhaps because it had also been a 5.30pm BBC Alba game and at the break we'd been 2-0 up on a synthetic surface.

Exasperatingly, we were a little slack at the start of the half and lost a goal on the hour. Spence got in front of Pallardó and seemed to shoulder home Donaldson's cross. Robbo, at half-time, had made the point about Alloa being two down to Rangers at half-time in the Petrofac semi, only to come back strongly. The point being we needed to be vigilant. A mad five minutes of copious sweating ensued until, thankfully, our two-goal advantage was restored.

Walker ghosted in to intercept a loose ball from Simmons and side-footed home for 3-1. Barry Smith, the Alloa manager, said that at 2-1 he felt his side were in the ascendancy but that mistake killed their chances. In light of the result last weekend that was a big five minutes for Hearts. Their character emerged, though and they even found time for a fourth goal to wrap up matters, Paterson bulleting home a King corner.

Rangers were preoccupied with the following lunchtime's League Cup semi-final versus Celtic which meant our lead at the top stretched to 16 points having played two more games than Rangers.

The night closed with questions from the floor and the topic inevitably turned to when the panel thought we might win the league. The hard facts are that with 14 games left to go 11 wins puts us on 90 points and uncatchable. Robbo reckoned that the likelihood of us playing our rearranged Ibrox fixture over the Easter weekend – he was proved correct – played right into our hands. 'We'd go there and win the title,' he declared. 'Na, Robbo,' Wilson interjected, 'we'd want to win it here.'

'No we wouldn't,' persisted Robbo, 'we'd win it there and GET IT RIGHT UP THEM! In fact that would be my team talk that day [alluding to a slightly odd question from earlier that no one had known how to answer]: GET IT RIGHT UP THEM!' The place was on its feet with that. I stayed up, a little worse for wear, got my coat and stumbled out into the chilly night.

The subject of Robbo's scorn, Rangers, folded quicker than Superman on wash-day against Celtic in that semi the following day. For its intro, *Sportscene* had this wonderfully dreamy, soft focus sequence in which two small children – a boy and a girl – re-enacted key moments from Old Firm games of yore. The wee girl was Scott Brown while the wee boy was El Hadji Diouf (mercifully the BBC stopped short of blacking him up). The girl was Jimmy Johnstone raising an arm and Larsson wheeling away, tongue out. The boy was Davie Cooper, then Naismith running away cupping his ears. Footage of the wee boy doing Gascoigne playing the flute mercifully ended up on the cutting-room floor.

Life then imitated art in the streets around Hampden as a different, sadly far less fortunate, ten-year-old was involved in another faithful Old Firm re-enactment: the riot after the 1980 Scottish Cup Final. This ten-year-old Rangers fan, sitting at the lights in a minibus, was smashed in the face by a bottle thrown from a mob of Celtic fans. The poor little guy suffered a hairline fracture to his cheekbone and lost three teeth, apparently.

With numpties like that, chucking bottles at innocent little kids, the transfer window really is just something they lick.

73

Livingston away,
7 February 2015, 3pm

THE transfer window wedged shut on the Monday prior to this re-scheduled league clash at Almondvale. Alas, the desire for regular, first team football saw us lose a fine young talent in Jason Holt who left for Sheffield United and big, bad Brad McKay who signed a pre-contract with St Johnstone. As a replacement for Holt, half-Dutch/half-Scottish Kenny Anderson arrived from Dutch second-tier side Waalwijk.

But the real story of the January transfer window was unfolding through at Rangers where Mike Ashley sent five reserves in the direction of Murray Park. The sullen, normally introverted Kenny McDowall then almost fell over himself in eagerness to tell the world he'd had instructions to play all five loanees, if fit. The ex-St Mirren man may have been working his notice but it seemed a clear attempt to distance himself from any fall-out should this peculiar Newco'castle hybridising experiment go pear-shaped. At the unveiling, one of the five – Haris Vučkić– said of Hearts' lead at the top, 'I think, realistically, we can catch them up.' Deluded sense of entitlement? He'll fit right in.

This weekend was free for both Livingston and Hearts due to neither having any more involvement in the Scottish Cup. So a fixture destined to clash with Livingston's Petrofac Cup Final on 4 April was very sensibly brought forward. It gave Hearts a chance to get more points on the board while Rangers were on Scottish Cup duty. Victory here would move us 19 points clear (having played three extra games).

Hearts came bursting out of the blocks and from the opening minutes of a turbulent and, at times, bad-tempered clash you could've been fooled into thinking we were in for another one of those gloriously stress-free turkey shoots we specialised in during late summer/early autumn. We raced ahead inside four minutes courtesy of the booming right foot of Zeefuik. The moment the Fridge picked up a pass from Walker on the left it was clear he had only one thing on his mind. Ignoring the forest of raised arms, he advanced, shuffled inside and blasted a swerving ball home from the edge of the box.

From my seat in the front row of the east stand – which was 'restricted view' in all but price – I shifted nervously as that eagerly anticipated goals avalanche never materialised. This was due in no small way to Livingston's predicament at the foot of the table focusing their minds and lending their performance a gritty, borderline nasty edge.

More telling, however, were the three enforced changes to our side. McGhee filled in at left-back in place of the injured Eckersley and we sorely missed the Englishman's constant willingness to drive up the left channel. McGhee defended resolutely enough but not having a natural left-footer as an out ball, was a big miss. Sow and Buaben were the two other absentees; the former nursing a slight thigh strain and the latter suspended.

This was also the fourth time we'd played Livingston this season. They'd worked out their best chance lay in stifling our creativity by snapping into tackles and getting up close and personal. Siege mentality borne out of a points deficit leaving them cut adrift meant fair play went out the window. It was win-at-all-costs and they were guilty of gamesmanship on an irritating scale. White was booked for a laughable attempt at conning the referee with a dive in the box and then Talbot flagrantly play-acted in order to get Zeefuik in trouble. Writhing around in agony, hobbling off and then turning and sprinting back on in order to take a throw-in on the far side.

The Livi left-back was then lucky to stay on the pitch after a horrific head-high kung fu kick on Nicholson who was lucky he wasn't decapitated. A bleeding, barely coherent Nick was helped off and didn't feature again yet Colvin bewilderingly felt the assault warranted merely yellow. This sparked ugly scenes and Ozturk was booked for steaming in to confront Talbot.

Last January, Colvin's ineptitude marred our 3-3 draw at McDiarmid Park. That day he gifted the home side two nonsensical penalties. So, when I saw him book the Livi striker for diving it raised my hopes that perhaps he'd just had an off day up in Perth. But, no, still a dud.

There was widespread astonishment at the call in Sunday papers awash with images of the tackle and Nicholson's ravaged face. Talbot had apparently been guilty of a similar head-high assault versus Dumbarton the other week, too. Probably asking too much for Colvin to have been aware of that. Or that Talbot holds the dismissals record at Port Vale, with five in 47 matches. In the days following the game the SFA ended up doing Colvin's job for him and Talbot was hit with a two-match ban for serious foul play.

A nervy and ever-so-slightly careless showing was carried on into the second half. Wilson's cool, unruffled, Hansen-esque demeanour is one of his finest attributes. However, when he's slightly off his game – as was the case today – he can seem casual and a little slapdash. He was guilty a number of times of giving the ball away when under little pressure.

New signing Anderson had come on (for Nicholson) but was taking time to get up to speed. Stationed out wide he struggled to get into the game, at one point treading on the ball in his eagerness to create a good impression.

Then, seven minutes into the second half, Livingston pulled level. They'd been sniffing around Alexander's goal but without creating any clear-cut chances. So when the goal arrived it was a real rabbit punch to the kidneys. There was a slight hint of offside as Sives slotted in from close range and Paterson totally flipped out, adamant there'd been a huge miscarriage of justice. Play was on the verge of restarting and C-Patz was still remonstrating with anyone foolish enough to make eye contact: players, officials, stewards, spectators.

In the context of the title race and our remaining fixtures this one had definitely been filed under 'must win'. Thankfully for us, Livingston's points deduction has them adrift at the foot, which meant a solitary point didn't really suit them much either. It felt like win or bust for both sides and play swung back and forth.

Livi's bargain-basement Scott Wilson had been chuntering on brainlessly about 'making more noise' to their couple of hundred supporters at half-time. Maybe he has to pay the real Wilson royalties if he says '**some** noise'. Myles Hippolyte, who'd scored against our reserves in the Petrofac Cup back in August, was thrown on by Livi to cries of 'let's feed the hippo' from this imposter. A comment that caused most Hearts fans to go, 'Eh? What did he say there? Was he speaking about Zeefuik? Is that his new name?'

I was started to get a bad feeling about this one. Hearts were faltering and making a lot of basic errors and the edgy crowd were starting to get on the players' backs a little. Wilson and then Paterson both miscued passes out of play within a few seconds of one another as the agitated support began furiously checking then double-checking their watches and phones.

I watched Keats jog across to Anderson and instruct him to move inside more, I presumed so he'd see more of the ball. But then, moments later, Keats's number came up and he was trotting off with Billy King stripped and ready. So it was another example of how well-drilled the side is and how strategically astute. Keats knew he was about to come off and what the switch would entail tactically – King went out on to the left wing with Walker switching to the right.

The reshuffle was inspired and, not for the first time this season, tinkering with the tactics and personnel swung an evenly poised nail-biter our way. Anderson, King and Walker, between them, were the three principal architects of the turnaround: conjuring the requisite magic to claim a desperately precious victory.

On 82 minutes, King terrorised the Livi back division, surging for the line and then checking back inside. His pull-back was met beautifully by Anderson who powered a firm diving header low into the corner. Another January signing with a debut goal to his name and our 19th different league scorer of the season.

The Hearts support that had been, for the most part, sitting and silently fretting, leapt to their feet, warmly applauding the side and finally the singing started again. Two minutes later there were Hearts supporters hurdling the wall at the far side of the pitch and celebrating like crazy as Walker made it 3-1. King played him in on goal and Jamie hared into the box, smashing a low, pinpoint finish across the keeper and into the far corner.

With the last kick of the game Jacobs made it 3-2 from the penalty spot after McKay (on for Ozturk) had pulled back Hippolyte. Perhaps it was because only a few days earlier he'd signed a deal to leave but Brad looked distraught on receipt of his straight red and trudged around the back of the goal close to tears.

The chips were down yet the side had come through. At this stage of the season, with wins at a premium, you just take this and move on. The end is in sight now. As the games count down and what we need to do to secure the title comes into ever-sharper focus, a clear divide in attitude from supporters is becoming evident.

A decent segment of the Kilmarnock 65/Dens Park 86 generation are fearful of jumping the gun, lest they jinx themselves and re-open old wounds that still fester. While the younger breed of fan looks at bookies offering odds of 1/33 on Hearts for the title and 11/1 for Rangers – not to mention Rangers' dismal state – and proclaim the league to have been done and dusted since Christmas.

Our 'bridesmaid' reputation was founded on losing the title on the last day to Kilmarnock in 1965 and Celtic in 1986, aided in no small measure by semi-final disappointments against St Mirren in 1987, Celtic in 1988, Airdrie in 1992 and 1995 and Rangers in 1993, not forgetting the 7-0 against Hibs. You also had Scottish Cup Final defeats in 1968, 1976, 1986 and 1996. Quite a catalogue of misery.

However, 7-0 was blown out of the water by the twin Hampden thrashings of 4-0 and 5-1, easily the two biggest derbies in our lifetime. The semi-final disasters have been swept away by victories in the last minute against Aberdeen in 1996, Falkirk in 1998 and Celtic in 2012. Yes, we lost four cup finals in a row but we've now won our last three in 1998, 2006 and 2012.

Our players have shown they handle pressure well, it's the supporters who need to be a little less anxious. Unwelcome nerves are jangling and you can see, at times, them being transmitted on to the pitch. We need ten wins from our last 13 matches and that's assuming a badly damaged, listing Rangers side win all 16 remaining fixtures. It's in our own hands, we just need to stay calm and put our trust in the management and in the players.

As Neilson said after the match, 'All the games we play now are going to be really tough. The majority of games will turn into a battle and we need to show character and strength. We didn't play great football today but the three points will prove crucial, I'm sure.'

74
Livingston home,
14 February 2015, 3pm

SO, in the end, Jason Talbot was missing, courtesy of a retrospective two-match ban for going kung fu fighting on Sam Nick's face. Playing Livi back-to-back meant, for once, the side that suffered through incompetent officiating actually benefited from the belated punishment. Well, I say 'benefited', last week we were denied the undeniable advantage of playing against ten men for an hour but, still, I'd rather it was us playing Livi minus their club captain than some other completely random side in the division.

In a perverse kind of way, though, I'd been quite looking forward to seeing Talbot take to the field. Mainly through idle curiosity as to which Hearts player would clean him out first. If pushed, my money would have been on Gomis but only because Ozturk would have had less opportunity. Also, if he'd played, he'd have been out warming up when Scott Wilson played 'Kung-fu Fighting' by Carl Douglas which would've raised an ironic chuckle or two.

The previous night Hibernian went through to Ibrox and brought the title three points closer to Gorgie with a 2-0 win. Their last game against Rangers (the 4-0) preceded a rather over-wrought 1-0 win for Hearts over Livingston – back on 27 December. And, in an odd quirk of fate, history repeated itself, but with the venues reversed: Jamie Walker's eighth goal of the season ending up being the difference between the sides.

On the day, little came off for a misfiring Hearts. Many misinterpreted the below-par performance as being wholly down to nerves. That may have been part of the story but I don't think it was even close to being the main reason.

Last weekend Livi got right in Hearts' faces from the off and it was obvious they'd done their homework. It would have been weird if they hadn't to be honest, given it was their fourth game against us this season. So, to try and steal a march for game number five, Robbie went with an attack-minded midfield diamond of Buaben, Pallardó, Anderson and Walker.

In order for that system to work properly, though, you need width to come from your full-backs. Unfortunately, neither Eckersley nor Paterson could be said to have brought their A-games with them. C-Patz, in particular, had an unmitigated shocker. His first two forays forward saw him easily robbed and he seemed never to regain his confidence. Credit where credit's due, though, he kept at it. His goofy, out of sorts display was topped off with a shanked effort late on that nearly uprooted the corner flag. He'd later tweet, 'Very poor performance personally but great win for the team.' Got to admire the big man's honesty and humility there.

Another reason for Hearts' lack of effectiveness was summed up by Sam Nicholson in the match programme, 'Some teams think the best chance against us is by making it a battle. But if Livingston want to keep dishing out bad challenges, we shouldn't get involved and just carry on playing the way we know how.'

Those comments encapsulated Livingston's approach perfectly. Following on from last week they set out to spoil the game. You often hear about these aspiring young managers, earnest students of the game, who model their approach on the way a particular side from the past played. Rafa Benitez, for example, was obsessed with Arrigo Sacchi's Milan team of the late 1980s, poring over endless videos and drilling his players accordingly. Similarly, when at Aberdeen, Sir Alex Ferguson would listen attentively to cassettes about Bill Shankly to try and get inside the great man's head. You wonder what DVDs have been on Burchill and his coaching staff's playlist? Greece's triumph at Euro 2004? BT Sport's *The Crazy Gang*? *Karate Kid III*? They were lucky, in the end, only to have the one player sent off.

At one point Paterson, entirely in keeping with his bad day at the office, took a flying boot in the face from Declan Gallagher following a Hearts corner. The referee flashed a yellow at the Livi defender and then, nonsensically, gave a goal kick.

And I'd give Alan Muir's performance as a further reason why our game stuttered and failed to flow as we'd have liked. Muir seemed to totally miss the narrative of the game. Bearing an uncanny resemblance to the PE teacher in *Gregory's Girl* with his tentative attempt at a pubescent moustache, Muir ignored a raft of fouls on Hearts' players, not to mention a number of blatant attempts to con him by Livi's players.

Then, when he did deign to blow up for fouls, he'd often pick incidences where we were breaking away, denying us a clear advantage. You wouldn't mind so much if he was bringing play back to then book the player in question but he never administered as much as a ticking off.

Muir also fell into that common trap of referees the world over whereby if a striker is big and cumbersome, like Zeefuik, it basically precludes them from ever being fouled. We saw it last season when C-Patz was a makeshift striker and it happened repeatedly when Michael Ngoo was here. In certain games neither could buy a free kick. Note to referees: Just because one particular striker has a larger build than another it doesn't make smashing him off the ball any less of a foul.

Yet, despite a malfunctioning tactical set-up, rough-house opponents and a referee unwilling or unable to referee the game fairly, we still managed to carve out a few half-decent chances. Buaben, who began the game like an absolute world-beater on the left of the diamond, started a move on 18 minutes that lead to Walker setting up Keatings, Jamieson making a flying save from the number 19 to tip the ball away.

Keatings often came deep to good effect, switching over with Walker in a very fluid system, but then, twice, when balls with his name on them were fired enticingly across the six-yard line, he was nowhere to be seen.

The real shining light, though, was Walker. On 38 minutes he took control of the ball 35 yards out and juggled it forward like Jim Baxter at Wembley. His keepie-uppies took him to the edge of the box where all he was missing was a finish; his volley slamming against the keeper.

Two minutes later and Walker found that finish. His run at the centre of the Livi defence looked to have been halted but then a helpful ricochet landed at his feet and he had the presence of mind to take it on, round the keeper and fire the ball high into the net from a tight angle.

For the start of the second half King replaced Anderson. Irrespective of whether Kenny was injured or not this was the right call. King had looked highly accomplished when he'd come off the bench last week whereas Anderson never settled. He just needs to take a breath or two and calm down. At the moment he's running around all over the place like Wayne Foster on amphetamines. At one point, chasing a crossfield ball from Buaben, he was so pumped up he tripped over his own feet, falling heavily. He hobbled back to halfway to ripples of sympathetic applause.

The switch meant Hearts went to a flat midfield but that never really worked either due to our central duo of Buaben and Pallardo getting swamped. Livi were energetic and packed the midfield, disrupting us to good effect. It wasn't until midway through the half and Gomis's introduction, at the expense of Keats, that we began to win more of those battles. Up until that point Livi probably had the better of things in the second half and were looking threatening, especially from set pieces. Alexander tipped a Sives header from an O'Brien free kick acrobatically over the bar.

Livi began fouling with a degree of abandon perhaps because they could see Hearts were now bossing the midfield. Despite Burchill's ever-complimentary press interviews his players seemed hell-bent on nobbling the opposition. Finally, Muir joined the dots and, with 15 minutes left, Praprotnik cynically hacked down Buaben to earn a second yellow.

The scoreline could and should have been given a nice healthy sheen late on when a cluster of glorious chances were all spurned. We were unlucky when a bamboozling piece of magic from King ended with his cross being headed against the bar by a Livi defender. Then, in the final minute, a kamikaze back-pass put Zeefuik through one-on-one with Jamieson. The big man tried to be too clever for his own good, though, with an attempted Pirlo and the keeper was all smiles as he stood up and read it. Finally, in stoppage time, we saw the worst miss of the lot, King leaning back and ballooning over from ten yards when he was all alone in front of goal.

This is not the time to be sniffy about performances. These are the dirty, scrappy wins that earn titles. Hibernian and their six home draws from ten are testament to what can happen in close games such as these.

Then, you look at the table and see we're 22 points above Rangers who still have those three games and 20 clear of Hibernian. Speaking of our closest rivals, Liam Craig popped up on *Sportscene* and was asked by smiling assassin Jonathan Sutherland, 'Does it pain you to see Hearts 20 points clear?' Shame he never asked him whether he **still** felt Hibernian could win it.

Today you would not describe as pretty by any stretch of the imagination. But we only have 12 games to go now and I'd bite your hand off for eight more of these ugly beauties.

75

Queen of the South away, 21 February 2015, 3pm

DESPITE the footballing world's growing assumption that the title is as good as secured, the need remains for us still to go out and stick wins on the board. After Rangers eased past Raith Rovers on the eve of this match, Kris Boyd commented that all they could do was keep winning to put pressure on us. And there's the rub. A run of Rangers victories will mean we can't afford to waver. They win their three games in hand and our lead is reduced to 13 points. Then, you factor in the two games they have against us and our lead could potentially be cut still further.

Yet, all season, Hearts have been staunchly single-minded, their focus locked, unshakeably, on the next target: shutters blocking out forlorn attempts at mumbled psychobabble from elsewhere. 'So-called champions?' Call us whatever you like. 'Can you take the heat?' It's starting to look that way. You? Today was no different. The battle at Palmerston Park was more about the players assuaging the fears of their supporters than vice versa. The players were calm and unfazed yet the uptight, charged ferocity that greeted Queens' opener betrayed, from the stands, a genuine sense of unhinged anxiety.

It may have taken until the 85th minute and Zeefuik's deflected winner but the players faithfully delivered the panacea and relief continued cascading like so much Tennent's lager all the way back up to Edinburgh. The songs that rang out on overcrowded train platforms at Dumfries and Carlisle spoke volumes. Yet, only a tiny fraction of those decibel levels had been audible inside that desperately fraught ground.

A refreshed-looking Hearts side took to the field and straight away began mixing play up to good effect. Their fluid 4-3-3 with King and Walker either side of Zeefuik quickly became 4-5-1 whenever the Doonhamers had the ball. The wide players making a five with Gomis, Buaben and Pallardó: our midfield triumvirate forming a highly effective pyramid with Gomis and Pallardó holding.

What scuppered the fulcrum of our side were a sequence of heavy and infuriatingly unpunished fouls on Buaben that blunted his effectiveness, forcing him off at the interval. Referee Euan Anderson seemed to have raised the threshold for what constituted foul play and let much go in a hectic opening spell. The worst example being when Zeefuik was grappled around the waist as he ran clear. A straight red any day of the week, however the glaikit-looking assistant, two feet away, glanced fearfully across at his superior and kept his flag firmly by his side.

In any other season, while clearly less than thrilled, you'd be relatively sanguine about falling behind now and again. Not here, though, not in this division and not with victories at a premium to keep the Govan wolf from the door. There's too much at stake and Carmichael's routine finish, on 24 minutes, saw howls of discontent aimed at a side that had actually started quite brightly. Personally, I thought it went way too far: one boy, in the row in front of me, was up off his seat screaming abuse at first Wilson and then Gomis for having the temerity to play it square. Twenty points clear and you treat your players like **this**.

You know, I think it's more the idea of Rangers than the actual reality that's making people so jittery. As if, somehow, the footballing essence of Laudrup and Gascoigne will seep into the flaccid corpse of present-day Rangers, causing them to rise up, infused with the spirit of yesteryear. More and more we need to remind ourselves it's just a name: Rangers – the present incumbents have next to nothing in common with that giant behemoth we grew up fearing.

Zeefuik was available long and Hearts possibly found themselves looking to him more than they'd have preferred. Even more so when we fell behind and play briefly became a little frantic. If, as expected, these remaining games pan out as major slug-fests, Genero is going to become even more massive for us than he already is.

Mercifully, the side were behind for only nine minutes. King made a sweet connection with Paterson's cut-back and cracked the ball high into the net from around the penalty spot. The goal settled the support down. Being behind hadn't felt right at all. Not surprising when you consider it was only the second time we'd trailed at any point in an away league match this season.

Half-time saw Anderson take Prince's place and the system, on paper at least, remained the same. Anderson is no Buaben, though, and with Gomis lacking his customary awareness and touch it fell to the mercurial Pallardó to control the midfield. El Conquistador produced an immaculate, imperious performance.

Hearts may have gone for a slightly less-refined approach at times but it was telling that the two standout performers down in Dumfries were Pallardó and Wilson. Both these elegant ball-players persisted with passes out wide where, on either flank, we had a tag-team working tigerishly to feed the ball down the line: King and Eckersley on the left; Walker and Paterson on the right. C-Patz did his utmost to erase the memory of last week and largely succeeded, although his crossing remained a little patchy.

Nonetheless, the industry from the side was incessant. This victory, above all the others, showed Hearts' mettle. These points mattered and not many sides win down at Palmerston. Queens remained a viable threat yet Hearts persisted, repeatedly committing men forward. The raw desire and self-belief underpinning their staying power at the top of the league propelled them to all three points when a lesser side might have stuck on one.

With five minutes to go, Wilson, imperturbable, strode out from the back and angled an impeccably weighted ball down the line and into the path of the zooming Eckersley. The Englishman's first-time cross picked out Zeefuik who half-turned, then knocked the ball home off a defender. The ensuing celebrations spoke more of relief than jubilation. This was the Dutchman's fifth goal in his last five starts and he looks to have pepped up our attack, just when it was needed most.

The clouds parted and for the last few minutes of normal time Palmerston rang out to the tune of a Hearts support in full cry. A rising chant of 'fuck you Rangers, we're going to win the league' engulfed the ground as the paralysing worry lifted.

This ebullience was checked by a flurry of corners won by the home side in stoppage time, the fretting intensified by, once again, a board not going up. What's the deal with that? Are there not enough boards to go around so each week someone has to miss out? I'd be more than happy to bring along chalk and a little blackboard for the fourth official next time we draw the short straw. Seeing as the SFA have taken the unilateral decision that if we can't have the information delivered in high-tech mode then we won't be getting it at all.

Eventually, the referee blew up and we'd done it; our 21st victory in our 25th league game and 21 points from these last 11 fixtures will sees us safe. Rangers have a sequence of three matches coming up (Falkirk and Cowdenbeath away, QotS at home), during which time we play only the once: Cowdenbeath at Tynecastle next Saturday. Then, taking it further ahead, Rangers have a run of five games in 15 days in March which will be illuminating. Certainly, by the time Dumbarton come a-calling on 14 March, we should have a far clearer picture of how exacting a fight we'll have on our hands to secure that flag.

Certain elements of the Scottish press, disgruntled perhaps that there isn't really a title race to speak of, seem keen to inject some spice into proceedings. Maybe there's also an element of displeasure at seeing Rangers bested by an Edinburgh side. Either way, the *Daily Record* completely distorted the comments of Robbie Neilson, printing a baseless claim from him that the league was as good as won. This was disingenuous at best. What Robbie actually said was, 'I felt a win here would be a huge step towards the title,' which isn't really the same at all. The aim seems to be to stir up a little animosity, in the hope of provoking a reaction and making the run-in more interesting. *The Scotsman* also tried to talk up the battle at the top, describing Kris Boyd as being 'on the boil'. Given that Boyd's goal in Kirkcaldy was his first in the league since October I'd go as far as saying that that particular pot boiled dry months ago.

Soccer Saturday's Jeff Stelling has already made his mind up, it seems, 'Hearts first, the rest nowhere.' While, for me, it's still too soon. The fat lady is waiting for a cab to take her to the theatre.

76

Cowdenbeath home,
28 February 2015, 3pm

WOODEN spoon candidates and champions-elect mingled in the streets around Gorgie. And while the Murrayfield set may have had their afternoon ruined by visitors wearing blue, there were no such worries at Tynecastle: a mind-boggling 10-0 obliteration of the Blue Brazil had the home fans in absolute raptures.

Rory Loy's equaliser, the previous evening, for Falkirk against Rangers had already nudged the title another two points closer. This was before today's win meant 16 points from our ten remaining games would seal the deal. Again, of course, this is in the event of a shambolic-looking Rangers winning all 13 of their remaining games which, on last night's showing, looks dubious to say the least. Our players don't have their winners' medals yet but you'd dare to speculate that they're in the post. Until then, the cosmic ballet goes on.

Amid the increasing sweat and toil of this inexorable push towards the title, today was a luscious oasis. It was a game that saw Hearts finally unleash their full pulverising repertoire and doomed Cowdenbeath ended up slap-bang in the path of a maroon typhoon.

Zeefuik began the rout, with a hat-trick in three minutes and 35 seconds (tying with Andy Black v Arbroath in 1938, for Hearts' quickest-ever treble) which included two penalties and Sow ended it with a rapid-fire double. In between, Nicholson, Walker, Gomis, Ozturk and Wilson all got in on the act.

Strangely, the game actually started rather limply. For 20 or so minutes Cowdenbeath worked really hard at closing down the spaces and Zeefuik began to look isolated in Hearts' 4-2-3-1 formation. King, Nicholson and Walker all zipped around in lively fashion behind the Dutchman without managing to link effectively with the lone striker.

Then, suddenly, 25 minutes in, the rout began and in a 215-second blur, Zeefuik had bagged a treble (or, if your name's Ronnie Deila, a 'triple'). Nicholson was fouled in the box and, as they'd also done at Dumbarton, Walker and Zeefuik had a sharp debate on who'd get to do the honours. The Dutchman won – again – and rapped in his effort low, off the base of the post. Barely a minute later Walker showed there'd been no hard feelings, laying the ball crisply at the feet of the Dutchman who shifted it on to his right foot and slammed home from 20 yards. Amazingly, this mini-sequence wasn't yet over and a further minute later Nicholson flew into the box at high speed and had the ball whipped off his toe by the hand of Toshney. The defender simply had to walk and Zeefuik rammed the spot-kick past Thomson for 3-0.

We now had a good old-fashioned turkey shoot on our hands and Hearts looked in merciless mood. On 24 minutes, Nicholson made it 4-0, skelping a magnificent 25-yarder into the postage stamp. For Nicholl's boys the game had gone. You'd imagine their original game-plan still applied except, now, with the more modest aim of damage limitation.

Colin Nish summed up the extent of his side's attacking intent by needlessly slam-dunking C-Patz to the floor and getting booked. C-Patz took an age to get back to his feet and didn't quite look himself. Although that was due in part to him sporting a haircut last seen on Kenneth More when he played Sir Douglas Bader in *Reach for the Sky*.

The 103 Cowdenbeath fans began slowly drifting for the exits in their ones and twos, their egress triggered by Hearts' fifth on 40 minutes. Nicholson was interchanging with King and Walker to ruinous effect. He embarked on a jinking run before setting up Walker who pinged the ball past the hopelessly exposed Thomson.

Five-nil up at half-time and you wondered whether Hearts might come out for the second half and ease off the gas a little, settling perhaps for six or seven. However, if anything, the intensity was stepped up and the Edinburgh side continued their persecution of the demoralised Fifers.

Ten minutes into the half, Morgaro Gomis one-twoed his way into the box, only to be tripped. While the Cowdenbeath defenders remonstrated with referee Bobby Madden, Morgaro made a beeline for the loose ball and plonked it down on the spot. He'd decided he'd earned the right to take this one and neither Walker nor Zeefuik sought to dissuade him otherwise. Gomis's quick run-up was a subtle ruse and the cheekiest of Pirlos was dinked, casually, home for number six, by number six.

If 6-0 sounded more like a tennis score what happened in the ensuing 35 minutes took the result into the realms of rugby. Zeefuik, King and Walker were replaced by openly-salivating trio Sow, Keatings and El Hassnaoui. Walker knew there'd been the potential to really fill his boots out there and almost needed to be dragged physically from the pitch, his reluctance more than endorsed within 60 seconds of the switch.

Ozturk came prowling forward, the ball at his feet, and with the crowd bellowing 'shooooot' he was happy to oblige, crashing an angled 30-yarder into the far corner. Not sure how many of Stubbsy's '999 attempts' Ozturk's had but the deeply discourteous Hibernian manager was clearly in Scott Wilson's thoughts as he pointedly referred to the goal as Ozturk's 'third freak of the season'. Seven minutes later seven became eight as Alim's central defensive partner also muscled in on the act, Wilson firing home after a corner had only been half-cleared.

The closing stages became almost surreal to watch. Hearts were cruising 8-0 yet there was still a fanatical craving for more goals. None of the three substitutes had got on the scoresheet and it was clear all were eager for a piece of the action: scurrying after the ball and chasing down lost causes.

With 20 minutes left El Hass collected the ball from Sam Nick and clipped a nicely-weighted reverse pass into Sow who slid in number nine. Five minutes later Sow had another, smacking the ball into the corner from 20 yards with Thomson looking shell-shocked.

As the clock ran down Keats and El Hass began lashing at anything that moved in the hope of contributing to the jamboree but to no avail. The closest Keats came was from a 25-yard free kick that drifted over and the suspicion remains that he's happiest on his own up top rather than dovetailing with a second (and in this case, third) striker. El Hass, on the other hand, struggled to shine, even in the company of such drained and dispirited defenders and will probably need a full pre-season to show his true capabilities.

Despite the ever-expanding scoreline, Bobby Madden had done his utmost to nurse Cowdenbeath through the second half, allowing them to form walls only eight or nine yards from any potentially troublesome free kicks, penalising the softest of fouls and sparing them even one single second of injury time. The Blue Brazil shuffled off at the end, dishevelled and hollow-eyed. Yet you can't help feeling the true victims today weren't Cowdenbeath but another team in the division that plays in blue tops and white shorts.

We'd notched our biggest ever win in the league and the freakish nature of the scoreline meant the name of Heart of Midlothian reverberated around the footballing world. Heartbreakingly, it would do so again two days later as our beloved Dave Mackay passed away. A torrent of grief greeted the news that the captain of our 1958 title-winning side and the man viewed by many as Hearts' greatest ever player had been lost to us. Such a figurehead, so compelling a leader: a true colossus. He was so tough that it was hard to comprehend how death could've ever got the better of him, but he'd succumbed after a long and courageous fight.

That deftly skilled hardman: a player who could back-heel a half-volley into the goal from the centre spot yet still be picked out by George Best as the hardest player he'd ever faced. A ferocious, barrel-chested leader of men who, when managing Nottingham Forest, ensured Rob White – son of recently deceased former team-mate John White – accompanied him and his team to every single London fixture they played. That was our Mackay: silk and steel, ruthless but caring, charismatic yet unassuming. A giant, inspiration of a man who will be sorely missed.

77

Dumbarton home,
14 March 2015, 3pm

TYNECASTLE rose to acclaim Dave Mackay, first with a stirring round of applause from the 15,631 souls crammed into the ground, and then, heads bowed, in a sombre, deathly silence. His words adorn the first-team dressing room here, 'For as long as I can remember, all I wanted in my life, nothing else, was to play for Hearts, which is my dream team. And to play for Scotland. I had no ambition for anything else. Always Hearts.' In the enduring vacuum of sound – a striking image of Mackay gilding the centre circle – all you felt you could do was pray the great man hadn't suffered too much at the end and silently entreat the players to go out and win this title in a style befitting our fallen hero.

It felt like longer than two weeks since our last game. Partly, I think, because Hearts' matches this season have been a genuine treat and being denied the buzz of matchday leaves a noticeable void. Mainly, though, it was because over in Govan there had been a rash of activity as they'd sought to make up for lost time.

The Friday before we'd been set to play at Raith (prior to them being cup-tied), Rangers finally held their much-heralded EGM and ushered in a new era as Dave King's consortium won control of the Rangers boardroom. Side-stepping the mind-blowing irony of Rangers fans brandishing placards denouncing their plethora of boardroom crooks while simultaneously embracing a guy who'd pled guilty to 41 separate contraventions of the Income Tax Act, this should, ultimately, lead to an upturn in Rangers' fortunes. You'd imagine it's come slightly too late to influence the destiny of the title but should it invigorate the club in the short term those play-offs could get quite spicy.

Fraser Aird must have been happiest of all with King's arrival. Not only was his club now entering a fresh era of unity and boardroom stability, but the figurehead of this new regime also bore an uncanny resemblance to his all-time hero, Ken Barlow.

The woozy optimism and impassioned pledge to return Rangers to their 'rightful place' failed to kick-start an immediate upsurge in form, however. The day following their EGM Rangers could only draw at Cowdenbeath and then repeated the trick at home to QotS three days later. The spectre of those games in hand had, in theory at least, allowed them to retain their sense of menace. But three draws in a row has frittered that away and, once more without us needing to kick a ball, the title edges ever closer.

Four wins now guarantees it and all the tickets for Queen of the South's visit in a fortnight were snaffled as a large, metaphorical circle was scrawled around that date in the calendar. In order for us to ensure the title is winnable that day we required victory at home to Dumbarton, followed with away wins at Raith (on Tuesday night) and Falkirk the following weekend.

Dumbarton were stodgy and wilful, a team built very much in the image of their manager, Ian Murray. They frustrated Hearts early on but most teams do when they come through to Tynecastle and the crowd were quite content to indulge a slightly off-key strike force.

Sow replaced King and played in a three behind Zeefuik and alongside Nicholson and Walker as Hearts went 4-2-3-1 again. Not for the first time it was a position that failed to get the best out of the Swede, especially when he drifted wide and ended up hugging the left touchline.

Yet, even despite failing to properly catch fire, Hearts still created a barrow-load of chances in the first half. First Walker and then Sow both saw shots bounce off the woodwork and Rogers in the Sons' goal was kept hard at it. Half-time came and went and Hearts kept on creating chances. It was obvious Dumbarton were being tenderised like a good fillet steak and it was hard to imagine they'd be stout enough to shut us out for the whole 90.

Sure enough, the breakthrough came on 53 minutes. Sow, who'd got noticeably closer to Zeefuik, blasted the ball in from close range following a corner. Dumbarton had actually done pretty well to keep us at bay as long as they did and, here, only Rangers have shut us out for longer.

As expected, the goal altered the whole tone of the match and Sow found a new gear, petrifying the Sons. Moments after scoring he took off on a lolloping, mazy run, leaving defenders in his wake. He exchanged back-heels in the box with Eckersley before the ball fell to Nicholson who lashed it wide. Hearts were playing with purpose and panache and a double switch on the hour mark served only to cement their domination: Keatings and King replacing Sow and Walker.

Minutes later, King and Wilson recreated Hearts' opening goal of the campaign – at Ibrox – the skipper smashing in a powerful header from the substitute's sweeping corner. The points were in the bag but Hearts had no intention of letting Dumbarton squirm away with a piffling 2-0.

This team simply never lets up and Billy King tore into the opposition box twice in the last three minutes, rifling in a brace of crackers. This brought the season's tally up to 78 and Hearts are now on the cusp of becoming only the third team in the last 20 years to hit 80 goals or more in Scotland's second tier.

Hibernian struck 84 in 1998/99 and Falkirk got 80 four years later. By contrast, Dundee (1997/98) and St Mirren (2005/06) won the title with just 52. Even Gretna, who amassed a remarkable 130 goals in their procession to the Third Division title ten years ago, could muster only 70 on their way to winning the First Division two years later.

Aside from Gretna, Celtic (2003/04 and last season) and Rangers (2002/03 and in League One last season) are the only Scottish teams to have brought up a century of league goals in a season over the past two decades. The fact Hearts are even contenders for such an accolade is amazing considering how mediocre their scoring stats have been in recent seasons.

The 2014/15 Hearts side – having struck at least four goals on ten separate occasions – is sure to be remembered as one of the most lethal in the history of Scotland's second tier. As former striker Kevin Kyle put it, 'When they get a goal, they always look like they're going to kick on and get a few more. They're fearless and they play attractive football. They just want to attack, attack, attack. They don't want to sit and accept a 2-0 or 3-0 win, they try and get as many as they can, which is good to see.'

Kyle's comments appeared in direct response to a piece about Hibernian by David McCarthy in the *Daily Record* after their Scottish Cup quarter-final win over Berwick, 'Boss Alan Stubbs has them playing the best football in the Championship. That might seem daft when Hearts are romping to the title but in the past few months they've been grinding out results until they went goal crazy against Cowdenbeath on Saturday.' Well, these 'past few months' McCarthy speaks of have seen a 5-1 at Dumbarton and a 4-1 at Alloa. And Hearts have now scored 25 more goals than Hibs despite having played one game less, conceding six fewer goals into the bargain. I guess it boils down to what it is you think constitutes the best football.

The side Stubbsy now reckons are 'on the cusp of something' won 2-0 away at Cowdenbeath keeping them 17 points behind us having played that one game more. This result, coupled with Rangers' latest implosion – a draw at home to Livi – promoted Hibernian to the role of our nearest challengers. Winning all their games would see them on 79 while we're currently sitting on 72 and eight points from a title that could now be won even before QotS visit.

Rangers, with new manager Stuart McCall at the helm until the end of the season, can now only reach 78 having drawn their last four matches, dropping eight points into the bargain.

Dave Mackay must be looking down and loving this.

78

Raith Rovers away, 17 March 2015, 7.45pm

THE Hearts machine rolled into Starks Park and executed their now habitual unwavering and incendiary performance. The BBC's Jim Spence tweeted, 'That Hearts team has an energy and fitness level that borders on the manic,' and a 3-1 win had them tantalisingly close to clinching the title.

As he'd intimated beforehand, Robbie switched things around after Saturday: Keatings, King and McHattie replacing Sow, Walker and Eckersley. Hearts lined up in a straightforward 4-4-2 as Keatings paired with Zeefuik up top and King and Nicholson took to the flanks either side of Gomis and Pallardó.

From the outset the game had the feel of an exhibition match to it. Raith are stuck in Championship no-man's land: not quite good enough to fight for a play-off place but not so poor to get sucked into a relegation dog-fight. The lack of any pressing incentive was clearly evident in their performance.

Whereas Hearts, whenever they extended themselves, looked prone to score and the awareness of this seemed to make them a touch sloppy. Keatings, King and Paterson all had McGurn – sporting a quite horrendous salmon-pink goalie kit – scurrying across his six-yard box to keep the league leaders at bay. I watched, patiently, from the back of the Railway stand, close to halfway, and awaited the inevitable breakthrough. Zeefuik, sauntering around like a beach-football Eusebio, was a magnet for the ball and held it up staunchly as opposition defenders bounced off his frame.

A whole tranche of chances had come and gone when, on 26 minutes, McHattie marked his return to the side with a goal. To be honest there was more than a hint of offside about it but given Hearts' unquestionable superiority it seemed daft to quibble over it. Not that Raith's fans saw it quite like that.

They're normally a fairly placid bunch but they had a right strop at the officials which suggests they may have had a case.

But, thankfully, it stood. And not simply because it was a goal for us but the build-up play was just a joy to behold. Ozturk was breezing through the match like a PE teacher joining in with a lesson. Faced by two snarling attackers, he nonchalantly side-stepped both and fed Keatings midway inside his own half. The little striker tenaciously held off the defender before spraying a cross-field pass out to Nicholson. The winger exchanged passes with Zeefuik before playing it back to Keats who'd sprinted upfield to reach the corner of the box. His shot had the sting taken out of it by a defender's half-block and McHattie was in the right place to steer it in.

Before celebrating he glanced, coyly, over to the assistant but, whichever way you cut it, Raith were lucky it had taken Hearts so long to score.

Other than a cross that Christian Nade had not quite been able to get on the end of, the first half had been one-way traffic. Although that never stopped Raith going in at the break level. The right type of delivery into the box can be almost impossible to defend and, from just such a ball, Barr powered a header aggressively into the top corner.

The second half saw Hearts more-or-less set up camp in the Raith half. 'Relentless' was the word used by Richard Gordon on *Sportsound*. Raith, to their credit, were admirably stubborn and got every single player back behind the ball.

A constant reminder that time was passing came with the regular passage of trains juddering by the back of the stand. Although, with Nade and Zeefuik both charging around like a couple of enraged rhinoceros you sometimes weren't quite sure whether it was a train or not.

Our sentimental attachment to often fairly random former players, coupled with two big goals against Hibernian, have led to Nade being viewed with a fair degree of affection. That relationship became somewhat strained just past the hour when McHattie narrowly pipped him to a 50-50 and suffered a deep gash to the knee courtesy of a dangerously high lunge. The Frenchman was sent, chastened, from the pitch, like a big slobbery dog that'd been overly boisterous and knocked a vase over. 'No, Christian: NO! Go to your bed!' Thankfully, McHattie was able to continue after lengthy treatment.

The dismissal had a negligible effect, though, as Hearts were so far in control anyway. The *Sportsound* commentary team of Gordon along with Allan Preston and Derek Ferguson were wetting themselves over the performance of McGurn in the Raith goal. I wasn't that impressed myself. Most of his saves were from shots drilled straight at him and, besides that, he took time-wasting to a whole new level. Mark Oxley seriously needs to get this guy's number. And, if they ever turn fannying about with the ball at goal kicks into an Olympic sport, we're nailed on for gold with this guy in tow. Referee George Salmon didn't exactly help matters either, relying on a stern glower to make his point for him.

In the end it took fresh blood coming off the bench to once more coax three points into the bag. Robbie Neilson has just been flawless with his decision-making this season. On 73 minutes Jamie Walker replaced Keatings and within five minutes he'd put Hearts 2-1 up with his tenth goal of the season (drawing level with Sow and Keatings).

Faced by a crowded defence, Gomis and McHattie combined skilfully via a one-two that saw the defender back-heel the ball into space for the cross. Gomis cleverly pulled the ball back for Walker who curled an absolute peach right into the far corner from the edge of the box.

The singing from both packed away stands suddenly became deafeningly loud. Hearts were marching onwards, their 24th victory from 28 matches imminent and the title within touching distance. The icing on the cake came five minutes later. Walker was gifted a suicidal back-pass and fed the eager King. The winger has been an outstanding performer of late – whether coming off the bench or starting – and he finished well, sparking uproarious celebrations.

For the first time this season the Hearts fans allowed themselves a proper, wholehearted rendition of 'championees' and it felt wonderful, like the ghosts of 1986 no longer haunted our souls and the song could finally be reclaimed, despite all its unhappy connotations.

The win took us 20 points clear of Hibernian while Rangers, also in action this evening, achieved the dubious honour of a hat-trick of draws against the division's bottom three sides (and their fifth on the bounce) with a 2-2 draw at home to Alloa. Already, you listen to Stuart McCall and he sounds worn down and utterly beleaguered, like he's been doing the job all season. That pugnacious swagger has deserted Rangers and they look a sorry bunch. This is a team that have dropped ten points in their last five games compared to a Hearts side that have dropped only nine all season.

Their spectacular fall by the wayside now has them trailing us by a staggering 26 points and on Sunday they travel to Easter Road. Were we to have won at Falkirk the previous day then the title will be ours should Hibernian fail to beat them. Otherwise this moveable feast will shift to a sold-out Hearts v Queen of the South the following Saturday.

Regarding this, Robbie Neilson remarked, 'I'd like us to win the title in front of our own fans with a victory. We haven't needed any favours off anybody this season, and we don't want anyone doing us a favour now. However, we're under no illusions as to how difficult the Falkirk game will be.'

Either way, that fat lady is now gargling backstage.

79

Falkirk away,
21 March 2015, 3pm

THROUGHOUT last summer, a good number of Rangers fans had been adamant the Championship would be signed, sealed and delivered by the end of March. Well, thanks to their club's 2-0 victory over Hibernian at Easter Road this prediction came true. That result, in conjunction with Hearts' defeat of Falkirk the previous day, meant our effervescent powerhouse of a side were declared champions. So, come 2 May, it will be maroon and white ribbons adorning the very same piece of silverware the incomparable Dave Mackay held aloft when Hearts won the old First Division in 1958.

Before the evolution of television's symbiotic relationship with football and the scattergun approach to fixture rearrangement, our visit to Falkirk would have taken on a radically altered guise. It would have been your classic transistor radio game and we'd all have had half an ear on events at Easter Road. Like an even more enjoyable version of the Kris Boyd game there on the final day of last season.

Not that the 24-hour delay detracted anything from a weekend where our supremacy was finally rubber-stamped. After Hearts' authoritative dissection of a blunt Falkirk side it was win-win for us. A Hibernian victory would've afforded us the chance to clinch the title under our own volition, at home, in front of a bumper, sell-out crowd while any other outcome and the league title was officially ours. I mean, what's not to like? Plus, with the latter, we'd get the added bonus of watching habitual bed-wetters Hibernian get spooked as Rangers' big sweaty foreheads suddenly loomed large in the rear-view mirror.

Certainly, against Falkirk, we were all having way too much fun basking in the warm spring sunshine, watching the goals fly in, to worry too much about the subtle detail of our imminent anointment. And, as our players were applauded off, after a resounding 3-0 win, they took a bow as champions in all but name.

Hearts came into the match absolutely flying, having notched seven wins on the bounce since losing to the Bairns in January. Of that defeat Robbie said, 'It took the pressure off us. I felt that in the weeks building up to that Falkirk game when we got beaten, there was a tension in the team. Every time we spoke to the press or to the fans it was: can we go through the season unbeaten? It was a good thing. You never like to lose games but it took that away.'

Admiral Neilson, for his first managerial appointment, has delivered a near-faultless masterclass, imposing a culture and a philosophy that has been willingly embraced by a ferociously hungry side, 'There are targets we can try to get to that we've spoken to the players about. But also there's the motivation of our own pride. We should be winning games, we shouldn't be letting teams score against us.' And again, 'Our mindset is that we must win every game, a club of this stature must not accept less.'

Well, Hearts' win at Falkirk extended their unbeaten away record in the league to 17 matches, dating back to last March at Rugby Park – equalling their record of nine successive away league wins into the bargain. And Hearts' goalscoring ratio is officially now the best in all the senior leagues in the UK, standing at 2.89 goals per game. The next highest, incidentally, is Bournemouth with 2.08.

After making three changes for the midweek trip to Starks Park, Hearts switched back, more or less, to the same line-up we'd seen last Saturday against Dumbarton, except Nicholson – who rarely if ever starts games on plastic – was replaced by King.

Hearts took a while to gain a foothold in the game; a start Robbie attributed to them adjusting to an unfamiliar playing surface. Even so, Falkirk never did enough to present themselves as any sort of a threat. The focal point of their attack – Rory Loy – was absent and, as a result, they lacked the necessary firepower to take advantage of any half-chances that came their way.

Despite the slow start, Hearts wouldn't be Hearts without that constant undercurrent of menace and, on the half-hour mark, they picked Falkirk apart. Sow strutted elegantly down the left-hand side in a manner reminiscent of former Brazilian captain, Socrates, and pulled the ball back into the middle. Walker reacted quickest and slid into a shot that ricocheted high into the net off MacDonald's leg. The goal nosed Jamie ahead as Hearts' top league scorer with 11 and the near-on 4,000 away fans needed no further invitation to start serenading the runaway league leaders with a few rounds of 'championees'.

Jamma probably felt he could have dealt better with the strike but moments earlier he'd stood strong and denied Zeefuik as the big man rumbled through for a one on one and then, on 44 minutes, our old keeper made a quite breathtaking save from Sow, flicking the ball past from point-blank range, so any criticism levelled at him would've been harsh.

After the break Jamma received another warm welcome as he trotted over to the North Stand goal but other than a brisk handclap and a boyish grin he pretty much kept himself to himself. You wondered whether such diffidence was at the behest of his manager. If so, you couldn't really blame Houstie. The former Dundee United manager must still have nightmares about Rudi Skacel – wearing that 51 shirt – applauding the home fans from the edge of the centre circle while his United colleagues were fighting desperately to peg back a two-goal deficit.

Barely a minute in and Jamma was once more staring through the back of the net at the travelling support – forced as he was to dig the ball out having seen his side fall two behind. Eckersley came bombing down the left before linking cleverly with Walker. The ball fell to the feet of Zeefuik who thrashed it in almost disdainfully, as if putting his name to such an elementary finish physically pained him.

The word is that Groningen are looking for £300,000 to make the big man's move permanent. Hard to know if our budget will stretch that far. Last summer, by all accounts, Craig Levein devised a five-year strategy based on a recruitment policy representing economic value. As Robbie Neilson puts it, 'We must always remember the situation we got into and never get into that situation again. We want to make sure we live within our means. There are a lot of clubs out there who helped us when we were struggling, whether it be fundraising or other means of support. We must be sure we're respectful of where we are and where we've been.'

Yet again, Hearts were demonstrating that they are way too good for the division. That blend of ruthlessness, stamina and commitment overwhelmed their opponents. In the first meeting here, back in November, Falkirk grabbed the initiative at 2-0 down with a double substitution at the start of the second half. Today, they tried the same trick, but the switch barely registered, and it was another substitution – from the visitors – that put the seal on the victory and gave Hearts their 84th league goal of this epic, record-toppling season.

Keatings replaced King with ten to go and with his first involvement the bearded marksman pulled level with Walker in the scoring charts. He raced on to a routine ball floated over the top from Pallardó, cleverly evading offside. Jamma initially rushed out then, thinking better of it, hesitated for a fatal split-second and dithered in no-man's land. Keats eyed him pitilessly as a mongoose would a cobra before clipping the ball beyond him and ducking behind the goal to take the acclaim of the fans who'd spilled out of their north stand seats.

It's no coincidence that 25 of our 90 goals in all competitions have come in the closing 15 minutes of games. Neilson appears to have tailored fitness so that his side finishes matches strongly and it seems like every week one or other of our substitutes plays a starring role. The players piled over to celebrate number three, C-Patz – his latest barnet giving him the look of a young Clark Gable – giving it even more beans than usual.

So, by 3pm on Sunday 22 March, the title was officially ours and has never been won this early. Right at the top of his post-match interview at Easter Road, Stuart McCall made a point of offering Hearts his sincerest congratulations. It would be a trend that extended throughout the division as the official Twitter feeds of every other club followed suit. Every other club bar one: Hibernian. Additionally, manager Alan Stubbs stubbornly ignored Hearts' achievement during his interview, preferring to congratulate Robbie by phone. If anything, their smouldering resentment topped the whole weekend off.

After the Falkirk game Levein tweeted, 'We were v good today. Well done Robbie, Stevie and the boys. Great time to be a Jambo. Nothing but good news at the moment and more on the way.'

And then, the following afternoon, when the title was officially confirmed he nailed it, 'Ann Budge OBE...Over Before Easter.'

80

Queen of the South home, 28 March 2015, 3pm

I T had been a momentous week of pure, unabashed merriment leading up to this game. All we were missing was a focal point for the celebrations. Last weekend, we'd felt slightly detached from the physical act of clinching the title and it had been hard to comprehend we'd just won it like that. You had these blurry images, filmed on someone's phone, of the players dousing Craig Levein in champagne, and then little snippets of a sing-song in the Tynie Arms that the morally upstanding *Daily Record* had invited readers to take offence to but, beyond that, there'd been nothing tangible to show for it. The BBC Scottish Football home page went even further in the immediate aftermath, giving lead billing to Rangers' win at Easter Road.

Well, all that changed here, today. From around lunchtime there was a carnival atmosphere in and around Gorgie and Tynecastle felt like those gala Sundays back in 1998, 2006 and 2012 when the Scottish Cup was paraded to a packed house. The only difference with today was that the festivities would also include a game.

The title may have been in the bag but Neilson is a hard taskmaster. I half-expected to see an inadvertent drop-off in players' effort and attention levels but our sights have been set on the twin targets of 100 goals and 99 points and Hearts were unapologetically thorough throughout.

Two of our new signings to have made the greatest impact this year – Sow and Ozturk – settled the contest with a goal in each half as an unchanged Hearts powered their way to the points. Victory number 26 (from 30 games), coupled with Hibernian's 2-1 reversal in Kirkcaldy, hoisted us a whopping 26 points clear of our city rivals, with a goal difference +40 better off – having scored 30 more goals and conceded ten less.

Early on here last season we faced Queen of the South in the League Cup and I'd made the point that the half-empty ground, echoing with the audible shouts of players, could be a taster of what to expect should we drop down a division. Well, in the style of Chandler Bing, could I *be* any more wrong?

Today, Tynecastle was jam-packed, swelled to the rafters with 16,855 punters craning to catch a glimpse of the 2015 champions as they made their triumphant entrance courtesy of a guard of honour from the Doonhamers. The streams of ticker tape and copious balloons were a wonderfully apt reminder of how far we've come in one calendar year.

For, a year ago this weekend – in administration and in dire need of a quick resolution from Vilnius to stave off imminent liquidation – Tynecastle was also consumed with an air of celebratory abandon. Except, that day, it emanated from the away end. Or, to be more precise, it had initially emanated from the away end. Within ten minutes those inflatable palm trees had brewers' droop and those paper hats been angrily scrunched up and cast aside. The party had been gatecrashed; commandeered by the hosts.

And, like that game a year ago, six minutes was as long as it took the home side to breach their opponents' goal. Osman Sow joined Keats and Walker on 11 with a strike that epitomised that combustible blend of artistry, brains and brawn that make him so valuable a player to us. Taking a ball from King, midway inside the opposition half, he executed a slick drag-back turn and bore down on goal. His angled run opened up the goal and from the left edge of the penalty box he jabbed a precise, low drive into the far corner sending the thronging masses berserk.

With a vice-like grip on the tempo and flow Hearts radiated confidence. It looked like Sow had grabbed his and Hearts' second on 43 minutes as he fashioned the deftest of flicks from a Walker cross, but Clark pulled off an excellent stop to ensure the scoring was limited to one at the break.

Back in August, as a support, we'd all have kittens each time Alexander passed the ball to a team-mate while an opponent lurked in close proximity. 'Man on!' we'd bellow and shake our collective heads in consternation at the unnecessary risk being taken. It's funny, no one really bats an eyelid now. It's become the norm. It's automatically assumed that the recipient will have enough about them to retain possession and, if not, Alexander will get the ball back sharpish and no doubt present someone else with an equally dicey pass.

Throughout all levels and age-groups, this is how we now play; we're brave on the ball. Whether or not we'll flirt quite so openly with danger next season as we seek to build play, will remain to be seen. It may take some time to find our feet again in the big league but you'd imagine the club will do its level best to remain true to its principles; footballing and otherwise.

But, certainly, some things will change. With McKay definitely away and a permanent deal for Zeefuik looking less and less likely, Neilson reckons new players will come in, 'We do need four, maybe five possibly...I know what I want. There's contact been made and now we're waiting to see.' But the nucleus will remain the same and it's not difficult to see why. Winning the division at a canter is not something to be taken lightly and top six has to be the minimum target for next season. Personally, I look at the SPL and, out-with Celtic and Aberdeen, don't see many sides capable of replicating our run of results, had it been them down here instead of us.

In the second 45 Hearts persevered with their expansive, passing game. At around the halfway point Walker was in full flight only to be dumped on the seat of his pants 35 yards from goal. He wasn't even back on his feet before the crowd were summoning the ever-popular Ozturk to the head of the queue for the set piece.

Were this a documentary I'd be playing a selection of Alan Stubbs's post-derby comments from October, while [in slow motion], Ozturk set the ball down and prepared his short run-up, 'Well, when you look at the strike I don't think he'll ever score a goal like that again…The lad will hit another 999 shots and none of them will be on target…It's one of them freak strikes that's gone in, unfortunately.' Then [back to normal speed], boosh, 2-0! Have that. Granted, the big man's effort took a fairly meaty deflection off the wall but, y'know (as Stubbsy is wont to say), it's still the fourth time this season the big man has found the net from beyond the 30-yard mark.

The clock ran down as Queens became the latest in a long line of sides to play second fiddle to this well-oiled Hearts machine and by the time the whistle went all that was left was for them to congratulate the champions and vacate the pitch. Of all the play-off candidates, a good number of Hearts fans cling to the hope that it's Queens who prevail and that sense of goodwill appears mutual. Before the game their chairman, Billy Hewitson, presented Ann Budge with a gift and offered his heartfelt congratulations, 'Everyone at Queen of the South would like to take this opportunity to congratulate Heart of Midlothian, worthy winners of the league this season. Good luck in next season's Premiership. Maybe we'll see you there.' Classy club.

As the players disappeared up the tunnel for a few moments to compose themselves and get into their special commemorative T-shirts, Craig Levein and Ann Budge entered the field of play along with the rest of the board of directors to a truly stirring ovation. The meticulous Levein has found the role of a lifetime as director of football at Hearts and the role appears to suit him perfectly. As Hearts fans it's simply a case of being grateful both he and Budge are at the helm of our wonderful club, guiding its future with such care, diligence and clarity of vision.

And, finally, with 'Champions 15' emblazoned across their backs, the players re-entered the fray to a tumultuous, deafening ovation and completed an unrushed lap of honour as the throngs applauded and photographed and filmed their every antic.

As midweek beckoned and images of title festivities slowly disappeared from the back pages, Hearts again hit the headlines, this time with the announcement of an innovative new partnership with the charity Save the Children.

Next season, the Tynecastle club will become the first in the UK to carry the logo of a national charity on home and away kits (although Aston Villa were sponsored by a local hospice, Acorns, during the 2008/09 season). The tie-up, which sees a seven-figure deal funded through philanthropy – split evenly between the charity and Hearts – will last for three years. Budge commented, 'Through their enormous generosity they have agreed to provide funds at a level which more than removes the need for a commercial shirt sponsor…these business people believe that we are promoting true family values and they want to help.'

While a few people couldn't help speculating as to the identity of these mysterious benefactors, what is in no doubt is that the seven-figure sum will secure investment for Hearts on a par with that of Scotland's top sides. The aim appears to be to use the funds to repair key infrastructure at Tynecastle stadium and strengthen the academy programme.

Not so long ago we were a model example of how not to run a football club and, as Ann Budge put it, were truly broken when she took over. From a club struggling to get anything right, we now seem to be one that can do no wrong. Between this and being the first football team in Scotland to adopt the living wage, we're now an exemplary model of a community football club. The road to redemption continues unabated.

81

Rangers away, 5 April 2015, 12.15pm

ELEVEN weeks have passed since these sides' aborted attempt at fulfilling this fixture back in January. And, during the intervening period, both have enjoyed a considerable upturn in fortunes. For Hearts, this has seen them romp to the title with seven games still to go while Rangers look to have resolved their ongoing ownership issues and finally appointed a coach who knows where the training bibs are kept. In some ways the performance of each team reflected this: a mentally weary and rather jaded looking Hearts edged out 2-1 by a committed and well-organised Rangers.

In the days leading up to the game, beefy Darren McGregor addressed those disparaging comments about Hearts that have plagued him since last November, 'I need to take my hat off to them. From my point of view they had done great up until that point and it was interesting for me to see if we'd gotten to a point behind them to see how they would have coped.' Well, watching your side implode was certainly 'interesting' for us, Darren.

He went on, 'Obviously that never happened and I've been forced to eat my words because we drew against Alloa and they've kicked on. Sometimes these things come back to bite you. I've nothing but praise for the way Hearts have carried themselves this season and unfortunately we've been poor.'

Poor on the pitch, even poorer off it as Rangers this week announced losses of £2.89m for the previous six-month period. A state of affairs described as 'disappointing' by interim chairman Paul Murray. You'd imagine of equal disappointment for Murray and his cohorts was uncovering that clause in the loan deal with Newcastle United stipulating that they're due the Geordies £500,000 in the event of gaining promotion.

I mean, where do you even begin with that? The prize for second place is £342,000 so the best case scenario still sees them £158,000 down on the deal and for what, exactly? Haris Vučkić has featured regularly and looks handy enough at this level but beyond that? Remie Streete played the first 43 minutes when Raith Rovers emptied them out of the Scottish Cup, Kevin Mbaba has been seen strutting his stuff in the Development League and the other two – Shane Ferguson and Gael Bigirimana – are injured and yet to leave England. What a staggeringly inept piece of business: Rangers are essentially paying the wages of two crocked Newcastle players who seem unlikely to ever kick a ball for them and were signed without even a hint of a medical. As Tom English put it on *Sportsound*, 'Sounds like another example of Mike Ashley feathering his own nest at Rangers' expense.'

Drenched in baking sunshine, balloons and beach balls bobbing around, the singing was incessant. 'Down with the Hibees, you're staying down with the Hibees', 'We're only here for the party' and 'Fuck you Rangers the Hearts have won the league' rang out, seeming to boom around the whole stadium. The hosts had zero comeback and shuffled wearily from foot to foot, making eye contact despite themselves and then half-staring, bleary-eyed, into the middle distance.

Stuart McCall at least seems determined to fast-track a modicum of class and decorum into the new Ibrox regime, and it was at his behest that the Rangers players formed a guard of honour for the champions. Our cheering was almost completely drowned out – discounting the odd smattering of home applause, the champions emerged to an ear-splitting crescendo of whistling and booing. 'Bring it on' was my take on our reception. The coruscating antipathy felt like a badge of honour, revealing the true extent to which our supremacy has angered the blood through here.

Furthermore, lording it over the hosts felt like a measure of payback against this club's previous incarnation, since plenty of baggage accompanies the original organisation: the Andy Davies flag, the Gerry Evans four-card debacle, that whirring rolodex of arrogance, brutality and condescension.

The away end was heaving. There were clearly way too many Hearts fans for the designated number of seats. I'm guessing the reprinting of tickets had led to duplicates entering circulation. In the packed aisle-way to my side I overheard a crimson-faced senior steward informing a colleague that a fair few Hearts fans would need to be thrown out before the overspill could be cleared. Aye, good luck with that. It looked to me like everyone was having *way* too much fun to do anything that might warrant ejection.

Sandy Jardine, as he'd done back in August, momentarily brought both sets of supporters together as pictures of the grand unveiling of his commemorative bust were beamed across the stadium. Additionally, as the anniversary of his passing approaches, there was also an excellent piece about the great man in the match programme – showing him in his Hearts strip – which was a lovely touch.

Later, on the 22-minute mark, the fans would once again be united, this time with a minute's applause for Shaun Cole, the British soldier who'd attended Tynecastle High School and tragically died in Miami last week.

If the Rangers fans had been muted and a tad crestfallen as the ground was slowly filling to a healthy 40,521, they became hugely animated once the game kicked off. Their side was lively and driven, acting like they'd all been injected with monkey hormones in the tunnel. The calibre of performance that would be needed from us in order to live with the hosts immediately became apparent. Yet, from the off, we appeared destined to fall short. Instead of being bright and alert in possession – as Rangers pressed us high up the pitch – we were sluggish and persisted with a slow, laborious and at times slovenly build-up. We looked decidedly lethargic while Rangers, with admittedly far more at stake than us, were keen to play us at our own game.

We went again with one of Robbie Neilson's favoured formations – 4-2-3-1 – and, apart from Nicholson replacing King, the only other switch from last weekend saw McHattie come in for Eckersley. During last Saturday's lap of honour, the Englishman had tossed his boots into the crowd, a gesture interpreted by some as a sign he wouldn't be with us next year. Sure enough, pre-match, Robbie confirmed this was, indeed, the case and the likeable lad isn't to be offered a new deal.

As with Zeefuik, all we can do is trust the judgement of our club as regards personnel and budgets. Personally, I rate Eckersley and would rather he stayed on, but I've no insight into his contractual demands – assuming they're even the reason he's not getting a deal. I'm only guessing but would imagine Hearts feel that by turning their attention to the more-than-capable McHattie, funds would then be freed up for use elsewhere. Time will tell on that one, but I thought we missed the ever-reliable Eck at Ibrox, especially as McHattie looked ill at ease until subbed late on.

Rangers were rampant in the early stages and it came as no surprise to see them surge into the lead, just shy of the half-hour. Lee Wallace broke down the left and his pull-back was tucked in by Kenny Miller – the former Scotland striker celebrating his goal like a braying donkey gambolling and cavorting along Blackpool beach. The build-up to the goal had been most notable for referee, Bobby Madden, playing a clever advantage; waving play on after Pallardó had decked McCulloch.

Falling behind was the trigger for Hearts to switch to a 4-4-2. It was one thing playing Sow as a left-sided attacker away to Falkirk and at home against Dumbarton and Queen of the South, but doing so here was a different matter altogether. All the system did, in those opening thirty-odd minutes, was marginalise the Swede and accentuate lone-striker Zeefuik's lack of mobility.

While Madden should be commended for his clever use of the advantage rule during the prelude to Miller's goal, immediately following it he denied Hearts the right to profit in the same manner. Zeefuik was tugged back, 35 yards from goal, before the ball ran through for Walker who stuck it in the net. Yet, infuriatingly, Madden brought play back for the free kick. Stephen Craigan was quick to address this inconsistency at half-time, 'Only Bobby Madden can answer why he's done that – that's a big call.'

Ozturk took his customary two-step run-up before leathering a dipping ball over the wall. However, Bell had seen his attempt all the way and punched it out as far as Nicholson on the left edge of the box.

The Hearts number 11 controlled the ball and then fizzed in a great shot that whistled past the far post with only inches to spare. The switch to two up top meant Hearts were offering more of a threat and Walker half-hit a shot that Bell got down to and smuggled around the post.

That said, Gomis and Pallardó seemed to be operating on completely different wavelengths. That big Ibrox pitch swallowed them up and both were pale shadows of their usual selves. Before today, Pallardó had seemed immune to dips in form but, here, we were incoherent and slapdash in areas of the pitch where we're normally switched on and sure-footed.

Seven minutes from half-time the ball found its way out to Vučkić on the right for Rangers. The Graeme Sharp lookalike is all left foot but McHattie – instead of ushering the Slovenian down the outside – allowed him to shift inside with devastating consequences. The ball was swerved unerringly past Alexander's outstretched fingertips and into the corner for number two.

For a second time the stadium absolutely exploded with passion and fervour and Vučkić, along with Nicky Clark, made sure their goal celebrations carried them right down in front of the travelling fans – turning and openly inciting a support that was more than happy to wave back and applaud them sarcastically. Well-taken goal chaps. Maybe you'll get another one like that in the play-offs, eh?

You then had the curious spectacle of both sets of supporters bellowing 'so fucking easy' at each other across the barricades of stewards and police. Both had valid points, I guess: going two up inside 40 minutes is suggestive of an easy battle, however the war was done and dusted weeks ago.

Rangers' second goal had actually come against the run of play and from the restart Hearts continued to try and make headway with their re-modified shape. On 44 minutes, Madden showed he wasn't completely averse to playing advantage for Hearts when Sow got his head to the ball a nanosecond before McCulloch's flailing elbow pole-axed him. Annoyingly, Madden's enlightened officiating didn't extend to awarding Hearts a penalty as Wallace seemed to catch Walker just as he got a shot away.

This was all instantly forgotten in the ensuing bedlam as Madden unexpectedly and belatedly brandished the tenth red card of McCulloch's career. The Rangers captain would pop up, briefly, post-match, to be asked about his ordering off, 'No intent whatsoever, I can say that honestly. Yes, I've apologised to my team-mates, feel like I've let them down.'

BT's anchor, Darrell Currie, had then tried to draw some spurious parallel with McCulloch's conduct and that of Steven Gerrard last month. The Liverpool captain offered a dignified and unqualified apology in the immediate aftermath of his sending off against Manchester United the very same Sunday our title was confirmed at Easter Road. However

Currie's comparison contained the tiniest of flaws: the Rangers captain hadn't actually admitted any wrongdoing!

At half-time Mikey Stewart's eyes were nearly popping out of his head, 'Unacceptable! He could've caused Sow serious damage.' It was perhaps the only time fellow pundit Gary Locke deigned even to glance in Stewart's direction. Unsurprisingly, after Mikey's numerous caustic, derogatory observations regarding Locke and Hearts last season, relations between the two remained decidedly frosty throughout.

Rangers took an eternity to re-emerge for the second half and Neilson could be seen querying the length of the delay with the fourth official. Eventually, though, Stuart McCall's red nose could be seen bobbing up and down in the darkened tunnel, lit up like someone was playing a giant-sized version of the board game Operation.

The story of the second half was Hearts doing their utmost to break down an unyielding and uncompromising Rangers defence. Robbie tried everything within his power to come up with ways to achieve this, unafraid to re-jig systems and personnel.

After 15 minutes of fruitless attacking, King replaced Gomis and Hearts, at times, played virtually 4-1-5. Notwithstanding the threat from Rangers' occasional, sporadic breakaways, Hearts continually tried to piece together sequences of attacks despite a fair number of their personnel having dropped below their normal level of performance.

Hearts' cause was made all the tougher by the McCall factor imbuing his charges with added bite. Rangers were dogged and resolute in defence and you'd have to say – on this showing, at least – they'd be tough adversaries next season, were that £500k to need to change hands. They even had Cammy Bell booked for time-wasting, such was their wanton desire to see the win out at all costs.

With 15 minutes to go Neilson replaced McHattie with Keatings and Hearts ended up playing more or less a 3-1-6 formation. With all these attackers jostling for the ball in the box, something had to give and Rangers' stubborn resistance was finally broken on 83 minutes. Ozturk tossed one into the mixer and Zeefuik bundled in his tenth of the season after Sow's header had been saved.

In many ways our season has been defined by late goals with 26 of our 93 in all competitions coming in the final 15 minutes. Yet here, despite there still being seven minutes plus stoppage time on the clock, it never felt like a leveller was on the cards. Not only were Rangers' players heroically blocking shots as if their lives depended upon it but Hearts, for all their second-half slog, had been unable to get in behind Rangers often enough to hurt them. And, the few times they did, their crossing invariably left a lot to be desired.

Perhaps a slight drop-off was inevitable once the title was secured. Certainly, far better sides than ours have eased off the gas once that little letter C prefixed their name at the top of the table. All season long the players have pushed themselves to the very limits of endurance, thriving on the need to set and then achieve targets. Suddenly, no serious targets are left to be attained and, facing highly motivated, relatively even-matched opponents, any drop-off, however slight, had to impact proceedings.

The sheer anti-climax of the whole occasion created a flatness. Yet it needn't have done. Notwithstanding the title win, we only need recall events of exactly one year ago to the day – 5 April 2014 – to rejoice, irrespective of that no-show at Ibrox. For, that day, our relegation was finally confirmed. We may have won 4-2 at Firhill but the games had run out and we faced a horribly uncertain future both on and off the pitch. So to be where we are now is outstandingly good going.

I thought Robbie's words, post-match, were perfect, 'It was a difficult day for us but you have to look at the big picture. We're sitting 23 points clear and it's been a wonderful season. I was speaking to the players at the end and told them that when you walk out there today you walk out with your chest out because you're a champion. It doesn't matter about what happens today. It matters about the whole season and the whole season's been fantastic.'

Ibrox Loyal saw things differently and after the game tweeted, 'Today just proved: Hearts won the league because Rangers were mismanaged. McCall in from the start we'd of [sic] walked it.' Far be it from me to accuse them of perhaps reading a little too much into a 2-1 win against a side with nothing left to play for. And, besides, these guys don't call themselves 'loyal' for nothing.

As it happens not all Rangers fans share that begrudging attitude and selective myopia. At full time, as the home support unhurriedly vacated the premises and we were held back to ensure we wouldn't get attacked again, the odd bear poked their head over the parapet of the upper Broomloan and applauded down at us. A genuinely sporting touch. The rest either made a beeline for the exit or lurched over the edge, spraying us liberally with saliva and/or insults. Each and every one of the latter were greeted like long-lost friends; mockingly cheered by the enthralled audience amassed below.

Final words go to Craig Levein via Twitter as, like Robbie, he did his utmost to maintain a sense of perspective and lighten the mood, 'Great performance…by our fans. We didn't reach our normal high standards on the pitch today but will be better on Wed I'm sure.'

82

Alloa home,
8 April 2015, 19.45pm

ROBBIE Neilson freshened up his side for the visit of Alloa, making a total of seven changes. In goal, Jack Hamilton got the nod. Ahead of him, Paterson kept his place as did Wilson, who was partnered by McKay, and Eckersley replaced McHattie. *Kickback* man of the match Kenny Anderson sat alongside Gomis in central midfield with Nicholson and King to either side while, up front, Keatings linked up with El Hassnaoui.

Last weekend, a rolled-up newspaper in the form of Mark Burchill's Livi swatted the Wasps aside in the Petrofac Cup Final. And, even though, additionally, they came into tonight's game perilously close to the foot of the table, it never stopped our visitors becoming the third side in succession to applaud us on to the pitch. Protocol decrees that only the team you face directly after being crowned champions are beholden to carry out such an act, so it really was very generous of Danny Lennon's team.

Unsurprisingly, after such extensive tinkering, we saw a fragmented opening to the game as the players took a little while to become accustomed to each other. Also, I'd heard through the grapevine that as late as 6.30pm Danny Wilson had been unsure of his place while Robbie had pondered a few alternatives. None of which helped quell the disjointed feel to the game.

In truth, the game was rather turgid, sitting comfortably within that pantheon of nondescript dead rubbers from seasons gone by. A game where you could make out players' shouts and heard barely a peep from the 15,156 crowd. The misfiring hosts dug deep to try to reconnect with the work ethic and technical aplomb that had struggled to emerge at Ibrox.

It took until the 22nd minute, and another rapturous minute's applause for Shaun Cole, for people to perk up and for the ground to become a little more enlivened. In a season in which a resurgent Hearts have been irrepressible, the heady optimism and success have been tinged with a deep and lasting sadness. It's been full of joy but also heartache. From the opening day at Ibrox and the official unveiling of the Sandy Jardine stand to the indescribably sad memorials marking the 100-year anniversary of the outbreak of the Great War to the passing of Dave Mackay. This contrast was never more starkly illustrated than by the full squad attending the funeral of ticket office worker Elaine Spence a matter of hours after being officially crowned champions. Yet, throughout the revelry and the sorrow, the club's soul has been recovered from the detritus of the Romanov regime.

The half was drawing to a close and, other than Keatings slamming a shot against the upright after Wilson had hit the byline, we'd never really looked like piercing an industrious yet rudderless Alloa. Then, on 42 minutes, C-Patz broke the deadlock in spectacular style. Moments earlier, a heavy knock had seen the big man cast a distressed glance over at the dugout. But, when the ball came to him, wide right, he sidled inside and hoofed a 30-yarder with his left foot that skimmed off a defender as it blazed in.

If the first half been very much Hearts-lite as the players took time to gel, normal service was resumed in the second: that pleasing recipe of athleticism and power mixed with exuberance, pace and hunger. Three minutes after the restart Keatings pinged in an enticing corner and Wilson leaped commandingly to head number two.

The main difference from the first half was the briskness with which Hearts were winning the ball back from Alloa and this urgency set the tone for a rapid tempo, underpinning all their good work. Anderson, in particular, stuck tenaciously to his task and grew into the game the longer it went on. On 65 minutes Pallardó appeared on the touchline and it would've been easy for Robbie to have hooked the man from Holland but, instead, it was Gomis that gave way.

Pallardó had only been on the pitch a matter of minutes when he played a hand in Hearts' third and, arguably, best goal. The Spaniard was tackled stoutly on the edge of the box and with half-formulated appeals for a foul suspended mid-syllable, El Hassnaoui hit home a blurring piledriver before being mobbed by his team-mates.

A thoughtful gesture from the coaching staff saw McKay's number flash up with 15 minutes to go. And the big centre-half deserved every second of the generous standing ovation he received. The housewives' favourite always gave his all and had lived the dream playing for his boyhood club.

The three goals increased our tally in the league to 90, setting a target of ten in four games for the century. And in the end, despite Keatings and El Hass not really sparking as a double act, we could quite easily have scored more than these three unanswered goals. Not least when King was bowled over in the box and Andrew Dallas put his whistle to his lips but then thought better of it.

Meanwhile, over in Dumbarton, Hibernian survived a scare to edge the Sons 2-1 and put an end to their three-game losing streak. Next up for them, a visit from the champions.

83

Hibernian away,
12 April 2015, 2.15pm

THE portents weren't great for Hibernian going into this fourth and final derby of the season. They'd lost three of their last four league games and, historically, had only recorded one league win at home in April in eight years – versus St Mirren in 2008. Yet, despite all this, and the fact that next season might very well afford them another crack at the Buddies, they were way too good for a muddled, fatigued Hearts side.

Flat, spent Hearts were out-thought and out-fought by a Hibernian team that savoured every last second of their 2-0 victory. The season now can't end soon enough for a Hearts side which has lost its sparkle and edge. And, while a second, insipid showing in eight days doesn't come even close to overshadowing what has been an epic, triumphant season, there's no escaping how badly Hearts took this defeat. Adam Eckersley's four-word tweet summed up the mood in the camp, 'Awful day, awful performance.'

Our successful run to the title began last August with a double-header against Rangers and Hibernian. Both were sent packing by a breezy, innovative Hearts side that seemingly had all the answers. Fast forward eight months to the dying embers of the season and another pair of Sundays spent jousting with our two closest rivals reveals a drained and stuttering collection of individuals, scurrying around trying to recall what their secret was. Hesitant, tippy-tappy football led them up a succession of blind alleys where a lurking Hibernian mugged them at every turn.

At Ibrox, Robbie had had little choice but to change his system around the half-hour mark and he was compelled to do the same here. All the big guns returned and Robbie initially set them up as a 3-5-2/3-4-1-2 – following in the footsteps of Stuart McCall who'd tried a similar formation here three weeks previously. Who knows, perhaps Robbie looked at that and thought, well if I can't tinker with the system and go like for like when I'm 26 clear with four games to go then when can I exactly?

The problem was that the players appeared criminally under-prepared to play that way. All season long the coaching staff have drilled the players meticulously for matches with an attention to detail bordering on the mildly obsessive. However, as the season draws to a close, a slight hint of slackness has crept in.

The start against Alloa was disordered, with the final selection apparently still under deliberation until an hour or so before kick-off. Here, the players had from Thursday to become accustomed to a brand-new system against arguably our toughest opponents. Robbie gave it 37 shambolic minutes before mercifully reverting back to 4-2-3-1 and overseeing an improvement of sorts.

Still, the damage had been done. McHattie had looked befuddled in his role as left-sided centre-half and dawdled, playing Cummings onside for his opener on 30 minutes. The number three was hauled off not long after to be replaced by Nicholson.

If Robbie wanted to play that way at such short notice, surely including a recognised centre-half in Brad McKay would have made more sense? And, instead of hanging McHattie out to dry in that unfamiliar role, why not just switch over the left-footed Wilson? He could then have used McHattie as a wing-back – a role that would actually really suit him. Any argument against playing McKay on the grounds that he's on his way cuts little ice, too, given we had Eckersley in the side – dying a thousand deaths at wing-back.

Hibernian, thus, were gifted the initiative and by half-time we were fortunate to be only one down. Having gone ahead, the Hibernian fans were keen to spin the narrative of the occasion as some sort of warped mirror image of last season's relegation derby, stealing our 'oh this is some fucking party' line. The inference was tenuous to say the least. I mean, it wasn't as if we'd all arrived at the home of our rivals with the sole intention of revelling in their demise; first and foremost we'd come to salute the league champions. Furthermore, for the result to share even a hint of last season's piquancy, we'd somehow need to shed 20-odd points and blow promotion. Good try, though.

But, fair play to them and their side. Despite it looking as if referee Kevin Clancy had accidentally discharged his vanishing spray into the main and Famous Five stands, their East Stand was packed out and noisy and I guess there would have been a sense of injustice had Hibernian not registered at least one derby win this season.

There's a creeping suspicion that these last two big games have, to a degree, seen us found out. This stems from the fact that in both matches the opposition sussed out how best to combat us. While it's difficult to argue that against the so-called better sides this season our passing game has faltered, surely of at least equal significance here is the number of Hearts players who have reverted to end-of-season mode.

Even so, you'd imagine Robbie's plans for next season will take heed of the lessons of all four derbies. From the outside his remit would seem pretty clear: formulate a more coherent Plan B so that when teams work out how to scupper our short-range, passing game we're not left aimlessly hoofing the ball to no one; and scout new recruits who constitute an upgrade on existing key players and will thus be better equipped to implement the passing style we've seemingly set our heart on.

For me, most heartening of all has been our mental fortitude. This, above all else, will stand us in good stead next season when times inevitably get tough. This year that durability ensured our focus was retained when it mattered most, enabling us to hoover up the points week in, week out. This, in many ways, set us apart from our city rivals, held back as they were by that perennial flakiness. That, and a dreadfully fickle home support.

Over in Gorgie, the fans have been made to feel valued and, accordingly, have backed their club to the hilt, creating an uplifting rush of momentum. Testament to that would be the Foundation of Hearts garnering over 8,000 happy to pledge each month. Whereas in Lochend such reciprocity is wholly alien. There, despite the snazzy PR smokescreen, fans subsist on meagre scraps – SPL-priced season tickets two years running despite the growing possibility of a Championship encore next season; and the carrot of fan ownership dangled, cynically, in a derisory share issue not worth the paper it's printed on.

We're undoubtedly in a great place right now. Even if our jubilant campaign runs the risk of petering out with a whimper rather than a roar. As we saw last Sunday at Ibrox, the mantle of acclaimed champions sits rather uncomfortably within the psyche of our club. Showboating simply isn't in our DNA. Certainly, as far as derbies are concerned, we're often happier – as last season showed – being written off as the underdog. It allows us to plug away, under the radar, free from pressure and expectation. Perhaps, then, it was for the best that Hibernian's grudging and embittered response to our title win precluded us another guard of honour.

Almost despite myself, I felt a tinge of sadness as this last derby of the season slowly ticked away and, as things stand, the occasion of our next rendezvous remains distinctly hazy. Each summer, when the fixtures come out, it's always the derby dates that your eyes are drawn to first. Of course, a major factor in that is just how good that fixture has been to us. Even the odd defeat here and there – hard as they are to take – simply wakes you up to how good we've had it.

Don't get me wrong, the haste with which a fair quantity of their fans acted in trying to see us liquidated has altered the landscape of the derby for the foreseeable future. That groundswell of activism that lead BDO's Bryan Jackson to say to a friend of a friend, 'You would not believe the chaos Hibs fans caused sending bogus e-mail offers to the Lithuanian administrator,' sits uncomfortably with the manner in which we stood alongside our city rivals when Wallace Mercer's plans threatened the end for their club.

So, of course, seeing them consigned to another year of Raith, Dumbarton, Alloa et al would be, quite frankly, hilarious but the downside would mean missing out on the chance to add more great memories to the derby database. And, faced with a choice of away venues, I'd choose two trips back here next season over two Ibroxes, two Palmerstons, two Fir Parks or two trips anywhere really.

These sentiments even survived El Alagui making it 2-0 in stoppage time, not to mention a prickly, withering Stubbs drawing the curtain on this season's derbies with a cutting, 'It's OK playing three at the back but you need to know where to go…It's not just about thinking we'll go three at the back and **hoping** it's going to work.'

Clearly he's right, but did he really need to say it?

84

Raith Rovers home, 18 April 2015, 3pm

AT a sun-drenched Tynecastle, Hearts barely broke sweat in seeing off a bland and inoffensive Raith. The Fifers must surely be overjoyed at seeing the back of a Hearts side which has now inflicted four defeats on them, scoring ten and conceding two. Hearts' 2-1 victory may not, in itself, have caused anyone to bat an eyelid – although the Jambo in front of us who took the ball full in the face from a Keatings block tackle may beg to differ – but the lead-up was hugely eventful with potentially wide-ranging ramifications.

Midweek finally saw Rangers catch up with ourselves and Hibernian in terms of games played. They sweated out a dour 1-1 at Livingston leaving them on 62 points – 22 behind us and one ahead of Hibernian. Principally, this lent an air of inevitability to that fight for second spot going right down to the wire.

All of which meant a furious reaction greeted the announcement that Rangers' final-day trip to Tynecastle was to be moved to the Sunday to accommodate Sky TV. Both Leeann Dempster and Ann Budge were quick to issue statements condemning the late timing of the switch and the wholly unsatisfactory state of affairs that would allow Rangers to kick off a full day after everyone else. Budge once again played a blinder, saying, among other things, 'On learning of the change, I immediately attempted to contact the SPFL and objected in strong terms to the proposed late change to this fixture on the grounds of it having a total disregard for the interests of supporters of both clubs and an apparent disregard for sporting integrity.'

On *Sportsound*, a rabid Tom English set about the SPFL in typical fashion, 'Grossly unfair…looks to me like a league bending over backwards to give Rangers every advantage.' Mark Wilson, also on Wednesday night's show, queried what was stopping the Hibernian game being switched to the Sunday too and the team agreed events would probably pan out that way. English hadn't finished, though, especially as the SPFL had neglected to mention anything about the other fixtures that weekend, 'It's illustrative that they haven't announced that **all** matches that weekend will be on the Sunday. Why haven't they done it? It looks like they're trying to give Rangers a leg up here.'

Then, live on air, a pompous and hopelessly out-of-touch statement from the SPFL was read out, 'Unreasonable to expect all Championship fixtures that weekend to move to Sunday when number will be unaffected by Hearts v Rangers. Hearts v Rangers is scheduled for Sunday 3 May to be broadcast on TV. It is not clear to us why this has caused so much surprise. To date, the only feedback we have received is from one Championship club [Falkirk, due to host Hibernian] which has asked for match to remain scheduled for Saturday. For the avoidance of doubt, we have had no request from Hibernian FC to move its fixture to the Sunday at the time of writing. Police Scotland confirmed to us that there were no security issues with the scheduling of all Championship fixtures that weekend. Regret any inconvenience to supporters…the circumstances surrounding the matches on the weekend of 2/3 May are in no way unusual.'

The wording was ham-fisted at best. Leaving aside the fact that Falkirk's stance would have negated any request or otherwise from Hibernian, the statement totally ignores normal, accepted, final-day protocol. Indeed, the final day of the 2012/13 season saw every League Two fixture moved to 12.45pm because Rangers were on TV, irrespective of whether teams were directly affected or not. Unsurprisingly, English was soon back on the warpath, 'In terms of misunderstanding the mood of fans that one takes the biscuit – that's an embarrassment to the SPFL. Inviting teams to apply to move their fixture? Where is the leadership here?'

The following day common sense prevailed as it was announced that all Championship fixtures would kick off, simultaneously, at 12.15pm on the Saturday. Hearts and Ann Budge, inundated with calls from supporters who'd switched tickets, travel and accommodation to the Sunday and then needed to change everything back again, lodged an official complaint at the farcical handling of the whole episode.

When Hibernian's Leeann Dempster was asked whether she too intended to take the matter further, she replied, 'I think we have to sit back and reflect on what has happened in the last 24 hours. We've a cup semi-final on Saturday, as have Falkirk, and we have to switch our minds to that.'

The intriguing prospect of Hibernian winning said semi-final and setting up a potential fixture clash between the Scottish Cup and play-off finals had vexed many a Hibee in recent weeks. Well, Craig Sibbald's 77th-minute header in the lunchtime clash spared them any more worry and Stubbsy's troops are now officially available that last weekend in May should their participation be required.

All season long the Stubbmeister has been the sorest of losers and, here, he was nothing if not consistent, 'There's only one team who deserves to be in the final – unfortunately it's not us. I just wish we had some of the luck the opposition had today.' However, instead of choosing, once more, to rise above the Hibernian manager's conspicuous lack of grace (as Neilson has on more than one occasion), the normally unflappable Houstie bit back spikily, 'After every game we've played against Hibs this season, they've deserved to win, according to Alan. What he should maybe think about is where we're getting our goals from – crosses into the box. Deal with it. That's what I would do. As a coach, I'd be saying to my team that we need to stop crosses because every time they put one in they score goals. Go back and look at the videos – they can't deal with crosses into the box. I'd say that's his problem and not mine. Rather than say only one team deserved to win he should think about how the team beat you. That's three times we've beat Hibs this season and we drew 3-3 after being 3-1 down at Easter Road. So I'd be concerning myself with losing goals, the way Hibs lose them to us.'

The ginger prince went on, 'Of course, Hibs were unfortunate not to win the match. I'm straight up on that. They put a lot into it...they were the better football side today but don't disrespect us by saying we didn't deserve to win – we put a lot into the match defensively.' Well, well. Someone was bound to say it, but I never expected him.

So, by the time Hearts took to the field it felt like we'd already had enough excitement for one week. Robbie continued experimenting with a nod towards building for next season. He picked a strong starting 11 which, with the exception of Gallacher in goal, you could quite conceivably see starting in the big league. McHattie returned to left-back after Eckersley's retrospective two-match ban for butting Scott Allan in the derby. Anderson was restored to the midfield after missing out at Easter Road and Sow was reunited with El Hassnaoui in a fairly loose-looking 4-4-2. On hearing our side it was hard to envisage Raith's honest plodders doing much to upset the apple cart.

Another bumper crowd of 15,405 packed out Tynecastle and all around the ground little spontaneous chants of 'you've no' won the big cup since 1902' were struck up to general hilarity. The atmosphere positively radiated mellowness and bonhomie; so it really does say something for the antagonistic and divisive nature of referee Willie Collum that he still somehow managed to puncture everyone's good mood.

Collum littered his performance with a flurry of fussy, contentious calls. When the match was still goalless he was quite happy to let Craig Barr send El Hass flying in the box. Then, later in the game, Ozturk was waiting to come back on after having received treatment and Collum blanked him just for the sheer hell of it, leaving him stewing for an age on the touchline. I think we have an official here who takes genuine pride from the racket a whole stadium makes protesting at one of his duff calls. It's like he feels he hasn't done his job properly unless one support (often ours) is hurling absolute dogs' abuse at him.

Hearts circumnavigated his transparent incompetence and strolled to victory. The first of their two goals came a little past the half-hour mark. Sow had been a peripheral figure, happy to step back from the limelight and let El Hassnaoui continue to audition for next season, but he perked up sufficiently to set up Nicholson. The winger ran off Sow, seizing control of his neat lay-off and finishing confidently.

At the other end, the shaven-headed Gallacher was more or less a spectator. Alexander's finger injury had signalled a premature end to his season, offering Gallacher the chance to impress. Observing him idly, it was hard to shake the image of a plucky outfield player corralled into donning the shirt and gloves after the keeper had been sent off. Not sure why exactly. Might have been his stance, and the way he had his shirt hanging scruffily outside his shorts. Your Buffons and Neuers don't carry themselves like that. This guy looked more like Jonjo Shelvey.

Hearts barely needed to engage second gear and had as much of the ball as they pleased. On the hour, persistence finally paid off for a languid C-Patz as Hearts notched a second. He thrashed his way down the wing like Bear Grylls cutting a swathe through the rainforest thicket. El Hass was on hand to finish off the big man's handiwork, for his fourth and Hearts' 92nd of the season.

El Hass putting us two up was Neilson's cue to mix things up a little. Firstly, Sean McKirdy replaced Anderson who'd looked the part once again. The young number 34, making his Tynecastle debut, was a little pocket battleship, tackling fiercely and firing neat little passes right, left and centre.

Raith pulling back a goal minutes after the change was in no way a reflection on the little midfielder. Calum Elliot finished sweetly at Gallacher's near post before a rather muted celebration that hinted at feelings he still had for his old club. He'd have been heartened by the round of applause that greeted the announcement of him as goalscorer.

Then, with 20 to go, Sow and Nicholson were replaced by Keatings and Oliver and Hearts edged more towards playing 4-3-3. The arrival of Keatings triggered the warmest of receptions. Earlier in the week the club had announced they'd be open to offers should the role of bit-part player next season not to be to the wee man's liking. The club had had their say and now it was the fans' turn to make an announcement: that they rate him and hope he sticks around.

A year ago those irascible, tattooed old warriors Hamill and Stevenson, not to mention MacDonald, were all informed they were surplus to requirements. Last month, more tough love saw Eckersley denied a new deal. And now Keats. Personally, I hope he decides to stay and fight for his place but, like a lot of players, the end of the season is often the time for a good deal of soul-searching.

85

Cowdenbeath away,
25 April 2015, 3pm

I N the week leading up to our final away match of the campaign it emerged that Danny Wilson would be triggering the release clause in his contract and leaving on a free despite still having a year left to go on his deal. Suspended for the trip to Cowdenbeath, his replacement Brad McKay converted an injury-time penalty to not only seal a 2-1 victory for Hearts but also set a record points tally for the division.

Instrumental in our successful promotion campaign, Wilson leaves us in far better shape than he found us. He signed from Liverpool knowing the future was bleak and pledged to get us back where we belong. Along the way he dug deep to buy shares, played for half his wages, bought season tickets which were donated for charity and attended many fundraising rallies.

That's not to say the captain doesn't polarise opinion among supporters, though. He has his critics who gripe about slack passing and a lack of leadership. The best analogy I can think of is Alan Hansen picking up only 26 caps for his country. As a nation we like our footballers to scurry around a lot and get stuck in. Languid, unhurried players tend to be viewed with a degree of suspicion. The suspicion being that they're not trying hard enough. I think it stems from an inferiority complex. Like, we're not good enough to have a player who's that laid back. It goes against the grain of Scottish puritanism.

Liverpool, on the other hand, knew they were plenty good enough for a player so laid back and, to this day, still revere the silky, composed Hansen. If Wilson's own Liverpool move didn't quite pan out as he would have preferred he's only 23 and still has plenty time to fully live up to that promise he displayed at an early age.

Neilson paid homage to Sir Alf Ramsey and the boys of 1966 by unveiling his wingless wonders at a bright and blustery Central Park. He pioneered what looked suspiciously like a 4-2-2-2 formation in Fife to try and counteract the hosts' unsophisticated approach. C-Patz, as was the case here last December, was shunted up top. He was partnered there by Zeefuik and, playing behind them, were the duo of Walker and Sow. Neilson stayed loyal to Anderson and Gomis as the fulcrum of the side while, defensively, McGhee filled in at full-back and a shaven-headed McKay partnered Ozturk. Finally, Hamilton returned in goal, having sat out the games against Hibernian and Raith.

If anything, the Central Park chicken wire looked worse during daylight. I guess, last time, the glowing floodlights must have softened the appearance of the place but here it was all a bit *Tenko*. At half-time you had the surreal spectacle of a sponsored aerobics class taking place in the centre circle. It had this clunky musical accompaniment from the clapped-out PA system which only added to the whole concentration camp vibe. I half-expected someone to flip out and try to scramble over the top of the big fence like Ives in *The Great Escape*.

The Blue Brazil were in dire need of the points and keen to inflict Hearts' third away defeat on the bounce. The early signs weren't great for them, however. Straight from the kick-off Hearts gave a lucid demonstration of how their system was designed to work. C-Patz drifted in from the right to win a high diagonal and walloped the top of the bar with a half-volley.

Cowdenbeath's playing kit bore an uncanny resemblance to Portsmouth's which was fitting really as the fare they were serving up was classic English League One, kick and rush. Hearts had set themselves up to counteract such agricultural play on a bumpy, bone-hard pitch. But, the fact remains, this is Cowdenbeath's forte. They have far more experience of not only that style of play but also the surroundings and took a deserved lead after 15 minutes. Colin Marshall knocked the ball past Hamilton giving the home support – all crammed together in the same, tiny stand, like survivors in a lifeboat – something to smile about.

Grizzled Ulsterman Jimmy Nicholl paced agitatedly around the technical area like an expectant father in a maternity ward. At one point the ball drifted out of play towards him and he made to pick it up before changing his mind and letting it roll away beyond the giant tyres. That's one thing I definitely won't be missing about this division, the yawning chasm in talent that persuades opponents to kill time with practised impunity.

Of course, the tyres are there because this venue also caters for stock car racing. The bobbly, uneven playing surface makes you wonder why they don't also rent it out as a crazy golf course. They'd make an absolute killing. Hearts began navigating the bumps and gullies in fine style and equalised on 34 minutes. Walker crossed and C-Patz planted a textbook header low past Thomson.

Neilson loves to tweak a system. Not long into the second half Nicholson replaced Zeefuik and Sow joined up with C-Patz as Hearts pushed for the winner. The champions were desperate for the win in order to hit that magical 90-point mark and it took one further bout of tinkering to get us over the line. Keats came on for McGhee and C-Patz trotted back to his customary berth at full-back.

On our travels this season opponents have often been trounced out of sight yet it's never stopped the local PA guy nominating some hapless plodder for man of the match. 'Yep, excellent choice, he'd get my vote too,' you smirk as you head for home. Here was different. On the 90-minute mark Thomson in the Cowdenbeath goal got the sponsors' award and it was thoroughly merited. The keeper had fought valiantly to preserve parity, making a host of top-notch saves from Anderson, Sow and Nicholson.

Standing on the curved bank, slap-bang behind his goal, had made for thrilling second-half viewing. In the end, sheer weight of numbers in the box told. Stoppage time was ticking away when Walker ran on to a loose ball and was sent sprawling. Initially, he looked set to step up himself but then tossed the ball to Brad McKay. It was a truly magnanimous gesture. Foregoing the chance to become leading scorer in his own right he presented the housewives' favourite with the opportunity to sign off with his first career goal. The centre-half remained calm and struck his effort with too much power for Thomson to get down to.

The win lifted us on to 90 points, one more than the total gained by Hibernian in 1998/99. That tally of theirs had remained the record ever since three points for a win was introduced 20 seasons ago. Under Alex McLeish, that side won 28, drew five and lost three of their 36 games whereas Hearts – with one game to go – have won 29, drawn three and lost three.

Present-day Hibernian saw off Alloa, winning comprehensively 4-1. They probably wouldn't have anticipated the win having an effect on overall placings, but Rangers were deeply unimpressive at home to Falkirk – requiring an injury-time equaliser to snatch a 2-2 draw. Their latest gaffe allowed Hibernian to leapfrog them into second, handing the Lochend side the initiative going into the final round of fixtures.

A win for them against new best friend Houstie's Falkirk and whatever Rangers muster at Tynecastle will be an irrelevance. Meanwhile, for us, next weekend is all about finally getting our hands on the silverware.

86

Rangers home,
2 May 2015, 12.15pm

THE champions came from two down to salvage a point courtesy of a late double from Genero Zeefuik in a rowdy, cantankerous and superbly entertaining contest against old adversaries Rangers. That peculiar quirk of fixture planning which pitted us against the same opposition on both opening and closing weekends had surely been designed to wring every last drip of intrigue out of the Championship campaign. Thankfully, though, by matchday 36, we were but a speck on the horizon to our visitors, untouched and largely untroubled by a markedly one-sided display of officiating.

Pre-match, Robbie Neilson spoke of the need to ensure events on the pitch didn't render the trophy presentation and subsequent title party a damp squib. His words also sought to dispel the memory of those two recent blips against the sides jousting for that runners-up spot.

Rangers needed to win while hoping events went their way in Falkirk but Hearts got off to an absolute whirlwind of a start. The home side were snapping swiftly into tackles and Rangers were unable to live with the tempo. It felt brilliant, watching our side get stuck in among Rangers, not paying them even a smidgeon of respect.

After ten minutes, Pallardó eased Jamie Walker through one on one with Cammy Bell, but the keeper beat his effort away. Less than a minute later the roles were reversed as Walker laid the ball into the path of Pallardó. However, the crafty little Spaniard, making a welcome return to the side, saw his shot clip a defender and drift out for another corner.

At the peak of his side's ascendancy, Sow found space in the box and ran across the path of Zaliukas (or Zaluskas, as an uncorrected Derek Ferguson insists on calling him), before tumbling, unconvincingly, to the deck. From where I was sat, it looked a clear dive and the retiring Calum Murray unhesitatingly flashed a yellow card at the Hearts number 20. The attempt to con the official was poorly thought out and the big man cut a fairly distracted figure throughout.

At or around this point Murray's grip on objectivity began to wane. Not for the first time we had to contend with the former Hearts season ticket holder over-compensating in his desire not to show favouritism. Having already paced out a Rangers wall eight steps from a nonplussed Ozturk, he then, half an hour in, ignored an obvious handball from Shiels. Instead, he awarded the visitors the softest of free kicks wide left. Law swung the ball over and McGregor shunted C-Patz out of the way to head powerfully in.

By this point Hibernian were already ahead but an oblivious Rangers partied like it was 1999. Shiels was gazing at the heavens and shaking his fists like he thought he was Gary Lineker scoring against West Germany at Italia 90.

The restart saw an unhinged madness creep over Tynecastle. It all began when Zal, for old time's sake, completely misjudged the flight of the ball and Sow found himself clear. Bell raced from goal and cleaned him out. It was impossible not to think back to the first home game of the season and the penalty Collum awarded Hibernian for a challenge where Hamilton got far more of the ball than Bell did here. The Swede was still appealing, arms outstretched plaintively, when Rangers broke upfield and a sniggering Kenny Miller fired his side two ahead.

You got the sense, rightly or wrongly, that having booked Sow for trying to con him, Murray felt the striker then lost the right to a fair hearing where fouls in the box were concerned. The atmosphere became rancorous and volatile. Usually calmness personified, the measured and softly spoken Neilson found himself sent to the stand. Of his dismissal he said, 'To be honest, I didn't think it was a penalty. But there were a few other things in the build-up to that goal that were dubious to say the least. If coaches are going to get sent up to the stand for shouting at opposition players, there will be nobody left in the dugout. I won't say who it was but it was one of the players who body-checked one of my players. It has happened a few times. It happened at Ibrox as well and it got let go. That is football. He is clever, players are clever, but you expect someone to see it.'

Bad blood has coursed through every single one of these clubs' encounters this season. Even the abandoned game had a nasty edge to it. Today was no different. Ozturk and Miller had been pursuing a running feud throughout the half and then, when the half-time whistle went, C-Patz had a nibble at Nicky Clark on the way up the tunnel – irked perhaps at having been sold a dodgy haircare product. Mohsni, too, sat on the bench, had earned a stern reprimand from the police for getting involved with home supporters.

Easy to say now but during the interval we were all pretty relaxed. Two-nil felt like a false scoreline as Rangers were clearly no great shakes and a stinging riposte from our side was anticipated. And, worst case scenario, we'd get handed the league trophy only the 20 points clear. C'est la vie! We were home-free and untouchable and took immense delight winding up our guests by loudly cheering news of Hibernian's half-time lead. The act burrowed beneath their collective skins like a parasitic worm, provoking the reproachful rebuke, 'Are you Hibees in disguise?' Bit of a daft question really: there were way too many of us for a start. Whether by accident or design we'd further debunked that tedious myth, pigeon-holing us as their subservient little proddie cousins.

Further fuelling this gaping disconnect they regaled us with an impassioned dirge about a flag they've formed an emotional attachment to, then another about a man who starved himself to death in a maximum-security prison near Belfast in the early 1980s. The returning players and a lusty chorus of 'championees' soon dragged us all back on topic.

In the same vein as the Ibrox clash, Rangers came back out and were quite content to sit on their two-goal lead. Although, having said that, early on Zal missed a free header from six yards for what would have been 3-0 after Ozturk and C-Patz had played 'after you, Claude'. Zal's hero status in these parts suffered a jolt not long after. After being bumped harmlessly by Gomis he incurred the wrath of the Wheatfield for waving his arms in the air and brandishing an imaginary card. This vignette riled me more than it should have and in the heat of the moment I was off my seat, bawling, 'Zaliukas! You were a shite captain!' Regrettable, but it's impossible to stay mad at Zal for long and, post-match, our 2012 cup-winning captain was happily posing for pictures with any number of Hearts fans.

Hearts' gutsy, tenacious comeback typified their season. A team bursting with big personalities, bloody-mindedly refusing to accept defeat until the referee inhales, whistle to mouth. Zeefuik was summoned from the bench on the 60-minute mark and drastically altered the complexion of the game.

Again, mirroring the corresponding fixture last month, Hearts' pressure told going into the final ten minutes. With eight to go, Bell had a brain fart; seemingly deciding that dodgeball would be more fun. He launched a throw-out at C-Patz's napper, nearly knocking the big man off his feet. The ball landed near McGregor who reflexively lashed a miscued clearance in the direction of the corner flag. C-Patz lumbered over groggily and, from his throw-in, Gomis clipped a left-footer into the box. Zeefuik pulled away from McGregor, arched his back and planted a quite glorious header across the flailing keeper and into the far corner.

The goal pulled the Dutchman level with Walker, Sow and Keats on 11 which is some feat when you consider he was making only his 15th appearance for the club. As Robbie said of him, 'We needed someone to come in and lead the line and score goals. That is exactly what he has done. I would like to keep a hold of him but I don't think I will because he still has a couple of years left with Groningen and is on good wages. He took a pay cut to come to us.' Our loanee hadn't finished there, either, signing off with a second goal and taking top scorer in his own right.

Trailing 2-1, going into the last minute, my first Hearts-Rangers game – back in February 1984 – flashed into my head. Probably because that day we'd also been two down before nicking one and entering injury time on the hunt for an equaliser. And, boy, did we find one that day, in the shape of an overhead kick from Robbo that triggered scenes of frenzied pandemonium on the old School End.

Joyously and bang on cue, history repeated itself. Just past the 90-minute mark, Zeefuik pulled a C-Patz head-flick out of the sky, outmuscled Zal and, with his weaker foot, rammed the ball home, sparking euphoric celebrations every bit as wild as back in Robbo's heyday. The modern-day equivalent of School End – the Roseburn Stand – saw a mass, blue-tinted exodus in both sections, accompanied deafeningly – magnificently – by the throaty refrain, 'That's why we're champions.'

Such an apt finale. As Robbie put it himself, 'I am really pleased. I think the way we did it, it felt like a victory. Coming back from 2-0 down and scoring in the last minute really summed up our season. Having that belief to keep going and trying to get that goal. I was just delighted. The players and staff celebrated that last goal as much as they have done all season.'

From there on in, the afternoon just got better and better as Ann Budge then came tottering on to the pitch with the trophy glinting in her arms. To chants of 'we love you Ann Budge, we do' Tynecastle absolutely bubbled over with joy and pride. Those maroon ribbons fluttering beautifully in the spring breeze, just as they'd done when Dave Mackay had got his hands on the trophy 57 years earlier.

The podium had been erected and, one by one, the players were announced, carrying a variety of selfie sticks. Neil Alexander even did a John Terry, coming out in full kit despite not having made the 18. It was too hard to tell from the Wheatfield whether he'd drawn the line at shinpads! Danny Wilson's last act as club captain was to hoist a trophy above his head. He said of it, 'It's been a joy to be part of this team this year. But I think I can leave with my head held high being a championship-winning captain. It's the way I wanted to leave.'

Through a blizzard of swirling confetti the players clambered down and, with their children in tow, took part in a jubilant lap of honour. The supporters warbled tunelessly along to 'We Are The Champions' and drank in every perfect second.

Epilogue

ONE week later and a full year on from Ann Budge taking the reins at Tynecastle, a number of us attended a fans' rally in the Gorgie Suite – the aim of which was to raise funds for youth development and the new museum via an auction.

It brought back memories of the last fundraiser we'd attended there, back almost two years ago in July 2013. That day had felt like the first tentative steps on an uncertain journey, the conclusion of which was cloaked in ambiguity. So returning here and seeing Ann Budge in attendance, not to mention the trophy, made it feel like a clear destination had been reached.

After the league was claimed, Robbo commented, 'Astonishing! Eighteen months ago the club was on its knees – saved by the fans! Phenomenal!' And, standing in a long, snaking line to grasp hold of that cold, gleaming trophy, it felt like the collective reward for sticking by the club through dire times: from taking six points out of a possible 54 to 54 points out of a possible 60; from finishing bottom to finishing top; and from being relegated before Easter to being declared champions before Easter.

Yet, of course, football being football, no sooner is one challenge out of the way than another begins and thoughts drift to next season. Be it departures, new signings, the new Puma kit, pre-season tours and fixture lists. As regards the latter the vicarious pleasure of the play-offs eventually ensured at least one visit to Fir Park awaits us. Rangers downed feisty Queen of the South and toothless Hibernian before having their mediocrity exposed by a Motherwell side that found form at just the right time.

Irrespective of the inestimable pleasure at seeing both Rangers and Hibernian consigned to another year in the second tier, we await the next instalment with bated breath. We would appear to have been truly blessed by the manner in which Budge and Levein have joined forces to lovingly craft a football club that we can all take pride in. After confessing to having suffered a bruising time as coach of Scotland, Levein spoke candidly of Ann Budge's regime, '[It's] different from the scepticism, the backstabbing and short-term thinking that goes on that really shackles our game.

'She's a fantastic person. She's a breath of fresh air. It is refreshing to have somebody who thinks about things completely differently. All she ever talks about is how the club will look in four or five years' time and that's the type of thinking that Scottish football needs. She's significantly better than anyone I have worked with.'

From the threat of liquidation to league winners; from Wonga to Save the Children; and from Vlad the Impaler to Ann the Saviour. The words of Tommy Walker hold as true today as they did the day he spoke them, 'There is no other club like Hearts. We don't have players, we have heroes. We don't have a stadium, we have a fortress. We don't have fans, we have the heart and soul of Edinburgh. This is a dynasty that will live on for eternity.'